PRAISE FOR *STAND-OUT*

'Based on highly credible, thorough research, this pragmatic book deals with an age-old problem of how to give customers something of stand-out value that they are prepared to pay for. I commend it to you.'
Professor Malcolm McDonald, Emeritus Professor, Cranfield University School of Management

'For organizations to stand out they need people to stand out. This book offers invaluable advice, based on credible research, about how your marketing and sales professionals excel now and into the future.'
Clare Kemsley, Managing Director, UK and Ireland, Hays Marketing

'After more than 30 years in B2B sales and marketing, specializing in business turnarounds for the last decade, it always amazes me how many companies fail to do the fundamentals of positioning their business in a hyper-competitive marketplace, let alone have the competencies to do so. *Stand-Out Marketing* makes you look in the mirror and identify some potentially uncomfortable truths, while providing some fantastic insights on sharpening your clarity and cut through to target customers. A book I would highly recommend and will often come back to.'
Tom Craig, CEO, Craig Roxburgh Consulting, former Group Director, Vodafone Business Services, former President, IP Networking, BT Global Services

'Customers today are overwhelmed with information to help them make choices. The fact that organizations all seem to offer the same things that don't appear to help customers, often means customers are paralyzed as the choice becomes too difficult. If you want to find out how to help your organization develop the competency to swim away from this "sea of sameness" and differentiate yourself, you *must* read this book!'
Colin Shaw, CEO and Founder, Beyond Philosophy

'Great to find a book that recognizes that to give customers something meaningfully different, you need the people competencies and the leadership to be able stand out from the crowd. A must-read for sales and marketing leaders who want to develop the talent to set their organization apart.'
Andrew Crouch, CEO, UniTek Global Services

'It's increasingly hard for businesses to differentiate themselves in today's hyper-crowded marketplace. Far too many companies are pumping out the same bland messages that fail to resonate with customers. This excellent book equips sales and marketing professionals with the capabilities to stand out in this "sea of sameness".'
Nick de Cent, Editor-in-Chief, *The International Journal of Sales Transformation*

'Top-performing companies that get ahead of the competition have great alignment between sales and marketing rooted in customer thinking. I commend this book as it provides great clarity for both marketing and sales leaders about the competencies required to develop and deliver outstanding customer value.'
Andy McFarlane, Enterprise Value Creation Executive, Telstra

Stand-Out Marketing

How to differentiate your organization in a Sea of Sameness

Simon Kelly
Stacey Danheiser
Paul Johnston

First published in Great Britain and the United States in 2021 by Kogan Page Limited

2nd Floor, 45 Gee Street
London
EC1V 3RS
United Kingdom

122 W 27th St, 10th Floor
New York, NY 10001
USA

4737/23 Ansari Road
Daryaganj
New Delhi 110002
India

www.koganpage.com

Kogan Page books are printed on paper from sustainable forests.

ISBNs

Hardback 978 1 78966 484 3
Paperback 978 1 78966 482 9
Ebook 978 1 78966 483 6

British Library Cataloguing-in-Publication Data

A CIP record for this book is available from the British Library.

Library of Congress Cataloging-in-Publication Number

2020041887

Typeset by Integra Software Services, Pondicherry
Print production managed by Jellyfish
Printed and bound by CPI Group (UK) Ltd, Croydon CR0 4YY

To our mothers, Mary Kelly, June Johnston and Phyllis Ekstrom – for instilling in us a love of learning and inspiring us to try new things.

CONTENTS

LIST OF FIGURES AND TABLES

FIGURES

TABLES

ABOUT THE AUTHORS

Dr Simon Kelly has 35 years' experience in the ICT industry in customer service, sales, and marketing. He pioneered the move from 'product push' to 'value-based' selling while he was Marketing Director (SVP) at BT. A 'pracademic', he has developed innovative marketing and sales skills modules at Sheffield Business School where he was a Senior Lecturer. He is currently CEO of Cohesion Marketing Services, a principal of Shake Marketing Group and lecturer in Marketing and Sales at York Management School.

Stacey Danheiser is CEO of Shake Marketing Group based in south Florida (US), where she helps B2B organizations tune into and deliver customer value to drive business growth. Prior to founding Shake Marketing Group, Stacey spent 15 years leading marketing strategy, field marketing and sales activation programmes inside of various Fortune 500 companies.

Dr Paul Johnston worked as a principal lecturer in marketing at Sheffield Business School, Sheffield Hallam University for 10 years. Prior to this, he spent 20 years in the gambling and electronics games industry with board-level roles in competitive strategy, key account management, marketing research, and product innovation.

FOREWORD

All products today are excellent, a fact that I have had confirmed by thousands of delegates at my conferences over the past few years (using computerized audience response systems to ensure confidentiality and honest answers). Let's face it, products have to be excellent today for them even to be considered by customers. It is, therefore, highly unlikely that functionality will be the deciding factor.

This, however, presents a major challenge for suppliers and they have to find some way of differentiating themselves.

The authors of this book cleverly spell out this dilemma by using the expression the 'Sea of Sameness'. In the fast-moving consumer goods domain, which I knew well as Marketing and Sales Director of Canada Dry, the big supermarkets used to refer to such products as 'pimply little me-toos' and guess what? Yes, they used to drive the prices of such products down.

The truth, of course, is that it is the depth of knowledge the supplier has of their customers and their business that matters today, as they are then capable of building trusting relationships that don't just help them avoid disadvantage, but which create advantage for their customers.

Is it worth doing what the authors call 'Stand-Out Marketing'?

I can tell you that after a long career in B2B marketing and in particular from my experience with my Key Account Management Global Best Practice research club at Cranfield University School of Management (sponsored by the likes of 3M, Siemens, Rolls-Royce and many others and still going strong), it most definitely is. Buying directors over the 23-year life of the research club always confirm that it is only a tiny percentage of suppliers who create advantage for them and for them they are prepared to pay a price premium of up to 25 per cent and often much more. All the others are subjected to severe discounting.

There are, of course, other books which promise to achieve the same as this one. This one, however, is different and lives up to its promise.

In a world where many see the destiny of marketing as the operational use of digital technology and software application skills, *Stand Out*

Marketing is a welcome call to refocus management attention on strategic marketing competences vital for achieving sustained competitive advantage and increased shareholder value.

I commend it to you.

Professor Malcolm McDonald MA (Oxon) MSc PhD DLitt DSc
Emeritus Professor, Cranfield University School of Management

PREFACE

Why read this book

On 19 August 2019, 181 CEOs gathered at the Business Roundtable led by the World Economic Forum in Davos, Switzerland to formally sign a declaration to recognize that the role of a company has evolved. This one-page declaration reads:

> Each of our stakeholders is essential. We commit to deliver value to all of them, for the future success of our companies, our communities and our country (World Economic Forum, 2019).

This is a big shift, as it rejects the previously held popular belief established by Milton Friedman in 1970 known as the 'shareholder theory' which states that a company only exists to make its shareholders money. This new charter recognizes that shareholders are just ONE of the groups of stakeholders that companies are responsible for and reminds organizations not to ignore their customers, employees, suppliers and communities.

We wholeheartedly agree with this new assertion, but there's one thing that you may subtly miss when you read the new declaration. The word 'value' assumes that companies know what their stakeholders value and how to deliver it to them. But, as we reviewed in-depth in our previous book, *Value-ology*, 'value' is often poorly defined and misinterpreted. We like to say that value is in the eye of the beholder because everyone gets to decide for themselves exactly what they value – and subsequently how they spend their time, talents and money.

Our latest research found that whilst 83 per cent of the B2B marketing and sales leaders we surveyed said that it was 'extremely important' to be able to clearly articulate what makes their solution different to prospective customers, only 24 per cent of organizations claim to be 'effective or extremely effective' at differentiating themselves.

Our belief is that many organizations are failing to differentiate themselves because:

- they don't fully understand the importance of having a unique value proposition;
- they have an internal-only view of what customers want.

And perhaps the biggest discovery that we made:

- their marketing and sales teams lack the competencies needed to develop and communicate value.

One of the most common questions facing today's business leaders is 'How do we get customers to choose us over our competitors?' At a time when only 54.3 per cent of salespeople are making their quota (CSO Insights, 2018), and only 11 per cent of B2B buyers believe vendor representatives are trustworthy (Trust Radius, 2019), it's imperative to demonstrate that you understand what your customers value and can communicate how your solution solves their problem better than anything else out there.

This book was written for you, the business leader, sales and marketing professional, to help you develop the competencies to set your organization apart, advance your career and feel job satisfaction instead of frustration. We wrote it because in our experience, and from the research we have done, we know that organizations are not good at differentiating in ways that resonate with their customers. And copycat marketing and sales programmes are not only ineffective, they leave your customers feeling uninspired, bored and unmotivated to take action.

While lots of books have been written about *how* to advance your marketing and sales technical skills, not many books focus on what you, as an individual, can do to develop yourself and your team to build long-term success in marketing and sales – no matter what new technology or technique comes on the market.

The competencies we've uncovered and are about to share aren't something that will quickly go out of style or be replaced.

About the research

When we wrote our last book *Value-ology: Aligning sales and marketing to shape and deliver profitable customer value propositions* (Kelly, Johnston and Danheiser, 2017) we wanted to give business leaders, marketing and sales professionals a framework and some tools to enable them to resonate with customers by tuning in to what customers value.

The detailed research we did for *Value-ology* included in-depth interviews with marketing and sales practitioners, a practitioner survey, and lots of analysis of credible third-party research. We found that B2B organizations were clearly having difficulty living up to our definition of a value proposition – 'A promise of expected future value, illustrating that future relevant and distinct benefits will outweigh the total cost of ownership' – and it was costing them in lost sales, failed bids, and fruitless marketing.

We sensed that there was a lot of 'sameness' out there and we saw that lots of organizations were saying the same things as each other, making it difficult for customers to choose, and leading them to choose to do nothing. In order to test this hunch, we developed a new research programme.

Stand-Out Marketing is based on research we conducted from 2017 to 2019. We sought to understand:

- the current state of how organizations are communicating their unique value proposition;
- why there seems to be a 'sameness' problem in customer-facing communications;
- competency gaps and priorities within the marketing and sales functions.

In the first phase, we compared websites and Twitter feeds for the largest organizations in three industry sectors: Telecommunications, Data Centres and Higher Education. Our research showed that the customers are left swimming in a 'Sea of Sameness' where all the companies are saying exactly the same thing to them. We explore the results of the 'Sea of Sameness' research in-depth in Chapters 1 and 2.

In the second phase, we conducted 1:1 interviews with over 20 business and sales and marketing leaders across a variety of industries. The combined experience of the individuals we interviewed spanned 119 companies and 54 industry sectors. We discussed the competency gaps that exist within today's marketing and sales professionals and what organizations are doing to differentiate and stand out from the competition. We also ran an online survey consisting of over 50 global responses to further understand competency gaps and organizational priorities. Our research was conducted using academic ethical research protocols to ensure participant anonymity and consent for the use of interview quotations.

Getting the most out of this book

Through a mix of explanations, case studies from our interviews, thought-provoking questions and plenty of practical advice and exercises to implement, this book was written to help you:

1. diagnose where/if your organization is stuck in the 'sea of sameness';
2. understand the implications of not making a change;
3. provide a competency framework with ideas and strategies you can use to get out of the sea of sameness and differentiate your business.

Since the bulk of the book details the competencies that you, as an individual, can develop and prioritize for your team and company, let's be clear that competency is much more than skill. Skill is readily trainable and focused on learning how to do a specific task, such as creating ads on Facebook. Competency, on the other hand, requires the ability to draw from knowledge and experience, blend thoughts, feelings and actions to make sense of situations and act effectively. Competency is evidence of professional insight and wisdom and involves demonstrating a high level of ability in interpretation, pragmatism, judgement and decision making.

Higher-level competency is your source of competitive differentiation. Without it, your pursuit of sustained competitive advantage will be at best hit and miss and at worst an ongoing miserable journey of below-average performance. The right people with the right abilities, working together in the right culture is the only path to sustained successful performance: after all, business is and always will be about people.

Ultimately this book is here to help you answer two questions:

1. Do our business leaders, sales and marketing people have the competency to help your organization stand out?
2. If you are a marketing or sales practitioner this becomes a much more personal question: do *you* have the competency to help your organization stand out?

Good luck in your quest to be meaningfully different for your customers and your own company.

References

CSO Insights (2018) *Selling in the Age of Ceaseless Change: The 2018–2019 Sales Performance Report*

Kelly, S, Johnston, P and Danheiser, S (2017) *Value-ology: Aligning sales and marketing to shape and deliver profitable customer value propositions*, Palgrave Macmillan

McClelland, D C (1973) Testing for competency rather than intelligence, *American Psychologist*, **28** (1), pp 1–14

Sanghi, S (2016) *The Handbook of Competency Mapping, 3rd Edition*, Sage,
Trust Radius (2019) The 2019 B2B Buying Disconnect: An in-depth study on buying preferences, vendor impact, and the persistent trust gap in B2B technology. Available from: https://go.trustradius.com/2019-B2B-Disconnect.html (archived at https://perma.cc/6L6T-LGK8)
World Economic Forum (2019) Davos Manifesto 2020: The universal purpose of a company in the fourth industrial revolution, 2 December. Available from: https://www.weforum.org/agenda/2019/12/davos-manifesto-2020-the-universal-purpose-of-a-company-in-the-fourth-industrial-revolution/ (archived at https://perma.cc/8QSL-SB22) [accessed 21 February 2020]

ACKNOWLEDGEMENTS

We would like to thank the many exceptional marketing and sales leaders with whom we have had the pleasure to work and learn from throughout the years. To our business colleagues and friends for sharing their time, thoughts and remarks – your insights and stories inspired us to bring this book to life.

To all the outstanding strategists and researchers for publishing reputable data about the state of our industry. And to the authors whose works spark ideas and motivate us to write. We thank you all.

Most importantly, to our spouses and families – we appreciate your unconditional support and encouragement throughout this book-writing journey.

Thank you to Kogan Page for allowing us to publish this book.

Last and not least, to our former, current and future students for your willingness to learn new concepts and approaches.

01

B2B organizations are stuck in a Sea of Sameness

In this chapter we will cover:

- the problem facing today's B2B organizations related to how they are communicating their unique value to customers;
- the results of our original research that led us to conclude that B2B customers are 'Lost in a Sea of Sameness' because vendors are telling them the same thing, providing no clear value.

Why should a customer choose YOU?

Imagine that you are a prospective customer for your company's product or service. Like most B2B buyers, you've conducted extensive research online to figure out what your options are and you have a pretty good idea about what you want. Google refers to this as the 'zero moment of truth' – the moment people research a product or service before buying something. Armed with this new intelligence, you've narrowed it down to a list of potential vendors, but you're confused about which one will be the 'answer' to your situation and solve your problem (Lecinski, 2014). You see, all of the vendors are virtually promising to provide the exact same thing: innovative products, access to the most experienced people, and customized solutions at an affordable price.

So how can a company set themselves apart in the eyes of the buyer?

This is the problem facing most B2B companies today. First, B2B buyers are confronted with an overwhelming amount of choice, which ultimately leads to choice overload. Behavioural economists refer to this as 'overchoice', when too many choices are available to consumers, making it hard to decide (Toman, Adamson and Gomez, 2017).

As Sheena Iyenger addresses in her Ted Talk, 'How to make choosing easier' (TEDSalon NY, 2011), while we like to be presented with a lot of options, *too many* choices lead us to become quickly overwhelmed when it comes to making a decision... which means we are more likely to:

1. delay making a choice, even if it's in our best interest;
2. make poorer decisions;
3. choose things that make us less satisfied.

Overchoice has negative side effects such as unhappiness because we end up wasting time researching all our options and eventually giving up if we don't see an obvious solution (Schwartz, 2004).

Can you think of a buying decision you've deferred or a situation where you've not made a purchase because of 'overchoice'?

Second, B2B buying has grown increasingly more complex over the years. Not only does your customer have to be convinced to buy your solution, but they also have to involve up to six other people across various roles, departments and geographies to gain their approval. CEB Research points out that companies are spending more time evaluating purchases, yet despite this extra time being invested, more than 40 per cent second guess their decision after they've made a purchase.

Lastly, while it is vital for your organization to communicate the unique value you provide to customers, we know that 'value propositions' are a widely misunderstood concept (Payne, Frow and Eggert, 2017). First introduced in the 1970s by Hanan *et al* (1970) in *Consultative Selling*, and further conceptualized by McKinsey in the early 1980s, there is still much confusion about what a value proposition is and how companies should be communicating it (Goldring 2017:1).

The definition of value proposition we like to use is:

> A promise of future value, illustrating that future relevant benefits and distinct benefits will outweigh the total cost of ownership (Kelly, Johnston and Danheiser, 2017, p 30).

But many companies are simply not telling the customer why they are different or better than a competitive solution, leaving it up to the customer to sift through their website and try to figure it out on their own. For example, Goldring's research into 24 financial planning firms in a large US city uncovered that:

> 16 of the 24 had no identifiable brand value proposition. Most of their assertions were focused on the company itself, using page navigation such as 'Our Company', 'Our Philosophy', 'Our Services', 'Who We Are', or 'Our team'.

So ask yourself – are you making it easy or hard for a customer to choose your solution over the competition?

Research reveals customers are stuck in a Sea of Sameness

'Sameness', according to dictionary.com, is defined as the lack of variety; uniformity or monotony.

As with most things in life, there are both pros and cons to being 'the same'. On the positive side, you could argue that it is critical for companies to deliver a consistent product and customer experience when launching into new cities or industries. Take Starbucks coffee, for example. You can walk into a Starbucks coffee shop in Germany and get the same cup of coffee that you would get in New York City. This level of consistency and 'sameness' has led to a loyal fan base and a healthy stock price.

On the other hand, 'sameness' has negative impacts in business when you use it to describe the products, services and experiences an organization provides compared to its competitors. When customers perceive that you are basically offering the same type of products/solutions/experiences as your competitors, with no real differentiated value, they view it as a commodity. When this happens, customers don't see any significant difference between their options except for price, and they will generally just choose the solution with the lowest price. On top of that, the way products are marketed within many industries is also the same – using the same promises, descriptions and statements.

This 'sameness' problem in communications is what we were interested in investigating after spending years addressing this at the corporations we worked for and later with our clients. We conducted case studies into how the top organizations are communicating their value in three separate industries: telecommunications, data centre, and higher education.

We also spoke to lots of practitioners in several different industries, and our conclusion was this: companies are communicating their value in the same way, using the same jargon, the same promises and the same reasons about what makes their company different.

Our analysis into these industries revealed, to our surprise, that what companies are communicating as their main differentiator doesn't match what the original idea and purpose of what a value and brand proposition should be. We found that almost every company is guilty of:

- **About Us – lots of 'we' statements that don't clearly explain the benefit to a customer**
  Examples: '*We have years of experience*' and '*We have a unique and innovative approach*'.
- **Generic claims – lack of proof points**
  Examples: '*We help your business grow*' and '*We save your business money*'.
- **Copycat marketing – saying the same thing as their competitors**
  Examples: '*Our solutions are tailored for you*'.

The problem with communicating the *exact* same story, benefits and promises as everyone else in your industry, is that you're putting all of the responsibility on the customer to figure out what makes you different. When every company sounds the same, your customers are left utterly confused as to which solution will best meet their needs. They may just avoid making a decision (ie continuing with the status quo), choose the one with the lowest price, or worse, choose a solution that is inadequate or ill-matched to their situation. We believe this is one of the main reasons why CSO Insights reports that over 50 per cent of forecasted deals don't close, and why only 56.9 per cent of sales reps are meeting their quota (CSO Insights, 2019).

So as you read through the following case studies, we challenge you to think about whether you are making the same mistakes in your marketing and sales communications.

CASE STUDY #1

Sameness in B2B telecom marketing

A large part of our personal job history and client work has come from the telecommunications industry, where we noticed a trend in marketing and sales communications. If you're not too familiar with the telecom industry, these are the companies that provide your internet, mobile, telephone and video connectivity to both your home and business. The industry has been around since the 1830s with the invention of the telegraph and has continued to evolve as new technologies are introduced: telephone, radio, TV, computer, mobile devices.

Because phones and computers need to be able to talk to each other, it is also a very standards-driven industry. As a result, telecom products at their core are not vastly different from one company to the next.

We were most interested in how telecom companies were communicating their business or enterprise value proposition, as words like 'digital transformation' and 'scalability' began to appear everywhere on websites, social media feeds, sales emails and analyst reports. It didn't matter how big or small a company was, if they were part of the telecommunications industry, it appeared that every company was telling the same exact story and using the same meaningless jargon to communicate what their company did and sold. It's almost as if the marketing professionals at each company got together and came up with a universal way to describe their offering, value proposition and 'why us' story!

So we decided to dive deeper into this issue and perform a thorough analysis of the top 30 global telecommunications company websites and Twitter feeds to see what was going on. We took a scrape of their marketing copy and ran it through a data analytics tool to see if there were any patterns.

The results were astonishing. Not only did they confirm our hunch that the same words were being used over and over again throughout customer-facing communications, but we also noticed a few other things related to the nature of the words being used (see Figure 1.1).

We published our findings in a whitepaper entitled 'Lost in a Sea of Sameness: Lack of differentiation dominates the telecommunications industry' (2018), and share the key points here.

Key findings

Generic business and technology terms dominate marketing communications

Sixty per cent of the top 10 most frequently used words across telecom company websites and Twitter feeds were generic business terms, such as 'services', 'businesses' and 'solutions'. The remaining 40 per cent were made up of general technology-related words such as 'networks', 'cloud' and 'security'.

What does this tell us?

First, none of these terms relates to specific customer benefits and they fail to elicit an emotional reaction. Instead, they are common descriptors of the products, services and technology that the organization offers. In fact, the word 'customers' comes in 10th place.

Second, considering that 48 per cent of IT purchase decisions are now made outside of the IT department (IDC), telecommunications companies are missing the mark by using techno-babble and not addressing the executive and business

FIGURE 1.1 Most overused words on telecom websites

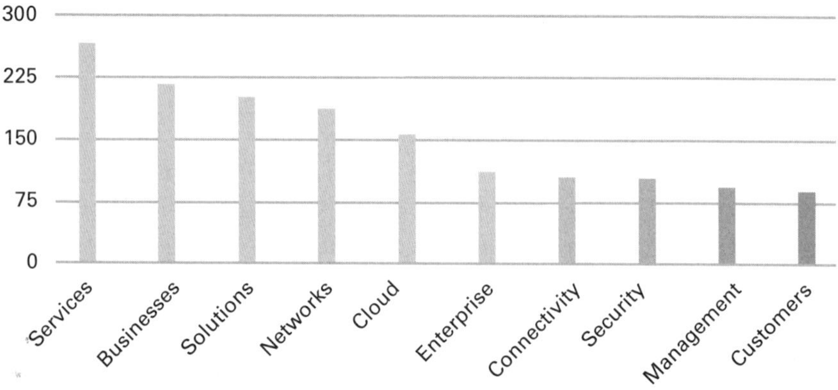

300
225
150
75
0
Services
Businesses
Solutions
Networks
Cloud
Enterprise
Connectivity
Security
Management
Customers

SOURCE Danheiser, Johnston and Kelly (2018)

decision maker with benefit-oriented statements that explain *why* their solutions are ideal for the customer. This approach puts an extra burden on the technical buyer to essentially translate and communicate how a new telecom solution will impact their business in terms that will resonate with the CEO, CFO and COO.

Further, certain words like 'networks', 'security', 'digitization' and 'cloud' are so casually and frequently used in the telecommunications industry, that it is assumed that there is a standard definition and interpretation, rather than a general 'catch-all' phrase. This assumption only leads to customer confusion, as all parties think they are speaking the same language, when in reality they may be misaligned. Take the word 'cloud' for example. A quick search for 'what is the cloud?' in Google produces over 4.2 billion search results, providing a wide range of explanations.

It's all about the company!

When attempting to differentiate itself and explain 'why buy from us?', we found that marketing content is packed with company-centric 'we', 'us' and 'our' statements, rather than customer-oriented 'you' and 'your' statements.

The examples below completely eliminate the customer from the story and don't explain the practical benefits a customer would receive if they choose to purchase products/services from that vendor:

'We have a large fibre footprint'
'We have really extensive geographic reach'
'We have transparent pricing'
'We don't throttle internet services'

'We provide a world-class infrastructure'
'We have a team of experts'
'We provide 24/7/365 support'
'We have extensive experience in both public and private sectors'

In other words, vendors are leaving it up to the customer to decipher how their claim that 'we have really extensive geographic reach' translates into the problem the customer is looking to solve or the benefit that they are hoping to gain.

In addition, we found that the 'why us?' story on every company website typically boiled down to three things:

- **Cost:** *'We understand your need to control costs'; 'We offer scalable solutions to match your budget and changing demands'; 'We can save you money by rationalizing your IT structure'.*
- **Product:** *'We offer tailored and customized solutions'; 'We offer robust and reliable solutions that ensure optimal uptime'; 'We provide cloud, hybrid cloud, VOIP, network, connectivity, and managed services'; 'We provide solutions that help you collaborate and give great customer service'.*
- **People:** *'We have extensive experience in the private and public sectors'; 'We have global reach and extensive resources'; 'We will be a great partner'; 'We have an amazing team of experts'.*

When every company in the sector claims to have the same 'unique' approach of providing 'tailored solutions… at a reasonable cost… developed by experts', this isn't differentiated at all, and customers start to tune out.

Empty promises and no real proof

Most of the companies we reviewed do attempt to explain how their product or service will affect their customer's business performance at a high level.

As you can see with the statements below, however, these claims are extremely generic and lack real proof and evidence that the company can deliver on their lofty promises.

'We will help your business grow'
'We offer customized solutions that are scalable'
'We can reduce your costs'
'We can reduce cyber threats and increase your security'
'We provide integrated business solutions'
'Our technology can transform your business'
'We can help you transform'

'We support your digital transformation'
'We help you accelerate business growth'
'We accelerate your digital transformation'

For example, 'We can reduce cyber threats and increase your security' leaves the customer wondering 'by how much?' and 'have you done this before for other companies like mine?'

Our favourite claim, 'our technology can transform your business', comes across as an arrogant and mammoth declaration when you discover that the 'how' behind this statement is to simply 'buy our products'. How can a telecommunications company claim to make such a significant change in a business's life simply by implementing a new fibre-optic connection? It's absurd and customers can see right through this!

We call these type of claims 'vanilla insight' – customer insight that is so generalized it could apply to almost any business rather than showing real understanding of your ideal customer's business needs. Of course, all businesses want to 'reduce costs', 'grow revenue', and 'improve customer experience', but our question is – which one of these is a top priority for your ideal customer? Many companies simply don't know how to answer that, so they include a laundry list of benefits on their website hoping that one of them will resonate with a prospective customer.

When our marketing and sales colleagues in the telecommunications sector reviewed our initial whitepaper, the feedback we received reinforced that the issue of 'sameness' was not only prevalent in the industry, but also somewhat accepted as the norm:

> *When I was a telecom salesperson there were no differentiators. It was all the same, and we focused way too much on product features. It was never: Here is how we solve your unique problem, Mr Prospect. But, on the one hand, that's where sales comes in. It's their job to understand the individual company. A marketer's job is to (hopefully) understand industry-specific applications (Tina, former telecom account director).*
>
> *Looks like there is a bunch of creative people working at Telcos :-) (account director, global telecom provider).*
>
> *Too often, the marketing strategy and communications strategy does a great job of discussing features and advantages, but NOT the benefit of using the technology/product. Maybe we could learn how to better use our ears and eyes, when in front of our customers, to understand exactly what the consumer/buyer really thinks they need (B2B sales consultant).*

What we found particularly interesting is that these comments were from Fortune 500 companies with large internal marketing departments, and significant access to resources. Despite all this, they were still unable to effectively explain what makes their organization different than all of the other players in the industry.

TABLE 1.1 Sea of Sameness research summary

Industry	Industry overview	Sea of Sameness?	Key findings	Our takeaway:
Telecommunications	• 150-year-old industry • Standards-driven	Yes	1 Generic business and technology terms dominate communications 2 It's all about the company, not the customer 3 Empty promises with no proof points	The telecommunications industry has reinvented itself many times as new technologies enter the market. That said, they seem to forget that it's not about the technology, but about what the technology will enable and equip someone to do.
Data Centre	• 20-year-old industry • Experienced significant and rapid growth • As technology changes quickly, companies are at a crossroads to innovate	Yes	1 In love with their products 2 Only addressing the IT decision maker 3 Same 'why us' story everywhere	The data centre industry is enjoying a growth curve and the need for marketing/sales innovation has been non-existent. As customer preferences and demands shift, the industry needs to wake up from its complacency.
Higher Education	• 500+-year-old industry undergoing a reinvention	Yes	1 Overpromising a cliché of human needs 2 Missing what's truly unique about their university 3 Only speaking to one audience	Universities are at a crossroads to reestablish the value they offer to prospective students.

Not just a telecommunications industry problem

After we published our findings, we wanted to know – was this just a phenomenon happening in the telecommunications industry? Or were other industries affected as well?

We performed the same analysis in the data centre industry by looking at the top 30 global players and in the higher education field, looking at 38 universities in the UK. Our research found that, yes, this issue is happening elsewhere, but with a few slight nuances, as depicted in Table 1.1.

CASE STUDY #2

Key findings in the data centre industry

Let's start with a little context about what's happening in the data centre industry. A data centre is basically a physical facility that helps businesses connect their servers (physical and virtual) in a centralized location to support business applications like email, CRM, collaboration services, etc. Data centre companies provide businesses of all sizes with the real estate, infrastructure, power, cooling systems, backup generators and connections to 'the cloud'. The current industry is relatively new, born out of a need for constant internet connectivity in the 1990s and early 2000s.

Since both consumers and businesses continue to consume large amounts of data, the industry is subsequently experiencing tremendous growth. For example, the latest Cisco Visual Networking Index indicates that annual global IP traffic will reach 3.3 zettabytes by 2021, a three-fold growth rate over five years. This staggering growth in data consumption contributed to 40 per cent growth in cloud infrastructure, worth $12 billion in 2018 alone (Danheiser, Johnston and Kelly, 2019).

So with all this rapid growth, you may be wondering why should data centre companies bother looking at how they deliver and communicate value to customers?

As Price Waterhouse Coopers (PWC) summarize in their report, 'Enterprise Data Centre Buyer Survey and Interview Insights' (2017), 'the role of the data centre has now changed from being an infrastructure provider to a provider of the right service at the right time and the right price.'

This means data centre companies can no longer sit back and wait for business to fall in their lap, but they must actively prepare for changing customer demands.

Our research into the data centre industry, which was published in our whitepaper, 'Caught in the Calms of Complacency: Why data centre companies need to get ahead of the next wave now' (2019) uncovered three key takeaways:

1 Data Centre companies are experiencing a false sense of security

We found that the top 10 most frequently used words across data centre company websites and Twitter feeds were 100 per cent product-focused terms, such as 'cloud', 'hybrid', 'security' and 'networks'. Similar to the telecommunications industry analysis, these words do nothing to explain the benefits of using such solutions.

This smells of what Ted Levitt, in his seminal *Harvard Business Review* article (1960) called 'Marketing Myopia' – when companies fall in love with their product, rather than what problem they are solving for the customer. Sears, Blockbuster and Kodak are all examples of companies that suffered and ultimately failed because they lost touch with what need they were filling for their customers.

Cheryl, product marketing director for a large data centre company, jokingly shared with us: 'If there's one thing we know, it's our products. We love to talk about our products and honestly, it's so much easier to talk about features than customer benefits.'

What Cheryl points out is that it takes a lot of work to understand what customers really value. When you are eating, living and breathing your product every day, you may be blinded into thinking that everyone else has the same level of obsession for your product that you do.

2 Talk business. Not just Technology

Also similar to the telecommunications industry, data centre companies are primarily targeting the IT decision maker. While IT departments undoubtedly wield significant influence when it comes to these types of purchases, data centre organizations are forgetting to address other influential groups such as Operations, Engineering, Business Development, Product Development, Finance and more.

Read through the statements below and you will see that they are filled with jargon that doesn't quite ignite a passion for change! Remember – data centre companies are selling complex IT solutions to various-sized enterprise customers. But these lacklustre buzzwords don't help quantify the value that the right data centre partner could bring to you:

> 'When your business demands unparalleled agility, scalability, reliability and performance, (our product) is changing how data centre networks operate.'
>
> 'The growth of Big Data is increasing demand for cloud-based high-performance computing.'
>
> 'From latency to accessibility, the benefits of having your data centre nearby are many.'
>
> 'We architect data centres with consideration for critical needs – responsiveness, agility, sustainability, and automation – with future scalability'.

3 An identical story

Companies are claiming to provide the same value to prospective customers using generic, unsupported and bland claims.

Figure 1.2 depicts the story we saw from nearly every company. On the left side, the data centre company promises to help their customer externally – meaning how they will help their customers serve *their* end customers and shareholders better. On the right side, the data centre company pledges to address internal operational concerns for the customer and their employees. The middle column explains why the data centre company is uniquely qualified to be able to provide such results. Unfortunately, the story is hardly unique, as it appeared in some shape or form on every website we reviewed.

FIGURE 1.2 Data centre marketing claims

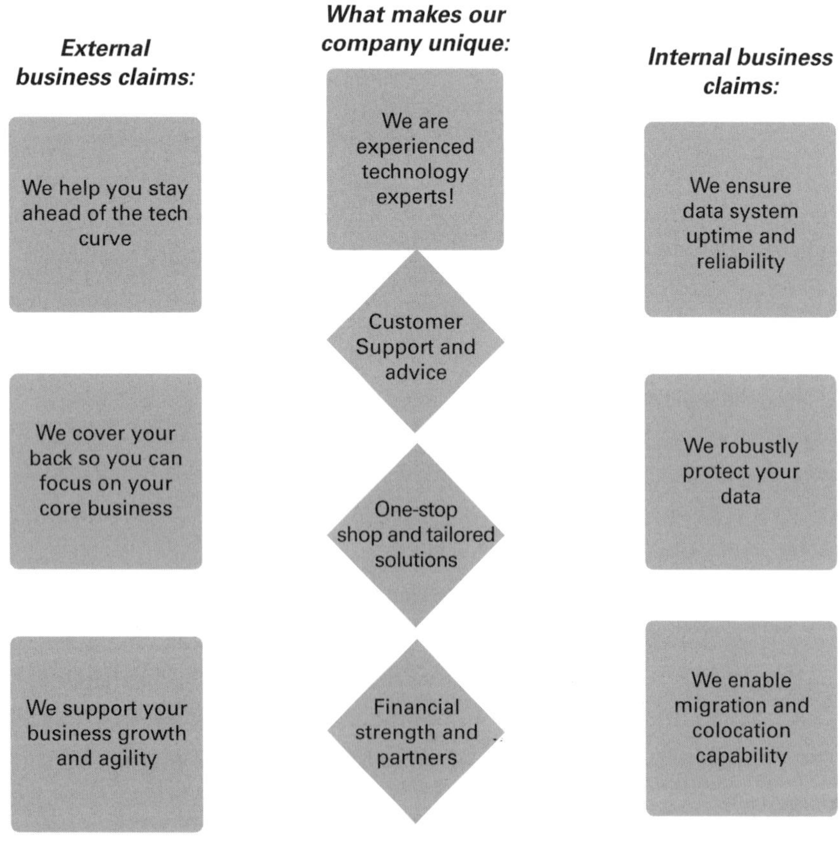

SOURCE Danheiser, Johnston and Kelly (2019)

CASE STUDY #3

University communications suffer from sameness

In this case study, we investigated 38 universities in the UK higher education sector.

The university as we know it today dates all the way back to the 1080s, with Oxford and Cambridge being among the world's oldest universities. In recent years, the university sector in the UK has focused on growing revenue streams by charging more tuition fees to full-time students and offering short-term sessions, seminars and workshops aimed at small business owners and corporate employees. As students are viewed as having a choice, university marketing spend on branding and differentiation has gone up in an attempt to attract more students. The driver of increased student choice was the higher education funding review of 2012, a process that is still ongoing as governments seek to ensure student value for money. Today universities are reliant on students fees with up to 47 per cent of teaching income coming from student fees and less than a fifth from government (Universities UK, 2016). Universities compete for student fees locally, nationally and globally. Today more than ever before student choice is influenced by explicit independent rankings of satisfaction and excellence that were not available to students in the past.

Furthermore, criticism for real-world relevance and applicability makes potential students stop and ask, *is this class/programme really worth it?*

Universities also compete for research and consultancy projects. Universities are uniquely positioned to help shape not only the lives of their students, but the communities in which they operate, the corporate partnerships they form and policy makers. Thus, they have a complex marketing problem to communicate value to a variety of audiences with differing needs and criteria.

Here are the key findings from our analysis.

1 Big promises to transform lives and fulfil personal potential

There's no doubt that a student's life looks completely different from the time they enter university to the time they graduate.

The narrative on these websites to 'transform lives' seems to hit on all of the essential human needs and desires! We found this to be a cliché, as universities make high-level, generic promises to build tomorrow's leaders. They may as well be promising to give students the moon.

For example:

'We care about health and wellbeing'
'We provide a great student experience'
'We have state-of-the-art buildings, learning spaces and resources'

'You will develop original ideas and thinking'
'You will belong'
'We have a vibrant student community'
'You will be inspired, stretched and challenged'
'You will fulfil your potential'

A small student focus group we did, however, didn't care or relate strongly to self-actualization, and instead focused more on the basic functional need of getting qualified for a job/career after they graduate. Research has shown that human brains aren't fully formed until the age of 25, so these lofty, rational messages about transformation and self-fulfilment are likely missing the mark.

2 Universities talk too much about themselves

Businesses and universities alike generally attempt to differentiate based on their product and people. But very little is done to showcase what makes the people and product so special. In the case of universities, we found several websites highlighting their campuses using similar photos and virtual tours. While this does give a feel for what the view is like around campus, the connection to the greater community in which they reside seems to be weak and contrived.

'Every single university has to sell the city that it's in and show how the student will be employable when they graduate', said Siobhan, University Marketing Director. Showcasing the facility, the course guide and the campus environment is considered table stakes in university marketing. 'Every single university runs a course that people are interested in. It's just that the building's different, and the academics are different people. But the product or service that we're selling isn't necessarily different.'

The line 'it's just that...' is telling, as these could be the very things that are the difference that set one university apart from another in the eyes of students. Surely these are the 'academics' and other people that students will come into contact with and can be what makes one university stand out from another.

3 Focus on student life

Tweets using the terms 'Student' and 'University' are student interest-focused in a way that differs from the generality and wide scope of information provided on main websites.

As depicted in Figure 1.3, the vast majority of tweets are chatter about ongoing campus life and events, research the institution is doing, and the activity of professors. Interestingly there are three values-related terms which stand out relating to respect, health, and the world. 'Respect' aligns with desire to portray an appreciative and welcoming brand image, 'health' resonates with an increasing concern with student and staff well-being, and 'world' reinforces the globally connected aspirations of the institution.

Tweet themes indicate textbook, careful control by central marketing to reflect a consistent impression that the university wishes to 'give off'. Whilst each tweet might be unique, the generic thematic impression means that every university is talking broadly about the same things; there is no difference from university to university.

Further, while some universities have sub-pages dedicated to serving other audiences, such as local businesses, these pages try to talk to everyone about everything all at once. As a business professional, you would essentially have to 'get lucky' to go onto Twitter and find something relevant to you.

FIGURE 1.3 Most frequently used words in university marketing

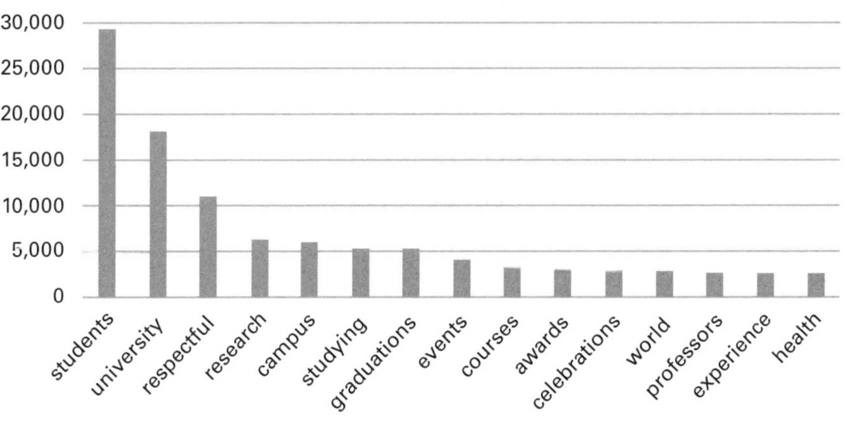

Recognizing the Sea of Sameness is everywhere

Once we started to recognize that this pattern exists across multiple industries, we reached out to get feedback from business, marketing and sales leaders across various sectors via in-depth interviews and questionnaires to better understand:

1 if companies realize this is an issue in their industry; and

2 how well they think they are differentiating themselves.

On the positive side, business, marketing and sales leaders aren't oblivious to the sameness problem happening in their industries.

One thing we did hear is that the sameness issue seems to be more prevalent amongst large companies operating in many markets, across many different product lines, versus the smaller, more 'niche' players who are able to hone in and provide one thing really well. Robson, former President at a large telecommunications company, observed that, 'Large companies that have a whole series of segments and markets to serve – from banks to government to hospitals – struggle with "Sea of Sameness" because they aren't as focused as the smaller, regional players.'

This makes sense; as companies expand their portfolio of services and enter new customer segments, they risk becoming 'jack of all trades, master of none'.

Companies that compete in more commoditized markets, like telecommunications, financial products and IT services, recognize the value of being able to differentiate their organization from the competition.

> Eighty-one per cent of survey respondents thought that it was 'extremely important' for their organization to be able to clearly articulate what makes their solution different to prospective customers.

So while differentiation is recognized as an important factor in business, many leaders admit that they struggle with HOW to differentiate themselves.

Siobhan, university strategic marketing manager, noticed that there are competing priorities which make it even more difficult: 'There have been so many initiatives that makes the institution more and more commercial, that instead of following the herd, I think every university desperately wants to be different. We just don't know how.'

> Only 5.4 per cent of survey respondents claim to be 'extremely effective' at differentiating their organization from their competitors, with the majority (54 per cent) stating that they are only 'somewhat effective'.

As Kristen, CMO at a financial services company, summarized:

> The Sea of Sameness is an issue not only on the communication side, which is how we ultimately end up using words in our marketing and sales materials,

but also on the product side itself. So our company is taking it seriously at the product development stage to inject something that makes the product itself completely different so that we ultimately use that point of differentiation in our messaging.

COPYCAT MARKETING

Jennifer, a VP of marketing in the technology industry, recently had her chief revenue officer approach her with a request to refresh their company website. They had just gone through a company acquisition, and needed to update the website to reflect their new brand and company offering.

When she asked what his timing was, he said 'ASAP'. He was getting pressure from the board of directors to increase revenue of the newly combined company, and he thought the website was certainly not doing them any favours to attract potential customers.

Now, if you've ever been through a website redesign, you know this project can take months of back and forth before the new site is ready to launch.

Jennifer jokingly told her boss that the only way to get something created quickly was to 'copy and paste' what was on their competitors' websites, since everyone in the industry says the same thing!

Following the herd

The core of this book aims to address the question: why is the 'Sea of Sameness' happening everywhere? And what can organizations do to solve it? Crucially, we will be exploring whether there is a people issue out there that is generating the Sea of Sameness phenomenon.

We look to early literature on the topic of 'herd mentality' to help shed some light. Herd mentality was a term first popularized by Wilfred Trotter, an English surgeon and social psychologist, during the First World War (1914–18). Trotter (nd) explained this phenomenon in his book, *Instincts of the Herd in Peace and War.* He found that humans, like herds of animals, can be influenced by the majority.

You've likely seen 'group think' happen at team meetings or in focus groups – when people set aside their own personal beliefs in an effort to achieve peace and consensus within a group. When this psychological principle is applied to the subjective art of marketing communications, which can often become a hotly contested exercise about what to say and how to say it, you can understand why some leaders may just 'give in' to keep the peace within the group and help move their projects along, rather than stand up and fight their point of view.

The bottom line is that we, as humans, have a deeply ingrained desire to be included – and this does not just impact how we behave in personal situations, but also in business.

As Tom, CMO at an advertising agency, put it: 'There's a great deal of safety in copying your competitors... After all, who is going to argue with your message if your competitors are also saying the same thing?'

> Herd instinct is a mentality characterized by a lack of individual decision making or thoughtfulness, causing people to think and act in the same way as the majority of those around them.

But being different isn't for the faint of heart. There's a significant risk involved in standing out from the crowd, and another psychological theory is at play here: *prospect theory*. This occurs when decisions need to be made and individuals evaluate 'will I gain more than I stand to lose?' As Herbert, former Sales VP for a mobile phone company wisely noted: 'Bravery and desire to be different can be killed by middle management (due to fear).'

So do today's marketing and sales leaders lack courage and bravery when it comes to taking a risk in what value they deliver to customers and how? *Or do they lack the competencies required to help their organization stand out from competitors in a way that's meaningful and valuable to customers?*

In the next chapter we will take a deeper look at why the Sea of Sameness seems to be occurring.

> CHALLENGE
>
> *Do you leave customers swimming in a Sea of Sameness?*
>
> Through our formal research, conversations with practitioners, and experience in a broad range of industries, we have a strong hunch that you and your organization leave your customers swimming in a Sea of Sameness, making it hard for them to make a meaningful choice between you and your competitors.
>
> Take a look at your own website and those of your top three competitors, and answer the following questions:

1. Do we clearly tell customers the benefits they will get from buying our products/services?
2. Does our 'why us' story explain why a customer should choose our solution vs the competition?
3. How similar is our 'why us' story to those of our competitors?
4. Do we use industry jargon and buzzwords to explain what we do?
5. Do we address all decision makers involved in the purchase?

References and further reading

CSO Insights (2019) All that glitters is not gold: key findings from the CSO Insights 2019 World-Class Sales Practices Study [online] https://www.csoinsights.com/wp-content/uploads/sites/5/2019/06/2019-World-Class-Sales-Practices-Study.pdf (archived at https://perma.cc/8XXT-ZU2M)

Danheiser, S, Johnston, P and Kelly, S (2018) Lost in a Sea of Sameness: lack of differentiation dominates the telecoms industry, Whitepaper [online] www.shakemktg.com (archived at https://perma.cc/4KV5-Z2KB)

Danheiser, S, Johnston, P and Kelly, S (2019) Caught in the calms of complacency: why data centre companies need to get ahead of the next wave now, Whitepaper [online] www.shakemktg.com (archived at https://perma.cc/GN5V-X2BS)

Goldring, D (2017) Constructing brand value proposition statements: a systematic literature review, *Journal of Marketing Analytics*, **5** (2), pp 57–67 [online] https://doi.org/10.1057/s41270-017-0014-6 (archived at https://perma.cc/RHE4-JS6C)

Hanan, M, Cribbin, J and Heiser, H (1973) *Consultative Selling*, Amacon

Iyengar, S and Lepper, M (2000) When choice is demotivating: can one desire too much of a good thing? *Journal of Personality and Social Psychology*, **79**, pp 995–1006

Kelly, S, Johnston, P and Danheiser, S (2017) *Value-ology: Aligning sales and marketing to shape and deliver profitable customer value propositions*, Palgrave Macmillan

Lecinski, J (2014) ZMOT: why it matters now more than ever, Think with Google [online] https://www.thinkwithgoogle.com/marketing-resources/micro-moments/zmot-why-it-matters-now-more-than-ever/ (archived at https://perma.cc/L4GD-VRA5)

Levitt, T (1960) Marketing myopia, *Harvard Business Review,* **38** (4), pp 45–56

Payne A, Frow, P and Eggert, A (2017) The customer value proposition: evolution, development, and application in marketing, *Journal of the Academy of Marketing Science*, **45**, pp 467–89

Price Waterhouse Coopers (2017) Enterprise Data Centre Buyer Survey and Interview Insight. Available from: https://junipernetworks.lookbookhq.com/c/Smart-Cloud-IntegrationEducation-ea4?x=Y3HmgD (archived at https://perma.cc/R24N-MG4U

Schwartz, B (2004) *The Paradox of Choice: Why more is less*, Ecco, New York

TEDSalon NY2011 (2011) How to make choosing easier with Sheila Iyengar [online] https://www.ted.com/talks/sheena_iyengar_choosing_what_to_choose?language=en (archived at https://perma.cc/UAM2-REFP)

Toman, N, Adamson, B and Gomez, C (2017) The new sales imperative: B2B purchasing has become too complicated. You need to make it easy for your customers to buy, *Harvard Business Review*, **95** (2)

Trotter, W (nd) *Instincts of the Herd in Peace and War*, Project Gutenberg

Universities UK (2016) *University Funding Explained*, p 4

02

Why does sameness happen in B2B marketing?

In this chapter we will:

- examine why sameness happens even when firms are trying to be different;
- explain how to distinguish between differentiation and distinctiveness and why this is important to you;
- share what experienced professionals tell us about their experiences of creating differentiation in practice

Introduction

Chapter 1 showed how sameness is a key factor that leads to 58 per cent of B2B deals ending in 'no decision'. Customers clearly find it hard to choose between one supplier and another when offers look the same. To get to the bottom of why this is the case, we had to find out what sales and marketing people actually meant when they talked about differentiation. We wanted to know if differentiation was a commonly used term. For example, did it mean the same thing to everyone? How did the idea of differentiation influence and shape sales and marketing practice?

Why does sameness happen?

The Sea of Sameness is the consequence of a lack of meaningful perceived difference between your value propositions and brand compared to your competitors. A key feature of sameness is the herd mentality of supplier organizations in a sector. As markets develop, company offers converge over time and start to look alike in terms of products and services and sound alike in their marketing communications. For example, Apple were the first in the market with their unique iPhone design and now most phones follow the Apple design style. A similar thing happened with the Audi A5 car, when virtually every major manufacturer followed the A5 look. The sameness of offer and communication has been observed by Chris West (2020), CEO of Verbal Identity, in his white paper 'What happens now that neo-banks aren't new', in which he discusses the sameness of new FinTechs like Revolute and Monzo. Best practice soon becomes bland practice. Indeed there is a real commercial downside to sameness, with several research investigations such as those undertaken by Banker, Mushruwala and Tripathy (2014) and Parnell and Brady (2019) showing that it is only through differentiation strategies that a positive and enduring effect on performance can be achieved.

So why does sameness and herding happen? The people we interviewed told us there are six principal reasons that drive sameness and the herd mentality:

1. The comfort blanket of success.
2. Risk aversiveness to try something new.
3. Inexperienced executives.
4. Inward-looking executives.
5. Being locked in the organization's mindset.
6. Laziness.

The noticeable thing about all of these factors is that they are about personal competency rather than the performance of products and services in the market. They all refer to things that relate to the way people think, and make business choices. Let's look closer at each one and bear in mind that each one can appear as a combination in your organization.

The comfort blanket of success

This is a typical company reaction seen in mature markets where early competition has been shaken out or acquired, leaving a few dominant suppliers. Herbert, managing partner in a consultancy, saw this as commonplace:

> ... we've gone to a point now, where in a lot of markets, it's difficult to tell the difference because markets are so mature... whereas I think you can be very differentiated when you are just going into a new market.

Success dulls market and customer intelligence-gathering senses and encourages a sense of misplaced confidence in the company's ability to keep winning. The comfort blanket of success creates conditions where executives believe they are on top of the job so they expect few if any surprises from competitors and the way customers buy. Norman, head of marketing, recognized this as a very common problem:

> All the lessons are learned the hard way, because when things are going well people just cruise along, and don't ask themselves why it's going well; senior staff only ask themselves why when things go badly wrong.

Risk aversiveness to try something new

Jerry, a marketing consultancy owner, said sameness indicates risk aversion, and saw playing it safe as:

> Just sticking to what marketing executives routinely know and what marketing school told them was necessary to know.

Of course, we all have different attitudes to risk and our attitude to risk is also influenced by the situation in which the business finds itself. A business with deep pockets and a culture of experimentation and non-blaming for failures means risk taking is more likely.

Another paradoxical effect of success is that successful brands dominate distribution which means buyers are loathe to take purchasing risks on something new and so everything follows this success and sameness becomes self-fulfilling. Whilst buyers might find the idea of something new and innovative appealing, their buying decisions are actually risk averse and this encourages sameness even more.

Similarly, successful suppliers operate with an 'if it ain't broke don't fix it' attitude, preferring incremental rather than revolutionary product-service development. This leaves them vulnerable to challengers who upset the apple cart with sometimes radically new ways of doing things. Just like Uber changed the taxi business, or when Rolls-Royce changed the airplane industry by shifting their business from the one-off sale of individual aircraft engines to aircraft manufacturers to leasing airplane engines with their 'fly by the hour' business model. The fly by the hour approach meant the aircraft manufacturers saved on the capital outlay and only paid for the time the engine was in use. Both parties benefited from a service package based on real-time continuous monitoring of engine performance. In a virtuous circle, the manufacturers got more reliable engines and Rolls-Royce got data to support continuous design improvements.

Inexperienced management

This is related to risk aversion, albeit it is most prevalent with early career professionals. The operating mantra is, stick with what works. The mindset is one that thinks, 'If it works for the competition it will work for me'. That said, general lack of ability even at the leadership level plays its part too, as telecommunications company (telco) president Robson explained:

> I mean, if the leadership across sales and marketing don't have the wherewithal to truly flesh out the differential storyboard, then the easiest default is to make sure that you've got at least a competitive parity message.

Inward-looking executives

Everyone at the executive table should be customer oriented. When this isn't the case trouble is likely. When the marketing function (who you would expect to be very customer focused) lacks customer orientation the problem is made far worse. It was observed that some marketers judged their success by how well they project managed their marketing agency rather than how well they directly understood what customers need. These so-called 'marketing managers' rarely engaged directly with their sales teams and rarely spent time with their boots on the ground interacting with customers. The need for marketers to devote time and energy to looking outside the organization was essential in the opinion of Norman, head of marketing:

> If we're going to talk about 'differentiation' let's do so with substance, and back up its usage with a huge dose of well-researched, credible reality.

Being locked in the organization's mindset

Being locked in an organizational mindset is when you lack the ability to escape the beliefs and assumptions you have about markets, customers and competitors and the way your business works. Gareth Morgan (2006) in his book *Images of Organization* called it a Psychic Prison. It is the dominant paradigm of the company and is typically set by the CEO and leadership team. It refers to the idea that people can get locked into traditional ways of thinking about their business and find it hard if not impossible to take on new ideas and points of view. Everything is justified by the phrase 'we've always done it like this'. Christine, a VP of sales and marketing in the telco sector, presented a vivid picture of this:

> Basically all of the mainstream telecom providers are offshoots of the Bell System. They have those common roots, ancestry, mindsets, and physical telecommunications plant, network, things like that. What that means is that you've lots of people with sort of the same mindset and this means you get commoditization of product sets.

A similar observation was made by Herbert, managing partner in a consultancy, who noted:

> I think people can become institutionalized. The more you work in a particular environment, the more you become part of it.

Recruiting and keeping on people in your own likeness is a double-edged sword and contributes to reinforcing the traditional world view of the business. Sure, you get people who have similar values and approaches but the downside is lack of critical viewpoint and an undue reverence to current customs and practices. Recruiting from outside the conventional pool of candidates stimulates critical thinking because diverse perspectives are introduced (Amabile, 1996; Rigby, Gruver and Allen, 2009; Reid, de Brentani and Kleinschmidt, 2014).

Laziness

Herding is simply laziness. The attitude here is, 'I'll copy the competition and just tweak it a bit'. It's a 'couldn't care less' attitude that seeks short cuts and easy gains. Robson, a telco president, was highly critical of what he called the cut-and-paste approach:

> People devote a nanosecond to defining what a valuable and differentiated proposition should be. They spend much more time on product collateral with lots of technical features. There is a lack of time devoted to articulating the true value proposition. People just cut and paste what everybody else is saying.

Herding means that suppliers are competing for the same market space, the so-called red ocean described by Chan Kim and Renée Mauborgne – a space where 'products become commodities, and cutthroat competition turns the red ocean bloody', a space where 86 per cent of product launches are line extensions, delivering 39 per cent of profits compared with launches in less competitive space that delivered 61 per cent of profits (Kim and Mauborgne, 2005).

We wanted to find out more about businesses fighting hard to get a competitive advantage, and what was going on inside firms that allowed markets to gravitate consciously or unconsciously towards sameness. Surely firms didn't want to be the same as their competitors, we thought. Based on our business experience and hundreds of business conversations over the years we concluded that sameness and difference in value propositions must have something to do with the capabilities, attitudes and behaviours of people inside vendor organizations, the very people responsible for making sense of markets, interpreting customer requirements, developing product-service solutions and designing value propositions.

Resolving the challenge of differentiation for B2B is made even more urgent as buyers do more and more pre-search and shortlisting online. When 60 per cent of the sales process is initially interacting with marketing channels, generic 'brand marketing' serves little purpose other than providing some evidence of credibility that the business is bona fide and serious. Deals will only be won through specific sales differentiation.

Differentiation and distinctiveness: what's the difference and why it matters to you

Two crucial marketing tasks play a significant part in business performance. These are what Mark Ritson, adjunct professor of marketing at the University of Melbourne, Australia and Lancaster University, UK, describes as 'differentiation and its more superficial, extrovert cousin called distinctiveness'. He discusses these concepts in his 2019 *Marketing Week* article, 'Distinctiveness doesn't need to come at the cost of differentiation':

1. **Differentiation** is ensuring the relevance and value of the proposition to the customer.
2. **Distinctiveness** is grabbing customer attention; cutting through competitive noise.

The so-called differentiation versus distinctiveness debate has generated controversy about which of these is the most important for sales and marketing effectiveness and gaining competitive advantage. The focus of much of this debate takes place in B2C marketing and relates particularly to the field of advertising. Central to this debate is deciding if it is customer awareness-making and repetition of advertising or product-service innovations that creates commercial success. We think the answer is that both are important to B2B but in different ways. You need to be distinct to be noticed and at the same time you need to be differentiated in a way that matters to the customer and the solution they are seeking.

Differentiation

Romaniuk, Sharp and Ehrenberg (2007) tell us that there is almost an unquestioning reverence given to the idea of differentiation in the world of marketing. Differentiation is accepted as such a commonsense idea that any challenge to it is marketing heresy:

> Differentiation is regarded as one of the core principles of marketing theory and practice. The near-universal exaltation is 'thou shalt differentiate' (eg Fulmer and Goodwin, 1988; Levitt, 1980; MacMillan and McGrath, 1997) – with the clear implication that marketers should be judged on how well they differentiate their brands.

Ted Levitt captured the differentiation sentiment in his 1980 article 'Marketing success through the differentiation of anything', which introduced the idea of three layers of solution: the core deliverables or 'table stake essentials' for being in business, the expected deliverables of any good supplier, and the augmented deliverables that set the supplier apart from the competition. And so, as marketers we've had it drummed into us that innovation is the key marketing priority and the only way to secure a lasting competitive advantage is by differentiation. As a theory for marketing success, differentiation works like this:

Differentiation:

- stimulates demand by offering improvements leading to more sales and profit;
- positions the product-service offer as unique in the mind of the customer;

- creates products and services that are valued;
- generates brand loyalty and reduces the costs of new customer acquisition;
- secures sustained competitive advantage.

All of these things mean you create more customer value and as a result sell more and make more money, which in turn justifies premium pricing and enables the vendor to resist the downward price pressure that comes from commoditization. The sources of differentiation can come from products, people who deliver the customer service experience, different channels to market, and brand associations and perceptions.

It's worth bearing in mind that we often use the word differentiation rather loosely. Over the years, a key part of the idea of differentiation has been lost and so many marketing people have lapsed into believing that it's just being different that matters and that difference is best communicated through distinctiveness. This often results in an inside-out, self-referencing view of what constitutes 'good marketing'; you can see this in the ubiquitous 'about us' pages on corporate websites. However, the critical part of Levitt's idea of differentiation is that differentiation has to be *meaningful* from the customer's perspective. Does the difference being proclaimed have some sort of value for them? That meaningfulness can be any or a combination of functional, perceived/symbolic, relational, experiential or societal value that is relevant to the customer.

Distinctiveness

Distinctiveness addresses the way buyers process information. Psychologist Hedwig von Restorff (1933) showed that the more distinctive something is, the more memorable it becomes. By grabbing the buyer's attention in some way, distinctiveness ensures that when the buyer has a need they will remember the distinctive offer above all others. This is the basis of the well-known AIDA marketing communications model – attention, interest, desire, action – which states that in order to get the buyer to act, you have to grab their attention first. The technical term for grabbing attention is *salience* and it is achieved in three main ways:

1. an amazing fact, such as that there are more mobile phones in the world than toothbrushes;
2. a shocking image, such as those used by fashion house Benetton; or
3. an unexpected contrast, such as a gorilla playing the drums to the Phil Collins song 'In the Air Tonight' in Cadbury Chocolate advertising.

As well as being memorable, distinctiveness also plays a role in switching the buyer's mind from Mode 1 thinking to Mode 2 thinking, as described by Daniel Kahneman (2013) in his book *Thinking, Fast and Slow.* Distinctiveness causes the buyer to move from a disinterested and ambivalent Mode1 mindset to a full attention Mode 2 mindset. This shift is a key part of what Petty and Cacioppo (1986) call Elaboration Likelihood, the likelihood that you will want to find out more about the thing that has grabbed your attention.

Distinctiveness is not without its downsides. Many B2B professionals downplay distinctiveness for being way too reliant on subjective emotional cues such as appeals to creating happiness, improving personal status or giving a sense of personal achievement, claiming these things have little real influence on sober, rational business people. Another problem with distinctiveness is that it can become very self-indulgent or lapse into poor taste just for the shock effect in terms of language and images that are used. Used uncritically, the end of 'attention grabbing' justifies the means of using anything to shock the customer. This is a dangerous situation in terms of corporate social responsibility and means that marketing communications creativity can't be allowed to carry on unfettered because there are ethical, brand image responsibilities to be accounted for. That said, B2B customers are human and so must be subject to the same principles of cognitive information processing and worries that keep them awake at night – what IBM described as their fears, uncertainties and doubts and a sense of professional identity. This means there is a role for a balanced use of emotional appeals in business-to-business communication. We will be returning to the idea of balance frequently in the following chapters.

It is worth noting that marketing communications and branding education in business schools is predominantly based on B2C cases, and B2C mass marketing methods; McDonald's, Apple, Google, Procter and Gamble and so on are the usual case study subjects. This means the unthinking application of a B2C distinctiveness approach in a B2B context is problematic because it assumes professional buyers think and act exactly like consumers. This assumption should be avoided in order to ensure that distinctiveness in B2B is appropriate to the market context.

What experienced B2B professionals told us about the pursuit of differentiation and swimming away from sameness

The background above gives a general picture of the issues and debates surrounding differentiation and our interviews allowed us to get a deeper grasp of what was going on in the pursuit of differentiation in B2B.

Some of the issues people told us about echoed theoretical debates such as the difference between differentiation and distinctiveness and the difference between professional competency versus using operational marketing skills. Other insights came as a surprise, such as discovering that differentiation and sameness have both good and bad qualities. We also learned more about the central role of face-to-face customer experience in B2B for providing vital insights into the specific value and differences customers were looking for from their suppliers. Crucially, it became clear that although everyone recognizes the importance of differentiation, it actually meant different things to different people in the organization. And above all, perhaps the most telling thing that people told us was that achieving differentiation is hard, very hard indeed, as Herbert, CEO of a consultancy firm, emphatically told us:

> I think it's really hard, actually. I work with a lot of clients and they all struggle... they struggle to articulate what the difference is really. Even though they've got a lot of slide ware, if you were to ask them, 'what makes you different from one of your competitors?' they do struggle a bit.

The pursuit of differentiation in B2B is hard work

When you pick up any standard marketing management textbook and look up differentiation, it will point you to a couple of paragraphs at most telling you what it is and why companies need it to succeed. This is typically followed by some straightforward advice on doing market research, segmenting customers by their psychological characteristics, behaviours and benefits sought. There is absolutely nothing about just how difficult it is to make differentiation happen in practice and the sorts of real-world challenges and obstacles that can get in the way. Five things that make the job of differentiation hard stood out from our interviews:

1. articulating the essence of what makes you truly different isn't easy;
2. addressing differentiation takes time, energy and commitment;
3. technical-product inertia diverts energy and attention from real differentiation work;
4. lack of deep customer insight dilutes differentiation effectiveness;
5. the bigger you are the tougher the job of differentiation gets.

Many of the professionals we spoke to commented on just how hard it is to articulate what is particularly different about what they do for the customer and get this across in a way that will change the buyer's behaviour. Tom, a former CEO and current advertising agency CMO told us:

> It is one of the most puzzling things I've seen in my career. Brilliant marketers walk into the room, yet their messaging falls flat or isn't differentiated. How can someone so smart and disciplined come up with something so bland?

There were a series of reasons why articulating your difference is a challenge. Firstly, it requires a significant commitment of executive time, effort and soul searching. Often, the time available to do this is scarce, and the issue is even actively avoided in the busy day-to-day life of organizations. Time is needed to carefully assimilate and make sense of customer insights, challenge current beliefs and assumptions about the way the business is done and really put a finger on what the source differentiation actually is. Secondly, there is the challenge of overcoming technology and product inertia where the focus of executive attention is on communicating the details of solution features and technicalities. This problem gets worse when the product catalogue is large and there are lots of things to say about the details of each product. Christine, VP of sales and marketing, explained how a technical obsessiveness can sap the attention and energy needed by sales and marketing teams as they wrestle with the details of defining differentiation from a customer rather than product point of view:

> Technologists and product marketers get enamoured with the actual technology. Whether or not that technical aspect is materially different than a competitor's technical aspect, is perhaps really not examined that much; they don't ask themselves, where does this really position me in the marketplace?

Thirdly, differentiation is hard because it is often hampered by a lack of direct customer insight. This results in generic value propositions and brand promises created from the desks of remotely situated marketing executives who rarely spend time with real customers.

Robson told us that:

> I think generally people don't have the depth of competitive intelligence to truly know what's differential or not from the other offerings.

The other problem that Robson brought out was that accessing customer insight costs money and is often something that gets cut back when belts are tightened. This short-term viewpoint can have a catastrophic effect on the quality of understanding about where opportunities for competitive differentiation lie.

You are in effect fighting with one hand tied behind your back when you lack competitive intelligence and this only fuels a further problem of generality. If you don't have specific customer insight you can only communicate in generalities. This means marketing communications teams energetically communicate to everyone in the market at the same time, but the only way to communicate with everyone is to do it at such a level of generality that it is virtually meaningless. This is problematic in three ways for organizations who want to differentiate:

- First, a generic understanding of the world of the customer means you provide bland claims of differentiation, for example, 'we can help you in the digital future', 'experience our difference', or 'we transform your business'.
- Second, you lack what Siobhan, head of marketing, called a signature strength – something that singles you out and you are self-confident enough to accept that in doing that you might push away some potential customers. A differentiated brand should actually push some customers away because the offer isn't directly relevant to their needs.
- Third, the way marketing materials are actually used in customer interactions by the sales team is overlooked. In Jerry's experience this indicated a lack of customer insight by the marketing team whereby they actively avoided 'delving into the real customer experience', which frustrated him hugely in the following way:

> ... and we're saying, 'Go back to sales because you need to know how it's being used? Who is going to use it? Who is it going to? What do they need to know?'... and they [marketing] can't answer these questions, they're not getting answers and I say, 'Well you can't create anything until you know these answers, because otherwise you are just creating stuff'.

'Stuff' can be a real problem when you are trying to differentiate. The brand-building urge to be distinctive drives the marketing function to generate stories and lots of them in the hope that something will stick. This problem seems to get worse if the organization is big. Global organizations lack customer sensitivity and responsiveness compared with their small and middle-sized, more focused competitors. Lines of communication are longer; there is more bureaucracy, more people with a say. As Katie observed:

> ... when you have big companies I feel like you have 'the too many cooks in the kitchen' problem around developing your messaging and your differentiation.

This point is something that Robson, telco president, agreed with:

> I see more sort of sea of sameness when I'm looking at the larger players versus when I see some of the pure play regional or more focused approaches... big telcos either regional or global, they just have so much to plan, they have so many products. They serve so many different customers, and they compete against so many competitors, that they don't have the fidelity to truly draw out the differentiation.

The idea of fidelity is crucial for the creation of differentiated value propositions. It's to do with how well your value proposition is tuned in to particular contexts and particular customers' needs. Fidelity enables you, and therefore, the customer, to cut out the rubbish and select only the really valuable things that are needed to make the offer stand out.

Differentiation means something different to people with different roles

When we asked people about the role sales and marketing played in the job of differentiation, we were struck by what Bob, Chief Commercial Officer at a large building services company, had to say. Bob pointed to a fundamental challenge in organizations that hinges on the differentiation distinctiveness debate. Simply put, classic marketers are trained to emphasize brand building and awareness at a generic level and salespeople are trained to seek and understand what specific solutions customers are looking for. Sales and marketing people operate at different levels of analysis. They actually have different world views. Here's what Bob said:

> In terms of differentiation, I think marketers just perceive it's all about building a brand and brand awareness. I see differentiation as knowing what you're doing and why you're doing it, and why you're putting something into the marketplace. I think a lot of marketers really do not understand that, they don't understand the customer base, or understand the true basis of differentiation despite what they will tell you.

We believe this difference of perspective between sales and marketing needs to be called out. If marketing has no role in market intelligence gathering, no role in customer-specific value proposition production, all it has left is the job of corporate communications and PR – worse still, it is pejoratively named 'the colouring-in department'. When that happens, it has been successfully branded as a junior player in the organization. This is not to argue that brand building and awareness should be dismissed and trivialized;

as we've explained above, what we are saying is, don't fall into the trap of thinking brand building and awareness is your singular and fundamental source of differentiation in B2B.

Don't use the word differentiation when you mean distinctiveness

Many of the people we spoke to recognized that the job of differentiation should not be confused with the job of distinctiveness. What is very clear is that differentiation means different things to different people and that often when marketers speak of differentiation they actually mean awareness and salience of the brand rather than the competitive difference of the value proposition. Martin, Chief Commercial Officer of a large building services company, emphasized the importance of getting a good understanding of what people in the organization actually mean when they talk about differentiation:

> Yes, very much so but I think you need to define what you mean by differentiation. And I think a lot of marketers talk differentiation, and it's all about differentiating the brand and everybody's reared on building the brand and all of that, without really understanding where and how you're actually competing.

In this case differentiation is seen as evidence of winning deals, rather than winning attention.

Recognize that differentiation operates at different levels of sales and marketing activity

Inconsistency of what is meant by differentiation was also seen as problematic by Herbert, managing partner at a consultancy. In particular he noted that there are different levels at which differentiation works – a generic brand level of difference and a customized account level of difference:

> I think the term is not used consistently. For me, differentiating in sales is very much about what's on the mind of the client and me differentiating what I'm trying to sell to them, in a very individualistic way... differentiation in marketing is more what I would perceive to be more your points of parity and points of difference... differentiation in sales, it's about the value in the eyes of the beholder. Otherwise, marketing is much more I think driven on a more general level.

Here differentiation in a sales context is understood as something unique that emerges between people during a sales interaction rather than something intrinsic to products that can be written down and generally communicated.

Make sure differentiation is at the heart of your business model, not just a communications afterthought

If marketing is seen as just the awareness-making and lead generation function, marketing are frequently left with no choice but to focus on, or are simply expected by the C-suite to create distinctiveness. In fact, some marketers recognize that achieving differentiation is not within their remit and this can create problems in terms of authentic communication, as Regina, VP marketing at a mid-size data centre company told us:

> Differentiation isn't created by marketers. It's created when you build the business. And if the business wasn't built with that in mind, then it's going to be very difficult for a marketing organization to make up that differentiation in a credible way.

Credible differentiation is central to successful business performance. Differentiation has to have a direct link to the substance of the proposition from a customer point overview. If marketing claims lack an obvious connection to the customer's real-world problems then you are heading for trouble, as marketing consultancy owner Jerry told us in no uncertain terms:

> ... with words you have to have substance in order to say something unless you are prepared to write nonsense. Lack of substance means you are prepared to write brochure-ware or mere blah copy... if there isn't enough substance behind the offer, there isn't enough difference, then it's vanilla and it's down to price. Nothing more than price or convenience.

Avoid mystical differentiation at all costs

Proximity to the customer is essential in the case of specialized market sectors and sophisticated buyers and as we have noted, mistakes often happen when marketers with a B2C background try to apply the same rules of emotional appeal communication used in B2C to B2B and ignore commercial realities. As Terry, CEO of a second-tier telco, explained, it was customer proximity that drove product superiority and differentiation rather than brand distinctiveness or what he calls 'mystical differentiation':

> I don't think we have differentiation challenges; I've got a lot of direct customer experience. Over the years I've tried to do mystical differentiation even down to selling the emotion of a phone call. In the end we sell hard on product superiority to very sophisticated buyers, and we try to make those sell at the point of compelling event.

The risk here is that companies become obsessed with issues of brand image at the expense of real customer needs. Jeff, a business unit president and former CIO, made this point clearly when he told us:

> Most companies that I've ever worked with or for... people don't understand that focusing almost exclusively on the difference or the things that set you apart as a provider are really what matters. A lot of times we want to communicate all the things that we do that may or may not be relevant to the differentiation question.

The complexity and challenge of avoiding value proposition Sameness can be shown using the idea of a Value Stack (Kelly, Johnston and Danheiser 2017). This means thinking about multiple value propositions as layers representing increasing levels of proposition customization and granularity. The base of the stack has to be a complete grasp of what is going on in the business life of the customer and only works when it is specific information from customers about their business pains and aspirations. From that basis value themes can be generated that bundle together combinations of individual product/service solutions. For example, an assortment of solutions can be arranged under, say, a business agility theme, future scanning theme, or a digital security theme. Individual solutions may sit in more than one proposition theme. These can then be targeted at verticals, specific accounts and further still specific decision-maker roles in the customer account. Thus:

> Stack base = deep customer understanding from face-to face-meetings.
>
> Thematic layer = products/services arrayed as themes that reflect key customer issues.
>
> Verticals layer = propositions targeted at different market sectors.
>
> Account layer = propositions targeted at customers within a sector.
>
> DMU (decision-making unit) layer = key influencers and decision makers within an account.

What is it that really makes you different from your competitors?

There was something very interesting that emerged when we explored this question. On the one hand people told us about the importance of *product differentiation.* However, even though this might deliver practical functional value to the customer, as we have mentioned, this can be a short-lived advantage and it can leave you prone to features-led communication. On the other hand, everyone mentioned that they believed the way they did business set them apart. We would call this *CX or customer experience differentiation*, and we believe it is central to the pursuit of B2B differentiation. CX was portrayed as inimitable, difficult to reverse engineer and involves:

- difference in personal face-to-face approach to customers;
- difference in the problem recognition and solving experience customers receive;
- difference in style of collaborative engagement;
- difference embedded in trust-building interactions between people.

CX differentiation is related to the cultural, personal and interpersonal nature of the organization. Jeff, business unit president for a large IT services organization, told us:

> Differentiation is not just what you sell but how you sell it. Get the best and most capable people you can to be able to understand the impact of your solution in business rather than the bits and bobs of the feature set.

What we are talking about here is a resource-based view of differentiation rather than a positioning view and it strikes at the heart of the difference in approach to differentiation taken by sales and marketing. CX differentiation depends on ensuring your business plays a meaningful role in the world of the customer. CX differentiation achieves a type of competitive difference that product differentiation can't. Tom, business owner, former CEO and advertising agency CMC stated:

> What I have seen in my career is that there isn't a ton of differentiation between one product or another but I have found that if you can find a spark and say what is different and meaningful about a company, then you actually live this out. For example, company X chose to make their brand promise all about customer support – fanatical support. They embraced it everywhere and lived it out compared to other brands in the space.

Differentiation and sameness come in good and bad varieties

One of the really interesting things that we noted from our interviews which came as a surprise was the fact that differentiation and sameness can come in good and bad varieties. Recognizing this and making the appropriate judgement calls on differentiation or sameness is a critical competency. Here once again we were being told about the abilities of people in the pursuit of differentiation.

- **Good differentiation** resonates with customer needs and gives value they will pay for.
- **Bad differentiation** mistakes distinctiveness and superficial image making for differentiation.

A critical approach to good differentiation is being able to ask tough questions about the true relevance of the offers you are making to customers. Robson, telco president with a sales background, talks about forcing the differentiation issue:

> I force the issue around clearly articulating your differentiation. This is about not pretending you've got something differential when all you really have is a me-too. I test if we truly understand what the customer wants and have we got something that's different and special and standout.

Good differentiation also cuts both ways. Unless the supplier can appropriate value from the deal as well as the customer then it is commercially impractical and leaves you prone to customer worship and giving money away. As Robson went on to explain to us:

> It is vital that you can truly identify differentiation, and make sure the customer values it and actually wants to pay for it. If you've got something unique but customers don't really value it to the extent they'll pay for it then it's not really valuable.

Bad sameness unthinkingly follows the herd and reverts to a commodity.

Good sameness reduces investment risk and saves time.

John, business investor and product development and strategic marketing director, explained that:

> Differentiation is affected by attitude to risk. Following the herd is for the risk averse. It does have a place though.

Good sameness means not reinventing the wheel and innovating unnecessarily. If sufficient market share and profits can be gained through being similar to the competition then it might be appropriate to follow the crowd in some circumstances.

The key takeout, however, is that commercial experience and wisdom are needed to make good and bad calls. What it seemed we were being told was that product and service differentiations were only surface manifestations of something much deeper going on that resided in the abilities of the executives responsible for differentiation.

Differentiation and distinctiveness don't happen by themselves

This might seem like a very obvious statement, but we want to emphasize that differentiation has to be grounded in customer reality. You can't make it up, it can't be so abstract that it doesn't resonate directly with real customers and their real needs. Differentiation is not an intellectual indulgence. It isn't word-smithery, you can't re-describe an undifferentiated offer into a differentiated offer because the customer will see through it.

From our interviews, a clear picture emerged that pointed to differentiation effectiveness being inextricably bound up with the ability of people and their ability to:

- differentiate in a good way;
- understand what differentiation means and how it differs from distinctiveness;
- recognize and manage the paradoxes they face;
- make judgement calls on when to differentiate and when to be similar;
- recognize the vital significance of social skills and having direct face-to-face interactions with customers.

This is a cultural issue and it seems clear that differentiation and distinctiveness become whatever the people in your organization assume these two concepts are for them. Differentiation will be shaped by the appetite of people in your organization to wrestle with knotty problems, push boundaries, challenge assumptions and take risks. This is significant. It means that the type of differentiation and distinctiveness you get has its roots in what your people think those concepts are about in the first place. So, in your organization what do these words mean? What do they refer to? What decisions and actions happen as a result? If you think differentiation is changing the colour of the letterhead, doing what you've always done, or following the herd because there is less risk of being fired – then guess what... that's exactly the sort of differentiation you will get.

Finally, one of the biggest traps to be avoided is assuming that differentiation only occurs with products. Of course, intuitively and from experience, many of the people we spoke to know this. That said, it's worth making it explicit, so here are some broad-brush considerations.

TABLE 2.1 Value focus considerations

What	Differentiated Value Focus
Revenue	Pricing and payment model
Products	Function and utility
Service	Relationship: trust, collaboration, commercial network access
Experience	Attentiveness, problem solving, helpfulness, seamlessness
Channel	Busines model, omnichannel integration

A final provocative thought comes from VP of marketing Christine:

> I define it in more classic terms. Differentiation is the concept of what is the discrete and tangible problem you're solving for the customer? Or what is the discrete intangible revenue opportunity you're enabling for the customer? It's a pain or gain question. What pain is your product or solution removing? Or what gain is the user getting from it?

It seems clear that the fundamental issue of differentiation means that it has to be grounded in reality, it has to address the real-world problem of the customer and to do that you have to deeply understand the business life of the customer. You can't do B2B differentiation from behind a desk. In B2B, you can't construct a realistic meaningful difference with words and images alone. This is an issue of organizational culture, leadership and professional mindset – something we will be addressing in detail in Chapter 10.

QUICK EXERCISE

Where do you score on good or bad differentiation?

Norman, head of marketing, talked about what he called 'legitimate' differentiation – this is differentiation that is based in the everyday reality of the customer's world. This is good differentiation. Bad differentiation lacks a connection to the customer's reality, relies on inside-out marketing, and emphasizes image over substance.

Thinking about differentiation in your organization, where would you place the approach taken in your case? You can separate the sales and marketing function by placing S for sales and M for marketing on the scale of 1 to 5.

What issues does this raise for the pursuit of differentiation in your organization?

FIGURE 2.1 Good differentiation–bad differentiation scale

Bad differentiation				Good differentiation
1	2	3	4	5
Remote from the customer's real-world problems				Very close to customer's real-world problems
Generic propositions				Customized propositions
Details extensive product range				Technically focused solutions
				Strong social interactions

Conclusion

- **It's VERY hard to differentiate** in a way that resonates with the customer, is better than the competition, and is something the customer will pay for.
- Differentiation is not the same as distinctiveness – both have a job to do.
- You need to invest **thoughtful** time, effort and resource into differentiation – this time can often get reallocated to firefighting everyday issues.

- **Differentiation is *assumed* to happen at the product level.** When asked about why this is challenging to create, nearly everyone said 'our products are the same' and the real difference happens in the way we interact and engage with our customers. It is a people thing, not a product thing.

We have now reached a point where we are interested in developing professional competency to create good differentiation and to look more closely at the question, 'What are the *people things* that make you stand out?' The next chapter looks at five key competency areas that are necessary for swimming away from the Sea of Sameness.

References and further reading

Amabile, T M (1996) *Creativity in Context: Update to 'The social psychology of creativity'*, Westview, Boulder, CO

Argyris, C (1999) *On Organizational Learning*, 2nd Edition, Wiley-Blackwell

Banker, R, Mushruwala, R and Tripathy, A (2014) Does a differentiation strategy lead to more sustainable financial performance than a cost leadership strategy? *Management Decision*, **52** (5), pp 872–96

Clift, J (2016) Millward Brown on why salience isn't everything – and magazines still matter. WARC Event Reports, *Magnetic Breakfast*, May

Fulmer, W E and Goodwin, J (1988) Differentiation: begin with the consumer, *Business Horizons* (September–October), pp 55–63

Kahneman, D (2013) *Thinking, Fast and Slow*, Farrar, Straus and Giroux, New York

Kelly, S, Johnston, P and Danheiser, S (2017) *Value-ology: Aligning sales and marketing to shape and deliver profitable customer value propositions*, Palgrave Macmillan

Kim, W C and Mauborgne, R (2005) Blue ocean strategy: from theory to practice, *California Management Review*, **47** (3)

Kowalkowski C *et al* (2017) Servitization and deservitization: overview, concepts, and definitions, *Industrial Marketing Management*, **60**, pp 4–10

Levitt, T (1980) Marketing success through the differentiation of anything, *Harvard Business Review*, January

MacMillan, I C and McGrath, R G (1997) Discovering new points of differentiation, *Harvard Business Review*, **75** (4), pp 133–41

Morgan, G (2006) *Images of Organization* (updated ed), SAGE, London

Parnell, J and Brady, M (2019) Capabilities, strategies and firm performance in the United Kingdom, *Journal of Strategy and Management*, **12** (1), pp 153–72

Petty, R E and Cacioppo, J T (1986) The elaboration likelihood model of persuasion, *Advances in Experimental Social Psychology*, **19**, pp 124–29 doi:10.1016/s0065-2601(08)60214-2.

Reid, S E, de Brentani, U and Kleinschmidt, E J (2014) Divergent thinking and market visioning competence: An early front-end radical innovation success typology, *Industrial Marketing Management*, **43**, pp 1351–61

Rigby, D K, Gruver K and Allen, J (2009) Innovation in turbulent times, *Harvard Business Review*, **79**, June

Ritson, M (2019) Distinctiveness doesn't need to come at the cost of differentiation, *Marketing Week*, 28 March

Roach, T (2019) The stupidity of sameness and the value of difference, *BBH Labs* [online] http://bbh-labs.com/the-stupidity-of-sameness-and-the-value-of-difference/ (archived at https://perma.cc/P6PX-Y46G)

Romaniuk, J, Sharp, B and Ehrenberg, A (2007) Evidence concerning the importance of perceived brand differentiation, *Australasian Marketing Journal*, **15** (2)

Sharp, B (2008) Differentiation vs distinctiveness, *Marketing Science* blog [online] https://byronsharp.wordpress.com/2008/04/10/differentiation-vs-distinctiveness/ (archived at https://perma.cc/2DTQ-CE35)

Sharp, B and Dawes, J (2001) What is differentiation and how does it work? *Journal of Marketing Management*, **17** (7–8), 739–59

Vandermerve, S (1988) Servitization of business: adding value by adding services, *European Journal of Management*, **6** (4)

Von Restorff, H (1933) Uber die Wirkung von Bereichsbilding im Spurenfeld [On the effects of the formation of a structure in the trace field] *Psychologische Forschung*, pp 299–342

West, C (2020) What happens now that neobanks aren't new? White Paper, Verbal Identity

03

The V.A.L.U.E. competency framework – core competencies for B2B differentiation

In this chapter we will:

- introduce the 'Value' competency framework – critical competencies to help you swim away from the Sea of Sameness, and connect to customer value;
- explain how the 'Value' framework was developed and the importance of each of the 'Value' competencies.

By now it should be abundantly clear that this book is all about the competencies, attitudes, and behaviours that business leaders, marketing and salespeople need to develop to help their organization swim away from the 'Sea of Sameness', and towards the 'island of uniqueness'. In order to be accepted on the island of uniqueness, you have to be able to demonstrate unique value to your customers. At this point you should be standing out from your competitors because you are differentiating in ways that matter to them, making it easy for them to choose you, rather than someone else. Arriving in the Nirvana we call the 'island of uniqueness' requires the demonstration of what we refer to as V.A.L.U.E. competencies.

We know that the definition of competency, like many other words in management, can be contested. The definition we like and will use throughout this book is:

> A competency is the set of behaviour patterns that the incumbent needs to bring to a position in order to perform its tasks and functions with competence (Woodruffe, 1993, p 29).

In other words, you have to be good at doing the things that you are paid to do in the role you have. We are compelled by an idea of British actor, Stephen Fry:

> We are not nouns, we are verbs. I am not a thing – an actor, a writer – I am a person who does things – I write, I act – and I now never know what I'm going to do next. I think you can be imprisoned if you think of yourself as a noun (Tim Lusher, *Guardian*, 2010).

In this book we present the competencies that people need to be good at to do their jobs as leaders, sales or marketing people as it relates to helping their organizations differentiate in ways that are compelling and meaningful to customers, while giving return for their own organization. This is what we call good differentiation.

V.A.L.U.E. competencies – what are they?

In the first two chapters we saw how through previous research we identified the problem of sameness and why we believe it is happening. In this chapter we will give you a framework that is memorable, practical, and in tune with the competencies needed to set your organization apart today, tomorrow, and into the future.

What better than a framework whose components together spell VALUE (Figure 3.1)? Here we will give just a brief introduction to what the competencies are, as in the chapters that follow each of the competencies will be discussed in detail. After we've introduced the competencies, we'll explain how we came up with them based on a combination of our own research, other credible research, through discussion with practitioners, sprinkled with our own experience in working in and with numerous organizations.

V = Visionary

Dictionary definitions of the word 'visionary' typically talk of a person with original ideas about what the future could be like. Visionaries are seen to have foresight and imagination, an ability to envision what might happen in the future. On the flip side, visionaries can be seen as dreamy or impractical.

When we use the term 'visionary competency', we think of someone who can provide a unique and insightful view of what the future might hold for their customer. Visionaries do need to be business savvy as they need to be

FIGURE 3.1 V.A.L.U.E. competency framework

Competency	Symbol	Description
V **Visionary**		Visionary competencies are needed to foresee potential changes in the broader business environment, and to paint a picture for customers about how the changing environment may affect them.
A **Activator**		Activation competencies are required to get buy-in to initiatives that are being developed to provide differentiation in the market and to drive growth in the business.
L **Learner**		How effectively people learn from changes in the environment, in what your customers value, and in what sets you apart from competitors.
U **Usefulness**		Usefulness competencies are about differentiating in a way that is relevant and resonates with customers. Tuning into customer needs to propose practical solutions.
E **Evaluator**		Evaluator competencies are required to make sense of the choices available to customers, potential profitability, and the ongoing success of marketing and sales campaigns.

able to paint a picture of a future world for the customer that they can help access. The future view needs to be in what Barta and Barwise (2017) call the value-creation 'V-zone', where future customer needs can be met profitably by the selling company.

Business leaders, marketing and sales professionals need to have vision, imagination, and to see the wood through the trees. Being a visionary requires the foresight and creativity to help you do something meaningfully different for your customers that separates you from competitors. By visioning you alert your customer to changes that are imminent, in the near distance, or on the horizon. To do this you need to be able to portray the future world in the customer context.

In today's environment there are lots of dynamically moving parts: there is the rise of US protectionism, the UK's exit from the European Union, there are questions about where the next international growth markets will come from beyond BRICS, and we have seen dramatic changes in societal attitudes to the use of plastics, waste, and global warming. We are currently witnessing a dizzying amount of technology that's currently out there: AI, blockchain, robotics, drones, 3-D printing... and, and, and. At the same time, many of us have dusted down our old vinyl record collections in a return to things nostalgic.

Who would have predicted a few years ago the rise of Uber or Airbnb? So, do you have visionaries in your own organization who have or can develop original ideas about what the future might hold for you and your customers?

WHY VISIONARY?

In research we performed for our previous book, *Value-ology*, in which we spoke in depth with a number of senior sales and marketing leaders, the need to be visionary for the customer to help create new value came through strongly. For example, Jeff, former MD of a global telco said:

> So, you must find ways to add value in your understanding of the client's industry, their business issues and how you can make them survive and thrive.

Like La Rocca *et al* (2016, p 55) we believe that:

> Renewing the offering and developing new ways to create customer value is a crucial issue for management in fast-changing contemporary markets.

In order to be able to do what Jeff is saying as a senior practitioner, you must have the visionary competencies to foresee where 'the client' and their industry are going. Without that you would not be creating the new offers La Rocca *et al* (2016) suggest.

Seventy-four per cent of the marketing and sales leaders we surveyed said that having the ability to be 'forward thinking' was very important. Interestingly, in line with how we view what Visionary competencies are, 92 per cent said that the ability to 'connect the dots' from customer needs to company solutions was very important.

We will explore Visionary competencies in depth in Chapter 5.

A = Activator

Once you get beyond the chemical and biological dictionary definitions, activation is all about making something or someone *active*, causing them to act. The dictionary definition we like best is 'to put (an individual) or unit on active duty' (Merriam-Webster dictionary).

To put an individual or unit on active duty gets right to the heart of what we mean by activation competencies. In order to successfully activate you need a bunch of competent activators. In order to get anything done in organizations large or small, you need to sell your ideas, create buy-in internally and mobilize the team. This requires collaboration, persuasion and negotiation. In addition, you need overall project management skills and an eye for moving the ball forward.

From a sales standpoint, it's long been acknowledged that you need to activate a whole range of people in the customer buying centre before you even consider potential users of the service you are looking to sell. We know that organizations are becoming more conservative in their buying behaviour and that the number of people required to sign-off a major deal is now running at 6.8 (Toman, Adamson and Gomez, 2017). There are clearly problems out there as we know that 58 per cent of deals end in no deal because the salesperson could not convince the customer of the value of changing (Qvidian, 2015). There are lots of books that have sold in big numbers that try to deal with the skills required by salespeople to activate customer buy-in leading to a sale. What seem to have had much less coverage are the activation skills required by sales and marketing people to get their own organization to create and develop solutions for their customers.

So, are your marketing and salespeople good activators? Can they mobilize people and teams towards their ideas? Are they able to put individuals or units on active duty to help deliver their ideas? Can they put themselves in their customers' shoes to activate and mobilize the rest of the organization towards giving the customer superior value to your competitors?

WHY ACTIVATION?

From our experience as practitioners who have worked in and with big organizations, we know that getting people with conflicting priorities to buy in to your ideas and mobilized to act is a big problem.

The challenge for marketers is in trying to activate salespeople to help drive through marketing programmes. Where marketing fails to involve sales in strategy development, sales view the initiatives as ineffective or irrelevant, which means they do not support the proposed plans (Rouziès *et al*, 2005).

In research we performed to understand how sales and marketing worked together to develop value propositions, practitioners were unanimous about the need to get buy-in and the positive effects this had on activation.

For example, Saskia, a marketing director with cross-industry experience in several different large organizations said:

> When marketing created customer literature with sales input it would be used in 100 per cent of sales calls. When marketing did things without involving the sales team you'd be lucky to find usage of about 20 per cent.

In short, we see activation competencies as key to deliver customer value and believe that activators can help your company swim away from the Sea of Sameness, towards the island of uniqueness.

We will explore Activation competencies more in Chapter 6.

> In our survey, 89 per cent of respondents said that the ability to execute was a very important competence, and 70 per cent said the ability to create buy-in was very important.

L = Learner = Learning

Of all the definitions of *learning* we have seen, the two we would settle on are 'the act of experience of one who learns' and 'to acquire knowledge or skills or a behavioural tendency'. There is a whole heap of difference between someone who sits in a training session and takes nothing on board and an active learner who will absorb the new knowledge and skills to make some behavioural changes in an effort to perform better: change behaviour, change results, as they say.

The field of business and marketing moves fast. We have already taken a brief look at some of a dizzying array of technologies that weren't even available a few years ago. If you are not dedicated to constantly learning and trying new things, you will find your knowledge, if not your job, redundant. Though, in the words of W. Edwards Deming (2000), 'Learning is not compulsory... neither is survival'.

A learner always wants to learn more about changes in the external environment, customers, competitors, new technologies, or business approaches. Being a 'learner' is at first a mindset and second a behaviour change. Customer research is not a once in a while thing you ask the market research team to do. It's a daily job that requires a cohesive learning loop between the customer, sales, and marketing. Especially in a world where customers now spend the first 60 per cent of the buying cycle gathering information from the internet and websites before they talk to a salesperson (CEB research).

So, how many learners, people that do learning, does your organization have? How many of them are in sales or marketing? How up to date are you and your team on what's happening out there?... and have you changed your behaviour or value propositions based on something new you've learnt?

> Only 63 per cent of respondents thought that 'a dedication to learn new things was very important'. But how can you be forward thinking, 'connect the dots' for customers or provide them with things that are useful if you are not constantly learning about what's important? Ninety-two per cent thought that connecting the dots for customers was an important competence.

From our standpoint, learning is at the heart of what sets organizations apart; that's why we have it as a key competency which we will cover in more depth in Chapter 7.

U = Useful

'Just because you are unique, doesn't make you useful.'

There are two definitions of the word 'useful' we like for slightly different reasons. 'Able to be used for a practical purpose or in several ways' (Oxford Dictionary) we like because we believe that practical communications that

FIGURE 3.2 Just because you are unique...

are developed for customers should help move a business problem forward, which in turn could make the lives of your own customers or employees better. This ties in nicely with the second definition, which is 'to be serviceable for an end or purpose' (Merriam-Webster dictionary). That means every time you communicate with a customer, they've got to be able to think that it was useful and that the information or advice they received can be put to use for their organization, customers, or for their personal gain. If you look for synonyms of *useful*, you'll land on actionable, applicable and practical. In order to be actionable, what you provide to the customer has to be relevant to them. You need a value proposition, which we define as 'A promise of expected future value, illustrating that future and relevant benefits will outweigh the total cost of ownership' (Kelly, Johnston and Danheiser, 2017) which demonstrates that by taking action they will get return. Crucial here is that what you provide is both unique and useful because if what you are offering is different but does not pass the useful test you'll be offering the customer a bent fork! You need to make it easier for the customer to choose you because you are offering something uniquely useful.

There is a problem out there, as we know that 94 per cent of customers say they have tuned off from organizations because they are sending them 'content' that is not relevant. On the flip side we know that 91 per cent of executives will forward useful information they receive on to colleagues (CEB research). Even armed with this knowledge, we recently spoke with a B2B marketing organization that expects to send out nearly 1,000 pieces of content to customers in the latter half of the year. If they followed the advice of our previous book *Value-ology* they would be communicating usefully through two or three themes relevant to what customers are trying to achieve – agility, productivity, or growth for example. But do organizations have the competencies to be useful... do they have people that understand and can do *usefulness*?

We can take a racing bet on the fact that your marketing and sales organizations are stretched. So, ask yourself: is what you are doing relevant and useful to customers? Do you have the competencies to help you answer this question and be useful to customers... to outswim your competitors?

WHY USEFUL(NESS)?

In research we performed to understand how sales and marketing worked together to develop value propositions, the sales and marketing leaders we talked with were very vocal about 'usefulness', by talking of its merits or citing examples of poor or bad practice.

For example, Erica, a marketing leader in a global IT company, said:

> So Global IT Co. has what I call a bunch of offerings which are bits of technology. So, let's go and sell them a bit of Widget X; let's sell them a bit of Widget Y. That means nothing to the customer if you don't put it in their context.

Erica seems to be suggesting the Global IT Co. is contributing to the 94 per cent of communications that customers tune out from because they are not useful or relevant. To make the communication about Widget X useful, the sales or marketing person has to be able to contextualize this for the customer in terms of how the Widget will help them.

Saskia pointed out that usefulness is a competence that applies to internal customers too, in this case highlighting what salespeople regard to be useful marketing work:

> What sales generally find the most useful are materials where the story absolutely resonates with our customer and where they have the ability to make small tweaks or customizations.

We are sure it will not have escaped your attention that the V.A.L.U.E. competencies are interlinked and need to work together to help you differentiate on customer value. Here we can see a close link between usefulness and activation; if the material marketing produced for sales does not resonate, customers will not be activated to use it.

And finally, practitioners recognize that usefulness is a difficult competence to master, especially as it relates to value propositions.

Terry, a seasoned sales vice president with experience in global mobile and technology organizations, said that producing compelling 'useful' value propositions required:

> a level of intellect and analytical capability that perhaps isn't always a requirement in an average sales force. I think it's still quite a rare skill in a way.

In Chapter 8 we will talk in more depth about the Usefulness competence and aim to shed some light on the 'rare skills' that a master in usefulness needs to possess.

> The 92 per cent of marketing and sales professionals who said 'connecting the dots' was a very important competence recognize this as an ultimate test of usefulness.

E = Evaluation = Evaluator

We see evaluation competencies as paramount at different ends of the marketing and sales cycle. The starting point for evaluation is linked very much to where visionary competencies sit. How do you make sense of what value a potential opportunity might be in the future? So, while a visionary would have to be the kind of person who can come up with an original view of where the future might take the customer, this has to be blended with more left-brain analytical competencies to assess the potential value of a future opportunity.

We have all seen the hype about 'big data', which runs to over 5 million articles on Google Scholar. Simply put, big data refers to the potential ability to collect and analyse the vast amounts now being generated in the world, from supermarket transactions to the photographs we put on Facebook and Instagram. With all the data that's supposedly available to marketing and sales teams do you and your team have the evaluation competencies to make sense of what the data is saying? Can your people provide unique interpretations of the data that competitors might not see?

At the other end of the cycle is analysing the results of marketing and sales programmes. We have all heard the saying mistakenly accredited to

Lord Leverhulme, 'Half of my marketing budget is wasted, I don't know which half'. Of course, this apparent fallacy does contain a very serious message because it is difficult to prove impact, particularly of marketing programmes. The advent of social media and internet technologies has made a number of things easier to measure: page views, click-through rates, etc… but these can be divorced from real sales and profitability numbers.

So, can you or your people really demonstrate ROI? The CMO traditionally is not highly perceived by the CEO or CFO because of the difficulty they seem to have measuring return. So, do you have the competencies to evaluate potential new opportunities, marketing and sales programmes? Or are you just guessing?

WHY EVALUATION?

This is not particularly a problem for salespeople, as generally if they hit their sales and revenue numbers life is good. That said, we do know that only 54.3 per cent of salespeople are on target at any point in time (CSO Insights, 2018). For marketers, this is a burning platform; there is lots of research out there which shows that marketers' apparent lack of ability to measure is perhaps the no.1 thing that damages the reputations and careers of CMOs. A recent CMO survey by Deloitte and Touche found that when asking what the top three success factors for the CMO were, the use of customer data came top, with proving quantitative impact coming in fourth. It's no surprise that CMOs have the shortest tenure of any C-level executives as they are increasingly being expected to take a more strategic role and deliver numbers. If they can't speak the language of shareholder value and operating margin they will not resonate with the CFO and CEO, which can only hasten their departure.

We've already seen that marketers often measure things in different ways to sales and we know this can cause tensions. Kyle, president in a global data centre company, when talking about a previous role as a sales leader, said:

> I can remember all the marketing scorecard being green while all mine was red; that just cannot be right.

Feeling the need to have to prove that marketing deliver value in order to have credibility conferred upon them can often lead to tension with sales. Davina, vice president of marketing of a global fintech company, and veteran of five blue-chip companies in different sectors, said:

> I think it's a very delicate balance between, you know, we're not trying to claim any territory but we are trying to prove the value and the ROI of what we're doing. And that I find is a tension point.

What Davina is hinting at here is that the pressure to prove value to sales and the broader organization can lead marketing to over-claim the role they may have played in bringing in business that might already have been in-flight.

The bottom line is that this is a problem specifically for marketers, affecting personal reputation, career prospects, relationships with other key players they need on their side, and crucially the ability to make coherent cases to ask for more money.

In Chapter 9 we will look at the Evaluation competencies needed to turn the reputation of marketers around and help them invest in programmes that help differentiate their organizations.

> The fact that only 40 per cent of our survey respondents viewed 'data analytics' as a 'very important' competency, is a reflection of this as an emerging competence that we believe will come to the fore in the future. The 89 per cent who saw 'ability to execute' as very important can only prove effective execution with robust evaluation in our view.

What's to come?

The rest of the book concentrates on the specific research we performed to understand the practitioner view on the competencies needed by sales and marketing people to help their organizations stand out in ways that resonate with customers… good differentiation. The competency research involved in-depth interviews with business leaders, sales, and marketing practitioners; a competency survey of practitioners; discussions with opinion leaders and experts (eg recruitment companies); and business conversations with practitioners.

Before we dive into questions about competencies we wanted to get an understanding of how the marketing and sales roles are perceived, which we cover in Chapter 4. Chapters 5–9 then look in depth at each of the VALUE competencies.

How do you fare against our competency framework?

So, now that you've learnt about our V.A.L.U.E. competency framework here's a simple competency self-assessment scoresheet for you to reflect on how you fare against each of the competencies. Firstly, think about how you fare personally against the five competencies. Give yourself a score out of 10, where 1 is poor and 10 is excellent, and make a note of what it is you do well in each competency area, and what you need to improve. At the bottom of the 'you' column total your overall score and make some observations of your strengths and key opportunities for improvement.

Next, think about the team you operate in and follow the same scoring process as you did for yourself. This time make a note of team weaknesses and strengths and call out any individuals on the team you think are strong in a competence area. After totalling the overall team score make some general observations of where the key opportunities for improvement are.

TABLE 3.1 Competency self-assessment scoresheet

Competency	You	Team
Visionary		
Activator		
Learner		
Usefulness		
Evaluator		
Total		

References and further reading

Barta, T and Barwise, P (2017) *The 12 Powers of a Marketing Leader: How to succeed by building customer and company value*, McGraw-Hill Education, New York

CSO Insights (2018) Selling in the Age of Ceaseless Change: The 2018–2019 Sales Performance Report

Deloitte and Touche (2019) CMO Survey Fall 2019: What insights can we gain from marketing leaders? [online] https://www2.deloitte.com/us/en/pages/chief-marketing-officer/articles/cmo-survey.html (archived at https://perma.cc/6N3V-ELNQ)

Deming, W E (2000) *Out of the Crisis*, MIT Press

Kelly, S J, Johnston, P R and Danheiser, S (2017) *Value-ology: Aligning sales and marketing to shape and deliver profitable customer value propositions*, Palgrave Macmillan, London

La Rocca, A *et al* (2016) Customer involvement in new product development in B2B: the role of sales, *Industrial Marketing Management*, **58** (1), pp 45–57

Lusher, T (2010) Stephen Fry reveals new BBC TV series, *Guardian*, 20 July [online] https://www.theguardian.com/media/2010/jul/20/stephen-fry-bbc-planet-word (archived at https://perma.cc/BD2K-E5PY)

Qvidian (2015) Sales execution trends. Research report [online] https://www.sellingpower.com/microsite/qvidian/sales-execution-trends-2015/?sp_src=WhitepapersRSS (archived at https://perma.cc/6KLK-JVNS)

Rouziès, D *et al* (2005) Sales and marketing integration: a proposed framework, *The Journal of Personal Selling & Sales Management*, **25** (2), pp 113–22

Toman, N, Adamson, B and Gomez, C (2017) The New Sales Imperative, *Harvard Business Review*, March/April

Woodruffe, C (1993) What is meant by a competency? *Leadership & Organization Development Journal*, **14** (1), pp 29–36

04

The role of sales and marketing in B2B organizations – what is important?

In this chapter we will:

- share our competency research – focusing on sales and marketing roles;
- outline what leaders saw as the most important facets of marketing and sales roles;
- provide a critical checklist to help you see if your marketing and sales teams are set up for success.

Before we turn our attention to the competencies required by sales and marketing people to help their organizations connect to customer value and 'stand out' from competitors, we wanted to understand how senior practitioners viewed the roles of sales and marketing, because from our previous experience and in earlier research we know that how the roles were perceived could be contentious, especially for marketing. While the task of selling is reasonably consistent across organizations the same cannot be said about the marketing function, which can range from purely tactical communications to full-service 'soup to nuts' marketing departments responsible for strategy, tactics, and execution.

After asking our research participants what they perceived the role of the named marketing and sales functions in their company to be, we then asked them to give a view on what the top three roles of each function were. Let's start with the less contentious one first – sales.

What is the role of sales?

From the wealth of input from our in-depth interviews, practitioner views centred around five key responsibilities:

- selling and execution;
- connecting the dots;
- balanced advocacy;
- customer experience;
- customer and market feedback.

We will look at each one of these in turn.

Selling and execution – it's all about execution

When asked the question 'What are the top three responsibilities of a salesperson?', a number of interviewees jumped to 'It's all about hitting the numbers'. This might seem trite, but we do live in a world where right now, according to the 2018–2019 Sales Performance Report (CSO Insights, 2019) only 53 per cent of sales reps are meeting their quota.

Robson, president of a global telco, took the execution role beyond just 'hitting the numbers' as more aligned to the market goals of the company. He described the primary role of sales as being 'the execution engine of the company to deliver the market plans that are set within marketing'.

Robson seems to suggest that marketing sets the go-to-market plan which the sales team executes, though hopefully not absent of sales input. At a more tactical level a number of marketers, such as Siobhan, a university marketing leader, talked about sales being responsible for 'converting leads into sales', often a point of contention. The need for alignment with marketing for effective sales execution featured in a number of our interviews. For example, Kristen, a CMO in the financial services industry, said a key role of sales was to 'complement marketing efforts to build a relationship to drive home the sale'.

From an execution standpoint, sales is seen to carry a joint responsibility with marketing – as Herbert, vice president of sales at a global mobile company put it, 'For being part of the marketing team and getting the message out there' – which builds on the point that Robson made, accepting that sales have a broader responsibility in executing the marketing plan. Other respondents believed sales had a joint responsibility in creating awareness of the offer, its difference from competitors, and setting the offer in the context of an individual customer.

'Connecting the dots' from customer needs to company solutions

It could be said that connecting the dots captures the whole essence of the role of a salesperson in an organization that seeks to grow and set itself apart based on customer value. By definition, here 'connecting the dots' means having a solid understanding of what problems your customers are facing and what their needs are, and being able to translate that into how your solution can *uniquely* solve their problem. The starting point requires an understanding of the customer's world followed by other key components for dot connecting identified by our respondents as:

- applying insight to the customer's world;
- understanding your own industry and company solutions;
- communicating your whole company offer;
- setting solutions in the customer's context;
- bringing partners to bear to enhance your solution.

Kirk, product management VP at a global telco, succinctly echoed what most of our interviewees said, that the sales team should 'Know their customer backwards and forwards', including whether the customer organization is

FIGURE 4.1 Connecting the dots

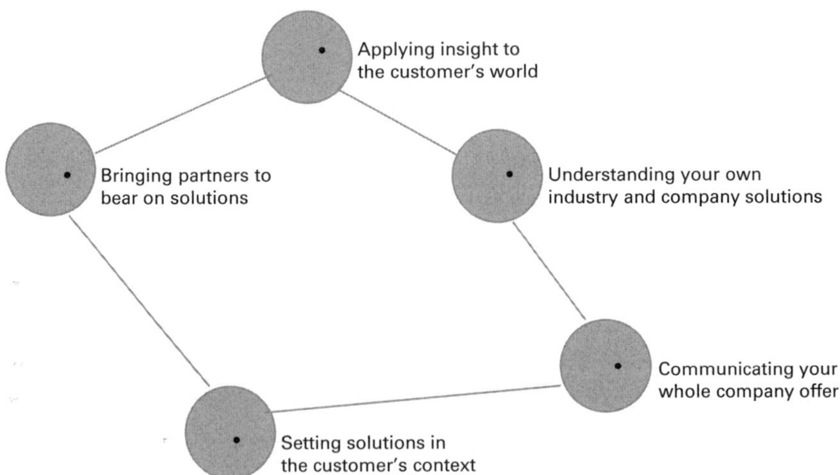

growing or shrinking, and who has decision-making power as facets of 'connecting the dots'.

A 2019 B2B buyers' survey showed that a prerequisite for 'connecting the dots' is being able to demonstrate knowledge of buyers and their needs (Demand Gen, 2019). Ninety-seven per cent of respondents agreed that it is important for sales reps to demonstrate a stronger knowledge of their needs and 95 per cent said that sales teams need to have more insights about their company needs. This level of understanding can be one thing that sets winning vendors apart and is essential for sales success.

Herbert saw providing context for the customer as a key element of connecting the dots, including 'applying your solution to the customer's world'. Before setting a solution in the client context the salesperson has a responsibility, as Siobhan and a number of others said, to 'make customers aware of the whole company offer' so they understand the overall scope of a potential range of solutions.

Kirk pointed out that bringing partners into the equation is sometimes needed in order to provide a customer with the required solution that solves a business challenge the customer has. What this could mean is partnering with other companies, so sales should be helping 'identify best-in-class partners'.

Here, as well as partnering as a sales role to provide better solutions for customers, Kirk is suggesting a broader role in providing feedback from the marketplace about who the best partners are.

Today's B2B buyers are more sophisticated than ever, with 67 per cent saying they prefer to conduct their own research online as a source of primary research (Wizdo, 2015). The flip side is that many buyers say that B2B buying is reported as growing ever more complex. In a buyer enablement study, Gartner (2019) found that 77 per cent of B2B buyers surveyed rated their purchase decision as 'extremely complex or difficult' due to the vast amount of information available and the growing number of people involved in the buying committee. Demand Gen's 2018 content preferences report (Demand Gen, 2018) found that 51 per cent of B2B buyers admitted to feeling 'overwhelmed' with the sheer amount of content available. A salesperson who can provide the customer with insight and 'connect the dots' is likely to get access to the customer earlier in the sales cycle as 48 per cent of buyers are open to engaging earlier with a salesperson who challenges their thinking (Aberdeen, 2019).

Balanced advocacy

Many of our interviewees put being an advocate for the customer across the whole of their own organization as a key responsibility of the sales organization. Traditionally a joint responsibility for marketing and sales has often been seen as keeping the organization customer-centric. For sales, this can involve ensuring that marketing, product management, customer experience, and the executive teams know what their customers want. Katie, chief executive of a software company, attached a high level of significance to the advocacy responsibility. She believed that 'advocating for what the customer wants is a key piece of how the sales team delivers the numbers'. Customer advocacy drives the salesperson to mobilize support for new solutions to customer problems leading to more sales and target attainment.

This can come in a number of forms: knowing what the customer wants and advocating for that across the business and taking responsibility for customer satisfaction.

The customer satisfaction element was something that Joseph, vice president of marketing, with a long track record in sales, called out:

> You can't be a successful salesperson and ignore customer satisfaction. You've got to sell the customer something that's working and meets their needs. If something is not working, you will often be the point person for helping the customer figure it out. I've seen over and over again – the best salespeople are great customer advocates too.

Joseph recognized that the salesperson does run the risk of getting in too deep and there's a line between advocacy and wasting too much time away from the sales numbers. In an environment where organizations are increasingly trying to gain advantage by superior customer service, this can be an increasing burden on salespeople who will have to balance the advocacy role with selling. We're sure this is familiar territory to many readers.

On the broader point of being the customer champion for all their needs, it was interesting to see leaders like Kirk, vice president for a product line in a global telco, with a long sales background, stressing *balanced advocacy* as a key facet of the sales role. While embracing the need for salespeople to advocate for the customer, Kirk believes that 'first and foremost, there should be balanced advocacy for your company' and that salespeople should not forget they 'do get a pay cheque from their own company'.

While sales and marketing have to be the voice of the customer to prevent inside-out product obsession, this has to be tempered with commercial realism. In their book *The 12 Powers of a Marketing Leader*, Barta and Barwise (2017) make a similar call for marketers to focus on issues that are important for customers and for their own business, in what they call the 'Value Creation Zone' or V-Zone. Kirk and other sales leaders seem to recognize

FIGURE 4.2 Zone of Balanced Advocacy

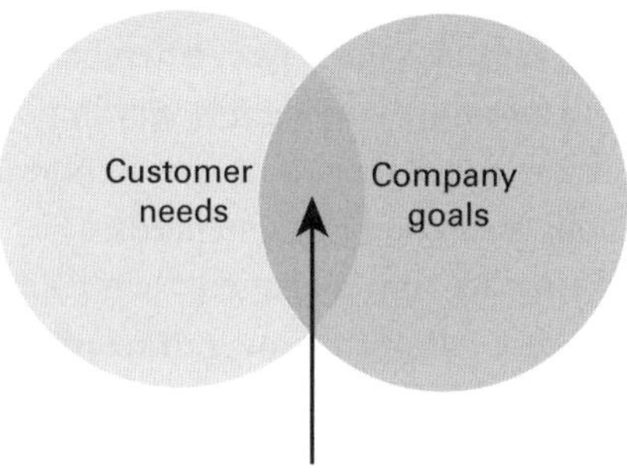

that advocacy should be focused in a sales advocacy zone where there is potential return for the customer and their own company.

We have all sat in meetings where we've heard a salesperson advocating for something on behalf of a customer that makes no commercial sense for our own company. We can certainly remember salespeople demanding faster service responses for their customers, which had not been paid for. This misguided type of customer obsession highlights the commercial need for balanced advocacy. Concentrating on things that can deliver benefits for the customer and your own company has to be a key ingredient for focusing on customer value to 'stand out', we call this the Zone of Balanced Advocacy.

Customer experience

We have already seen the importance attached to sales roles in advocating for the customer. Respondents certainly recognized the sales role in the overall customer experience.

Robson, for example, talked of the customer experience responsibility, specifically in relation to the customer interaction element of the job. In stressing that salespeople 'obviously have a customer experience responsibility, because they're interacting with the customers as much as anybody', Robson gives emphasis to the sales–customer relationship in the way he defines 'customer experience', which runs from pre-sale dialogue through post-sale service delivery.

So, how the customer feels about interactions with a salesperson can be integral to how they view the overall customer experience. Research by

Demand Gen (2019) found that the ability to demonstrate knowledge of their buyers and their needs is one thing that sets winning vendors apart; 97 per cent of buyers said it's important that sales reps can demonstrate a stronger knowledge of their needs, with two-thirds saying it is very important. Another 95 per cent of respondents also say that they think it is important for sales teams to have more insights about their company and needs.

If the customer is being account managed, then it's not just an individual interaction, it becomes more about the overall relationship and experience. For large organizations there may be lots of interactions between customers and different departments. Siobhan observed that 'One business could work with over 20 different people in the university'. She pointed out that this could be problematic for the business but cited a case where the university gave the customer 'A very good central point of contact, who could explain all the avenues open to him and sort of triage him in the right direction.'

In industries where account management is more well developed much more would be expected than to 'triage the customer in the right direction'. While there has been some debate over recent years, prompted by the publication of *The Challenger Sale* (Dixon and Adamson, 2013) about whether relationship selling has been replaced by challenging the customer with something new and insightful, practitioners still select relationship management as a key role for salespeople. This was writ large in our survey responses where respondents saw building long-term relationships with customers based on trust and delivering a win-win as fundamental to the sales role.

In a world where differentiation can increasingly be about customer experience the salesperson's role cannot be underestimated. Given that the salesperson sees the customer as much as anybody in your organization it is perhaps no surprise that the customer experience element of the role is seen by sales leaders as key to developing differentiation.

Customer and market feedback – the cohesive loop

Recent research has pointed to the fact that 67 per cent of a buyer's journey is now done digitally (Hauer, 2013). Often the interactions with the customer for the front end of the sales process are with your company marketing channels websites, direct mail, brochures, industry journals, twitter and other social media.

Our Sea of Sameness research covered in Chapters 1 and 2 tells us that there is a problem out there. If potential customers are looking at these sources and they all sound, feel, and look the same, how can this help but exacerbate the complexity of the buying process?

In the light of this problem it is heartening to see that many of our respondents, and especially sales leaders, called out bringing feedback from customers and the marketplace as a core responsibility for salespeople. Katie saw 'bringing back insight' from the market into the organization as 'a vital role for sales'.

Robson refers to the feedback loop as being important to 'keep the organization honest' about what customers really want. Interesting that he feels that the responsibility for providing the market and customer feedback to the organization may not be formally written into sales roles, even though this could be crucial to helping 'differentiate in a way that is meaningful to customers'.

Robson felt that by bringing customer and market feedback to the organization salespeople were 'Informing the organization to shake the proposition, so they can be more successful in the field'.

By doing this, the organization can provide something of value to the customer different from competitors, giving customers value to the point they are prepared to pay for it.

We see it as significant that the people with a sales leadership background we interviewed regard bringing back customer and market feedback from the field as fundamentally part of the sales role and one that can help develop 'meaningful differentiation'. Putting this customer feedback front and centre in the sales role reflects the increasing need for sales to bring customer intelligence to bear in a world where buying behaviour has changed and the front end of the buying cycle is spent by the customer interacting with marketing channels which can leave them swimming in a sea of sameness.

Sales roles – have you got them covered?

How does your organization shape up against the five key sales roles identified by our interviewees?

Here is a checklist (Table 4.1) of the five responsibilities and their components. For a role you have recently advertised, or may be planning to advertise, ask yourself if you have these responsibilities embedded into your sales roles.

TABLE 4.1 Checklist of sales roles

Role	Components
Selling and execution	• Hitting sales number • Executing company market plans • Getting the differentiation message out
Connecting the dots	• Applying insight to the customer's world • Understanding your own industry and company solutions • Communicating your whole company offer • Setting solutions in the customer's context • Bringing partners to bear to enhance your solution
Balanced advocacy	• Providing balance between customer needs and own company goals
Customer experience	• Recognizing role of sales interactions and relationship on customer experience • Owning experience from pre-sale through post-sale
Customer and market feedback	• Keeping company honest by bringing back customer needs, issues and trends • Provide insight to own company for better differentiation and new offer development

Marketing roles

And so… to the more contentious subject of marketing roles. 'Chunking up' from the wealth of input we got from our interviewees was not as easy as it was for sales. There is a stark contrast between the broad potential nature of marketing reflected in classical textbooks and the diluted role of the CMO to the tactical function we see in many organizations today. When we asked the question 'What is the role of your marketing organization?' often the instant response was, like that of Katie, 'It could be thousands of things' or Kirk, 'It's like a laundry list'. When we narrowed the question down to 'What do you think the top three responsibilities of the named marketing organization are?' there was one runaway winner which appears at the head of the top five roles below.

- brand;
- organizational alignment;
- strategy development;

- sales enablement or activation;
- demand generation.

We will look at each one of these five roles in turn, starting with brand.

Brand

While we didn't ask interviewees to define 'brand', it was clear that their views were in line with how we would see a brand as *associating a symbol and a name with a promise of and the experience of value*. Our participants, as we do, view brands as important, in line with what Naomi Klein (2010) said in her iconic book *No Logo*: 'Because they make choice easier, more certain and more rewarding'.

It was appreciated that the brand role was multifaceted, as Figure 4.3 shows; we are going to explore each element next.

We can see here proof that participants see brand as much more than a logo. The role spanned from strategic brand creation and development through to tactical communications. Importantly, for B2B organizations, mobilizing people to live and activate the brand in the marketplace were seen to fall within the marketing role. The overarching responsibility for brand management was set in the context of the outputs that good, or bad, branding could affect including reputation, credibility, and revenue growth.

What was interesting here is people with a sales background also called out the creation and development of the brand as key.

FIGURE 4.3 Branding – the role of marketing

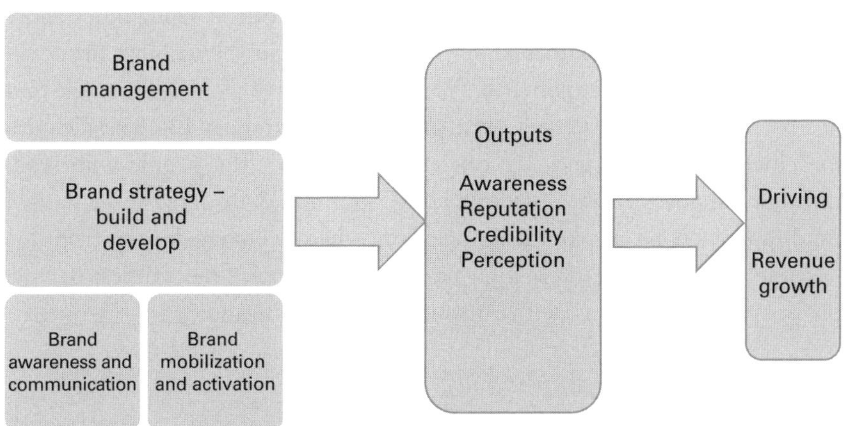

BRAND STRATEGY

Robson, a company President with deep experience in sales, saw marketing as having responsibility for brand strategy, in particular for 'the brand and the brand pillars of the organization', which encompasses what the organization wants to be seen as and extends to 'how it should look and feel externally and internally'. Brand pillars, the foundation a brand is built on, begin with Vision, Mission, and Values and include how the company should position itself it the market, and the tone of voice it adopts.

Jerry echoes Robson's view in saying that marketing's brand role is about 'how the organization is perceived internally and externally. The marketing team is responsible for how the company presents itself and appears'.

What Jerry is saying gives an output focus to the brand strategy element of the role; how a company presents itself influences how it is perceived. In the context of this book, does it help the organization stand out in a distinctive or differentiated way?

BRAND MANAGEMENT

The overarching responsibility for managing the brand was cited by a number of participants who used slightly different words depending on their context: while Siobhan, Head of Marketing for a university said the role was to *govern* the brand reflecting her role in an academic institution, Regina used *protecting our reputation* in line with her role as a marketing leader of an IT company. Overall, respondents saw the brand management role as being about consistent presentation, communication, and delivery of the brand in the market and externally, as succinctly described by Caroline, a CMO in private real estate: 'I would say to create a *consistent* brand and client experience across the organization.'

It's interesting that Caroline saw the marketing role as being much more than ensuring consistent messaging, incorporating a responsibility for creating a consistent client experience. From what we have seen, this is a role that has been increasingly taken away from the CMO and can often reside with the chief customer experience officer. In B2B, how the people who walk through the doors of the customer act is often not considered to be part of the brand. Having worked in universities where we consider the frontline lecturers as the brand, there appears to be no effective recognition of how the people who interface with customers affect the brand overall.

AWARENESS AND COMMUNICATION

There is certainly recognition from practitioners that you have to be well known or well respected before you can effectively sell anything.

For example, Siobhan saw the role of the marketing department as being 'To raise *awareness* of who we are as a university with people who don't know us; it's to drive people to a state where they are happy to give us their details.'

Interesting to note that raising awareness was often seen as coupled with strategies and tactics to win and grow business, while for Siobhan it was about helping to get students interested in her university. Kirk, vice president of product, linked awareness raising to demand generation in his technology world, placing brand awareness, thought leadership and demand generation 'into one category'.

Herbert, sales vice president at a global mobile company, hinted at a creativity competence required here that we will focus on in later chapters:

> To me, it's more about the creation of *awareness* and brand, of creativity around that, and the language that is used to communicate what the company does.

Other interviewees building on the importance Herbert attached to language placed a focus on 'tone of voice' which goes beyond making potential customers aware of who you are towards how you want them to feel about you. Terry, telco CEO, was a strong believer in the need for companies to spend more time concentrating on their tone of voice and being clear about 'What it is that you project of your company'. He contrasted his focus on developing a clear tone of voice with the obsession in his industry in using 'a lot of words with lots of syllables making yourself way less accessible'. The tone of voice you choose needs to set you apart from competitors in a way that is meaningful to the customers that matter.

Regina, marketing leader for an IT company, was keen to stress the link between awareness raising and strategy when she said:

> It's about promoting the brand and not promoting it to everyone, but to the ones who matter; this goes back to our targeting and segmentation.

In other words, we only need to make the people we think might be interested in buying our products aware of our brand. In Terry's telco world it's about trying to develop a strong brand reputation which can get him '100 true fans' as his laser-focused target segment.

BRAND MOBILIZATION AND ACTIVATION

In B2B industries with lots of sales and service people the importance of brand activation in the marketplace was reflected in numerous interviews. Jeff, a VP of strategic partnerships said that one method marketing should use to 'help create credibility for the company' is the production of whitepapers by an authority on the industry that the customer is in. Here Jeff is suggesting that customer interest can be activated through thought leadership aligned to the vertical market approach to industries often favoured in B2B markets. This means going beyond the surface-level 'Sea of Sameness' platitudes that we have seen on company websites to a deeper understanding of industry sectors and customers. Partnering with credible players in the particular vertical market is seen as a part of the brand activation process, and crucially in shaping the external credibility of the organization.

Robson, who spoke of the 'brand pillars' as part of the strategic brand management role was keen to stress the need to call out 'how those brand pillars get built on by all the employees'. So, to the point we were making earlier, while marketing has an overall responsibility for brand management, how it is mobilized and managed in the field has to be shared by operational managers running sales and service functions.

Organizational alignment

While the marketing role in getting and driving organizational alignment was not as popular a choice as branding, there were certainly some insightful views. Certainly, if pressed to answer the question 'How would you describe the role of marketing in one word?' we would always say *alignment.*

The definitions of alignment we would use is:

> Noun:
>
> 1 The act of aligning or state of being aligned; especially the proper positioning or state of adjustment of parts in relation to one another.
>
> 2 An arrangement of groups or forces in relation to one another
>
> Source: Merriam-Webster.com, 2019

We see the role of marketing as getting alignment from the organization with what customers value, that can help their own organization stand out and be successful in the market.

Bob, a classically trained marketer, and chief commercial officer in building services, was very passionate about this being the central role of marketing:

> For me what it should be is the absolute hub of the organization, it should be if you want to know where the organization is going, go and talk to the marketing team.

Bob clearly sees marketing as the creators and owners of strategy as they are the team who knows 'where the organization is going'. One of the major tensions for marketing leaders is driving a long-term plan while delivering on short-term gains.

Regina, sharing Bob's passion for marketing's important role in alignment, said that a key part of her role as marketing leader in an IT company was to:

> Align business strategy – promote the vision and mission of the company by understanding what we are trying to accomplish internally paired with what the customer needs.

Regina made it clear that her role is to align organizational strategy with customer needs. She does not shy away from the responsibility of being the one who has to drive internal alignment between company strategy and customer needs.

Herbert, amongst others, emphasized that before drilling down to discuss sales and marketing roles it was important that both were aligned to 'overall business goals and strategy' than focused on the more pragmatic need for alignment and integration with sales. In his experience, 'marketing works better where it has been integrated with the sales function'. By 'integration' Herbert does not necessarily mean that they have to physically report into the same leader but that they act in an aligned and integrated way. He recognizes that in a world where the customer spends the bulk of the buying cycle looking at company marketing channels, such as websites, marketing has to work much further down the marketing and sales funnel than it did in the pre-internet era, as we can see in Figure 4.4.

The reason why everything we focus on as authors relates to both marketing and sales is because we believe that these two organizations must align and be in tune with customer needs in order to connect with what customers value and help their organization stand out. Practitioners saw sales having an important role in the 'Cohesive loop' between the customer, marketing, and sales. Equally they saw it as important to drive alignment to the company vision and mission while being 'kept honest' about changing trends on what customers value, based on feedback from the market.

The role marketing has to play in getting organizational alignment, from the lofty goal of getting alignment with overall company strategy, to the more pragmatic role of alignment with sales, and crucially with the customer, is seen to be a core function of the named marketing organization.

FIGURE 4.4 The new marketing and sales funnel

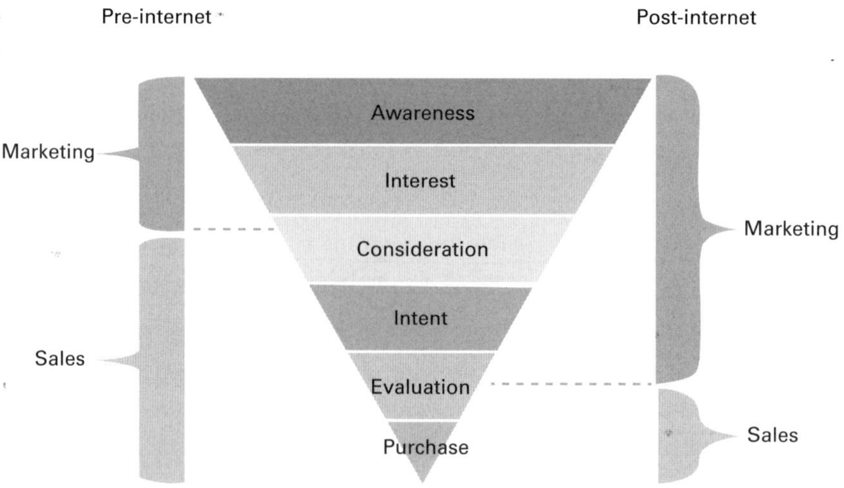

Strategy development

Building on the strategic need for better integration, we found it interesting that it was often people with sales backgrounds that placed some of the more strategic aspects of the marketing role in their top three. Marketers in B2B roles often feel they are under pressure to do lots of tactical things alongside providing golf balls and pens.

The specific ask from sales leaders, particularly where they had worked in organizations that were competing against large incumbents to win customers from them and take share, was for better segmentation, targeting, and positioning (STP). *Segmentation* is about chunking the market into sets of customers with similar requirements and buying characteristics into distinct subgroups. Following on from segmentation organizations need to decide which customer segments the company will actively pursue, otherwise known as *targeting*. Once these decisions have been made the difficult job of *positioning needs* to take place in order to decide the way in which a company wants to be perceived by its target market relative to its competition, against things customers consider to be of value

Kirk, based on a long career in sales, saw STP as the main responsibility, as the absence of targeting leads to a 'spray and pray approach'. What comes out strongly here is marketing's role to help sales focus their fire by pointing them towards the customers they really want to target, where they can have most impact. Without a clear steer on who these customers are you are left with a 'spray and pray' approach, which means try everybody and see where that gets you, strategy-free selling! Robson echoes the need for marketing to take on board the STP role and extends this on to a responsibility for building the appropriate product portfolio for the chosen target segments:

> Sales leaders see the STP element of strategy development as a key role of marketing that is much more than about providing 'golf balls and pens'.

As a marketing leader, Regina accepts STP as being a core part of her role as:

> Helping to position ourselves effectively relative to the competition based on those competencies of insight and understanding of our target segments and buyers.

We will come to the competencies required for effective STP in later chapters. From what we have seen in our 'Sea of Sameness' research it's fair to say that organizations are not typically doing a great job in setting themselves apart in the minds of customers. Given that salespeople can often fail to get deals over the line because the value in changing hasn't been effectively communicated it is no surprise that sales leaders are looking for more and better STP from marketing.

Sales enablement or activation?

It is interesting, though not surprising, that sales enablement showed up in the top five responsibilities for marketing. At the same time this has become a contentious space, with the enormous growth of sales enablement professionals over the last few years. There were 38,302 sales enablement job vacancies worldwide on LinkedIn last time we looked. Sales enablement roles typically roll up to a leader who works for the chief sales officer. For marketing practitioners these people can either be a wedge between them and the sales force or provide leverage for more success.

From our standpoint we strongly favour the term *Sales Activation* as much more dynamic than *Sales Enablement*, which feels like passively giving support to the sales channel, rather than helping activate salespeople towards driving more sales. Sales activation is what Robson sees as a key role that still sits with marketing, despite the growth of this separate sales enablement function:

> Marketing has an obligation to enable the sales channel in the field to go and deliver the corporate goals that we're looking for in the markets that we want to serve.

Robson sees marketing has an obligation to ensure that sales are enabled to meet their revenue and profitability goals on behalf of the organization. We know that this is a problematic area from previous research into how marketing and sales work together to develop value propositions. Kyle, president of a data centre company with a long sales pedigree, said that often material provided to sales by marketing was too 'sophisticated' or obtuse for them to use. He called this void between marketing and sales 'the sophistication gap'. Part of the marketing role is to ensure they know what sales need to feel effectively enabled. It boils down to the fact that B2B marketers can't be effective unless they understand both the customer's buying process and the sales process; very few marketers take time to learn one or both of these.

Regina, moving forward her view of marketing's role in developing effective positioning, sees this as key to effectively enabling sales, accepting that her role extended to:

> Enabling and empowering sales to effectively position and sell our services to the right companies and the right people within those companies.

So, the STP process makes for effective sales enablement and should help sales create differentiation on value and swim away from the Sea of Sameness, provided marketers understand the sales process and how to equip sellers with this information.

Caroline, CMO at a private real estate firm, sees effective sales enablement as crucial towards driving revenue, acknowledging that a function of marketing is working towards this by work with sales 'through an engagement, marketing and technology, sales enablement pipeline'.

Caroline sees the combination of effective sales engagement, marketing and technology taken together to be what she would call sales enablement. Clearly Caroline sees sales enablement as a core element of the role of marketing. Often the clunky nature of the technology the sales teams have to work with stands in the way of effective sales enablement. We would prefer to see this as *Sales Activation*.

Demand generation

The demand generation element of the job is at the most tactical end of the top five roles for marketing identified by our interviewees.

Regina accepts that part and parcel of the role of marketing is to take on board the tactical nature of some marketing work:

> A lot of B2B marketing is very tactical, right? Like go generate new leads. That's the only value. And if you don't generate new leads, you know, you're dead to me kind of thing.

How prominently this is regarded to be part of the role can depend on the context of the organization you are working for and the people that run it. Certainly, if you are a marketer in a company that needs to grow business by taking share from competitors or to get new customers then you will be expected to do a lot of demand generation work. It's telling that Regina used the phrase 'you're dead to me' as an extreme way of saying that to some senior executives who view marketing very tactically, if you are not generating leads you are not fulfilling what they perceive as the role of marketing.

We saw earlier how Kirk saw demand generation as an integral part of raising awareness. Robson emphasized the role of marketing in driving demand, which means effective demand generation is something marketers have to solve:

> Marketing is responsible for igniting the demand and bringing the demand to the sales team. So, it's got an awareness challenge to solve, it's got a demand generation challenge to solve.

In linking awareness to demand generation in this way Robson is accepting that you have to be known before you can sell something, again a challenge for smaller players in the market.

Marketing roles – have you got them covered?

We have seen what senior practitioners think the top five responsibilities of marketing are – have you got these covered? Table 4.2 gives a checklist for you to keep and consider whether you take these into account when designing marketing roles.

TABLE 4.2 Top five marketing roles

Roles	Component
Brand	• Brand Strategy – build and develop • Brand management • Brand awareness and communication • Brand mobilization and activation

(continued)

TABLE 4.2 (Continued)

Roles	Component
Organizational alignment	• Getting organizational alignment with what customers value • Align business strategy with customer needs • Get alignment to what helps you stand out
Strategy development	• Effectively *segment* customers into meaningful chunks • Decide which customers to target • Develop positioning strategy to stand out versus competitors in the mind of the customer
Sales enablement or activation	• Enable the sales channel to go and deliver the corporate goals that win in chosen markets • Enabling sales to effectively position and sell services to the right companies and the right people within those companies.
Demand generation	• Igniting demand and bringing the demand to the sales team • Generate new leads and follow-up business

In summary

By now you should be clear about the competencies that make up our V.A.L.U.E. framework which we used to shape the questions we asked senior practitioners in our research interviews. Before we asked them questions about competencies, we wanted to get a clear view about how they viewed the respective roles of the named sales and marketing functions in their organizations. The top five roles for each function are summarized in Table 4.3.

Clearly, what the roles are perceived to be affects the competencies required to perform them effectively, by which we mean to be able to help their organizations connect to customers, stand out in a Sea of Sameness,

TABLE 4.3 Key marketing and sales roles

Top five marketing roles	Top five sales roles
Brand	Selling and execution
Organizational alignment	Connecting the dots
Strategy development	Balanced advocacy
Sales enablement or activation	Customer experience
Demand generation	Customer and market feedback

and grow new business. What we saw is that salespeople often assigned importance to the strategic roles of marketing such as STP, organizational alignment and brand. This was often lost on marketers who can get deafened by the frequency of tactical requests from sales. On the sales side, although the core role of sales execution ('hitting the numbers') is uncontested there is definitely a need to more formally embed important aspects such as bringing back feedback from the market more formally into the sales role. This evidence provides us with a clear platform on which to develop marketing and sales competencies for standing out.

In the following chapters we will explore the competencies required by stand-out marketers and salespeople. Before you turn to the next chapter, on the basis of the top five roles for each function identified here, what do you think the competencies required are? Table 4.4 provides you with a notes page to consider this here.

TABLE 4.4 Notes page for key competencies

Top five marketing roles	Key competencies for role
Brand	
Organizational alignment	
Strategy development	
Sales enablement or activation	
Demand generation	
Top five sales roles	
Selling and execution	
Connecting the dots	
Balanced advocacy	
Customer experience	
Customer and market feedback	

References and further reading

Aberdeen (2019) Why do buyers struggle? The answer is data [online] https://www.aberdeen.com/old-resources/b2b-buyers-survey/ (archived at https://perma.cc/M36E-JD2C)

Barta, T and Barwise, P (2017) *The 12 Powers of a Marketing Leader: How to succeed by building customer and company value*, McGraw-Hill Education, New York

CSO Insights (2019) 2018–2019 Sales Performance Study [online] https://www.csoinsights.com/2018-2019-sales-performance-study/ (archived at https://perma.cc/46RJ-77KG)

Demand Gen (2018) Content Preferences Survey [online] https://www.demandgenreport.com/resources/research/2018-content-preferences-survey-report (archived at https://perma.cc/UAA9-UG8V)

Demand Gen (2019) B2B Buyers Report [online] https://www.demandgenreport.com/resources/research/the-2019-b2b-buyers-survey-report (archived at https://perma.cc/Y7Y8-HVAL)

Dixon, M and Adamson, B (2013) *The Challenger Sale: How to take control of the customer conversation*, Portfolio Penguin, London

Gartner (2019) Buyer Enablement Study [online] https://www.gartner.com/en/sales-service/insights/b2b-buying-journey (archived at https://perma.cc/LFQ6-UMWM)

Hauer, M (2013) Three myths of the '67 per cent' statistic, *Sirius Decisions* [online] https://www.siriusdecisions.com/blog/three-myths-of-the-67-percent-statistic (archived at https://perma.cc/53HL-QT4G)

Klein, N (2010) *No Logo: No space, no choice, no jobs* (10th anniversary ed.) Fourth Estate, London

Shaw, R and Merrick, D (2005) *Marketing Payback: Is your marketing profitable?* Pearson Education

Wizdo, L (2015) Myth Busting 101: Insights into the buyer journey, *Forrester Research*

05

The visionary – competencies for seeing the next competitive move

In this chapter we will:

- share our competency research – focusing on what sales and marketing leaders said about visionary competencies;
- explain what visionary competency is and why it is important;
- discuss what 'being visionary' in the context of B2B sales and marketing looks like;
- provide a checklist of the elements of visionary competency.

What do we mean by visionary competency?

We want to be clear what we mean by visionary competency from the start. As many readers will know, the common use of the word vision in business is typically connected to the overall aspiration of a company in terms of what it wants to be in the future. For example, Amazon's vision is 'to be Earth's most customer-centric company, where customers can find and discover anything they might want to buy online.'

It's the big picture or the so-called corporate vision. It is clearly an important statement that sets the aims and direction of the business. A vision statement is related to the idea of mission, which defines the competitive arena in which the business operates and the things that are necessary for it to compete successfully.

In this chapter, we are talking about something different. We are talking about personal behaviour rather than a top-level strategic statement. In that sense we are referring to the individual ability of sales and marketing professionals to 'see' what is happening in the world about them and notice what is happening in the market sectors they are competing in and customer accounts they serve. In that sense, visionary competency is closely related to the idea of deciding what is relevant and the process of determining what matters and what doesn't to the business. Clearly, the visionary competency of individual professionals will play an important part in the work that goes into strategic planning and the definition of the corporate missions and visions. Visionary competency has an inspirational quality. Many of us will be familiar with US President John F. Kennedy's 'we choose to go to the moon' speech delivered at the Rice Stadium, Texas, on 12 September 1962. The speech vividly invites the audience to see into the future and imagine things that are yet to come:

> ... if I were to say, my fellow citizens, that we shall send to the Moon... in a giant rocket more than 300 feet tall... and return it safely to Earth, re-entering the atmosphere at speeds of over 25,000 miles per hour, causing heat about half that of the temperature of the Sun – almost as hot as it is here today – and do all this, and do it right, and do it first before this decade is out...

Visionary competency is what precedes the details of mission and vision statement and strategic plans. This is what Jeff Bezos and his team had and this is what makes them stand out. They personally had the vision to see a future that combined internet technology, artificial intelligence, big data, cloud services, robotics, smart supply chain management and smart logistics that would enable them to sell you anything you might want to buy via an online portal.

Why is visionary competency so important?

Visionary competency is about what gets noticed and what gets ignored. It is about how people read situations and how people construct an image of the commercial world in their mind's eye to identify the factors that drive their actions. In particular visionary competency produces an integrated image of the following dimensions:

- markets;
- customers;
- competitors;
- your company and product-service solutions.

> Thinking about each of these dimensions in turn, can you list three factors for each that you believe will have an impact on the future direction of your business? You could compare and contrast this thumbnail sketch with different people in your company.

Because we are talking about interpretation and sense-making, you can't train people in visionary competency as if it is a technical process with a series of clearly defined and straightforward tasks to be followed and replicated. Visionary competency is an ability that develops over time. You often hear stories of the way seasoned police officers notice something that a novice has missed, something that doesn't quite stack up, something that raises suspicions. It was this ability that enabled the UK police to capture serial killer Peter Sutcliffe, the so-called Yorkshire Ripper, in 1981. During a routine police stop for using false number plates on his car, Sutcliffe distracted officers in order to discard his murder weapons by making an apparently innocuous request to step outside the car to go to 'the bathroom'. This request bothered seasoned arresting police officers and as they returned with Sutcliffe to the police station they sensed something was amiss. They went back to the scene of the arrest and found a knife, hammer and rope close to where the suspect had taken his comfort break, and when challenged about the murders, Sutcliffe confessed (Sheffield Star, 2018). This same ability to see things that matter was noted by head of marketing Norman, when he gave us an example of what happens at business exhibitions:

> At a trade exhibition the recent graduates would have seen dozens of things that would have made them all excited, and the more experienced Norman or Sarah would have seen just one or two things that made them excited. Norman would walk around saying 'that looks quite clever, of course, it's not going to work, because, because, because'.

Visionary competency has direct practical implications. It's not only about creating the big vision, it's also about directing everyday action. As Jerry, marketing consultancy owner, said:

> ... senior marketers see more than junior marketers. Vision is crucial. You need a vision to inspire an agency so they can go and deliver creatives for you.

Visionary competency therefore develops with experience and thinking, which means we need to consider what makes the difference between a novice and someone with competency. Let's see what Siobhan, head of university marketing, thinks about this:

> Not everybody, in fact most people can't see past tomorrow. Most people don't understand they are operating in a market that's highly complex. I look at many marketing professionals and they're just out of school. They don't have the experience or intuition to see, this is where we've been, this is where we're going to go. And that visionary competency is the ability to predict the future.

Why the difference between individual visionary competency and a corporate vision mission statement matters

We asked Katie, managing director of a software business, 'How important do you think it is to be able to build a vision of where you can take your customers?' She noted the connection between visionary competency and vision statements and drew out some important things to consider that relate to time wasting and customer relevance. Here's what Katie said to that point:

> ... building that vision of where the organization is going and how it's going to get there is hugely important. I would offer just a health warning on the term visionary... I have lost more days that I cannot get back in my life on time spent creating vision and mission statements and all of that.

The strategic planning task of writing a mission and vision statement can be a real-time vampire. Business academic Michael Raynor tells us that ATT took two years to produce a 250-word mission and vision statement – a task that for many organizations simply results in such generic statements that are no more than 'conceptual hand waving' and lack any meaningful substance for customers or co-workers.

Katie went on to say:

> ... that vision of where you want to go, with a clear understanding of why you're wanting to do it and the joining of the dots of how to get there is hugely important. If you can make that link between your vision and customers' needs, it matters.

It is practicality at the customer level that matters. There is a difference between saying something general such as 'we want to create brighter futures' compared to what the bike-sharing company Nextbike say – 'we want to make cities more liveable'. The Nextbike vision has a practicality about it. What will the world look like for the specific customer you are interacting with? We can see echoes here of the overall Sea of Sameness problem and the different outlook of the sales and marketing function where vision statements are so generic they become almost meaningless. Katie gave us this explanation for why vision statements don't live up to their promise:

> Very often they are tick-box exercises; they've read the textbooks and they know they've got to have a vision and a mission statement.

Likewise, Michael Raynor's review of vision and mission statements noticed that they often tried to sum up everything about the business in a few words. But to do this, they ended up being mere generalizations and losing the specifics. Vision statements have become taken for granted as best practice and many people have stopped questioning why they are doing them.

What does good look like?

The business outcome delivered by visionary competency is sustained competitive advantage. For sales and marketing professionals to be good visionaries, we mean that they must see beyond the obvious. They don't take things for granted and have an ability to connect things that others can't. They see things that lie under the surface and how things might be in the future. Being visionary is a leadership quality because it is about seeing where to go and painting a picture of what is necessary for others to follow. Business leaders, and marketing and sales professionals, need to have vision, use their imagination, see the forest through the trees, be agile and able to course correct. They have to use their wisdom to judge what is relevant to the business and what is not. Vision in this context is also an essential part of commercial creativity and the ability to avoid merely following what your competitors are doing. In the end, it is the essential first step in transforming the way your company operates. Those organizations that fail to notice the signals for change picked up from customers by sales and marketing and take action accordingly are doomed to fall by the wayside.

Let's develop a pen portrait of the visionary role model we'll call Victor the Visionary and connect Victor's competency to our research findings. First, we'll build up a general picture of enablers and derailers that make up Victor's platform for success. This will be followed by a detailed look at each of the competency elements he needs to be an ideal visionary in his business.

Enabling factors for visionary competency

The conversations with our interview participants revealed that three big factors are necessary for visionary competency:

1. Perspective – the ability to see things from different points of view.
2. Foresight – the ability to predict what will happen or be needed in the future.
3. Imagination – the ability to construct new possibilities in the mind's eye.

Organizational conditions must be right for visionary competency to thrive. Being receptive to and looking at the world from alternative points of view matters because as the saying goes, 'where you sit affects what you see'. Visionary competency indicates a respect for the subjective outlook of others and an ability to see the world as they see it. This is important because it reflects the openness of the culture and leadership style of the organization. At a practical and functional level for marketing professionals, seeing how the business works from a commercial position can affect the quality of co-working and credibility. As VP of marketing Christine said:

> Marketers also need to be business people. They need to understand what is the profit profile of what we're trying to do here? What is the capital intensity of what we're trying to do here? What is the revenue generation velocity and those types of things? So really beyond just those (4 Ps of marketing) pillars – how does the business work? How do these things make money?'

Visionary competency is therefore essential for understanding the many faces and contexts of value both inside and outside the organization. If your organization is receptive to new ideas and information that challenges the prevailing view of the business the conditions look promising for those people with visionary competency.

Derailers of visionary competency

Three factors inhibit visionary competency.

1. Lack of critical perspective.
2. Lack of time and resources.
3. Lack of diversity and inclusion.

Lack of critical perspective

Visionary competency involves an ability to make use of fresh and alternative perspectives. This presents a dilemma for talent recruitment in sales and marketing. This is because sector and customer knowledge is highly desirable in order for new recruits to hit the ground running. On the other hand it is well known that we have a tendency to recruit in our own likeness (Rigby, Gruver and Allen, 2009; Rivera, 2012; Ryan 2017). Similarity and familiarity might be good for common values but it is less good for the diversity of ideas and unsettling what we take for granted. This was something we first saw in Chapter 2 as part of the reason for lack of differentiation. Christine, VP telco marketing and Caroline, CMO financial services and real estate, gave us these interesting examples:

> We're willing to take people outside of the industry. If we're struggling to get an outside view, that's a straightforward way of doing it. We usually prefer people who have marketing experience in technology as opposed to, say, consumer packaged goods or something like that. But we've got a fairly liberal approach to who we recruit (Christine).

> ... we fired our ad agency who had lots of experience in the financial services industry. Yes they did what was asked of them, but they presented nothing new or innovative. The kiss of death is someone that has been with the same firm forever and has never seen anything different (Caroline).

A fixed organizational paradigm and dogmatic unbending leadership of the sort that uses 'my way or the highway' management will kill visionary competency. In 1982 Ron Westrum, academic and social researcher, described this behaviour as the 'fallacy of centrality', which is an unfailing belief in one's ability to be on top of everything that is happening in your field. It's the marketing director who believes there are no surprises in the market because she believes she has all the information. If she doesn't know about it then it's not happening. Victor the visionary is not as dogmatic and is also very likely to have so-called 'maverick tendencies'. As a result, Victor doesn't necessarily follow convention and possibly has unique sources of information; as such, a critical failing in organizations is ignoring the insights Victor can bring to the table.

Lack of time and resources

Like everything in business, the ability to do things well requires investment in resources. Regina, VP marketing, telecom and IT services, really emphasized this issue:

> Marketers need to have the tools and the resources to understand the segments that they serve and the buyers within those segments. There's way too little invested in that right now.

In this example we can also hear her underscoring the need for direct customer contact. It seems fair to say that without direct customer connection the organization is really flying blind.

Siobhan, head of marketing, faced similar challenges in terms of lack of time:

> When your resource is absolutely at the point where there is no time to spare, it's hard to pursue a potential opportunity. So, at the minute, especially within our sector, where you've got things like the Augar UK Higher Education Review which could have a massive implication, we are short of time to consider it in real detail.

Lack of diversity and inclusion

Lack of diversity and inclusion can also derail visionary competency; as Jeff, VP and business unit leader, pointed out, focusing on the input from one source can be problematic:

> They may have a piece of the puzzle but very few people have the whole puzzle.

Visionary competency will be derailed in an under-resourced, non-inclusive and closed culture. So ask yourself, does your company have the right conditions to encourage visionary competency? Peter Senge, in his book *The Fifth Discipline* (1993), pointed out that in any organization the conditions need to be right for a competency to thrive. To ignore the cultural conditions in the organization is akin to shouting 'grow!' to a flower and expecting it to happen without paying attention to environmental factors and soil nutrients.

Visionary competency elements

With the idea of enabling and derailing conditions in mind let's look more closely at how visionary competency is achieved. Victor the Visionary will perform to a high level of ability in each of these areas:

- outside-in;
- farsight;
- zooming;
- predicting;
- imagining.

Outside-in

An outside-in ability is a prerequisite for visionary competency overall. The outside-in view is central to market orientation and customer-centricity. In Chapter 1 we saw that Ted Levitt (1960) called the opposite of an outside-in perspective 'marketing myopia' or shortsightedness and with it came the accompanying risk of being blindsided by your competitors who understand the solutions nature of the business better than you do. If you have an outside-in perspective you are tuned in to what is happening in the world about you and how changes in that world might affect your customers and your business. As Christine, VP of marketing, explained, this is sometimes not as easy as it seems:

> ... it's also tough to not become only internally focused, as you continue to talk about your own products and your own customers and your own salespeople. It's very difficult to get exposure to things that are going on outside of your organization that may provide an opportunity.

There are serious consequences for your business if you lack this outside-in perspective. In his book *Leading the Revolution* (2000), Gary Hamel emphasized the serious consequences of not paying attention to the outside world when he reminded every business person that:

> Out there in some garage is an entrepreneur who's forging a bullet with your company's name on it.

Farsight

An enduring problem facing business is what organizational researcher Bob Garratt (1990) saw as managers getting 'hooked into firefighting the immediate rather than the strategically important'. The long-term perspective requires the C-level to make time to look into the future – and business leaders have to prioritize this. In their book *Competing for the Future*, Hamel and Prahalad (1996) said a long-term perspective is all about how far your headlights shine up the road. Here's what telco CEO Terry said about the challenges of ensuring the long-term perspective in their experience:

> ... it's often the least amount of time spent in the C-suite as well because it's a difficult topic and people shy away from it. Most of the time we are wrestling with next week's results and next quarter's results rather than truly having our radar up and looking at what the market is going to be like in three years' time.

This problem of overcoming a short-term focus was also identified by Regina, VP marketing, telecom and IT services. She observed that in her organization marketing had lost its long-term perspective, driven not only by a lack of time and attention, but also by commercial business forces in terms of potential company exit for the owners and shareholders.

This situation presents an all-too-real tension for many organizations. A balance frequently needs to be struck between the 'business as usual' activities of developing and serving current markets and customers, and the need to demonstrate company performance for a trade sale or flotation and justify an exit price to sales ratio:

> Marketing became about generating leads to help sales grow the business because there's so much short-term focus. What's really been damaging is so much short-term focus. Companies are built to be sold. Not many companies are being built to last, not in our space. There's so much consolidation in our sector.

For Regina, attention to the long term really matters:

> Marketing needs to be forward looking and they can't just look at the immediate opportunity. While it is important to be able to go in and dissect that, they need to be thinking three, five, seven, ten years ahead. They have to balance near term, mid term and long term.

The long-term perspective isn't something that necessarily comes naturally either. Kirk, SVP, product management, technology, explained that sometimes your role can lock you into the immediate and short term and this is a habit that needs breaking if you are to develop visionary competency:

> I spent the first almost 10 years of my career in operations before I switched to a sales and general manager-oriented role. When I first made that switch, I'd hear comments like 'competition drives behaviour' and I'd never had to think about that much – I just didn't appreciate it. A typical sales professional will only focus on the immediate month, the immediate quarter, or maybe the immediate fiscal year. So, many of them really don't care about that larger more strategic picture.

Having an eye on the long term was critical for Herbert, consultancy managing partner. In his opinion, any good sales and marketing professional ought to be aware of future trends as a necessary part of their remit. Using the electric vehicle sector as an example, Herbert saw where electric car demand was going a decade ago. The big challenge in leveraging visionary competency for Herbert lies in the ability to get the rest of the organization to act:

> Whether they were then able to drive that into their organization and prepare their organization accordingly depends on the remit and the role of marketing and the importance attached to marketing. Are they sanctioned to go off and drive new product development programmes, new technology platforms or is the organization based around what they're already doing and how they're doing it?

Zooming

John, business investor and strategic marketer, brought to our attention a very particular ability which he believed separated a novice from an experienced professional. Using the metaphor of an eagle's eye he said that the ability to simultaneously see the big picture at the same time as focus on particulars was significant. The Eagle's eye is designed to sweep the landscape from high up and focus on specific prey when it moves far below. In business you have to have a view of the general competitive landscape, who the key players are and how they are behaving; at the same time you might be pitching against one of those competitors for a specific deal and you need to understand the specific tactics they are using to win that deal.

Academic management researchers Julie Leroy, Bernard Cova and Robert Salle (2013) describe this as zooming in and zooming out, or the 'zizo' phenomena. We simply call it Zooming. Zooming gives us a clue as to how sales and marketing see the world differently too. Classically trained marketers tend to view the world from the zoom out position of broad trends and customer segments, whereas sales professionals view the world from the zoom in account and individual buyer perspective. The challenge that that zoom out perspective brings is the so-called 'black box' problem where analysis of markets is so generalized that the details of what is going on inside the black box at the local level is completely missed. This is a real challenge when it comes to understanding customer value because, according to Leroy, Cova and Salle (2013), zooming out:

> is becoming increasingly embraced by leaders in the marketing discipline, running the risk that the broad abstractions this approach generates will become the black boxes to which all future research will defer.

In other words, local customer knowledge and insight is treated as less important by marketing than big brand themes.

Predicting

Seeing where to go is an act of forward thinking or prediction. Kirk, VP of product and experienced sales leader, gave this vivid image of the importance of being able to predict what actions to take based on vision of where the market will be at some point in the future:

> You know I'm originally from a country that loves ice hockey. I always say you can't just chase the puck these days. You need to skate to where the puck is going... and how you're going to skate to anticipate the place on the rink you need to be.

The fascinating thing about Kirk's metaphor is the way it captures not only the anticipatory nature of vision competency, but also its dynamic nature. You, your organization and the market are all moving at the same time and it's how you ensure the trajectory you select will take you where moving target opportunities can be obtained. Michael Stanko and Joseph Bonner describe this ability as projective competency, which is the ability to understand and shape future customer needs with a demonstrable impact on the bottom line. Projective competency relies on an ability to predict and is more than being market oriented and keeping pace with expressed customer needs. It is an ability to anticipate customer needs and trends into the future and comes from:

> frequent dialogue, regular joint problem-solving sessions, and participative involvement of customers in order for a deep projective understanding to emerge (Stanko and Bonner, 2013).

Seeing where to go understandably depends on market scanning abilities. However, the mere collection, collation and sharing of market and customer information isn't enough on its own. Visionary competency requires peripheral vision. George Day and Paul Shoemaker (2005) explain that strong peripheral vision is essential for anticipating the things you don't see coming. Typically the first indications come in the form of what Igor Ansoff called 'weak signals' (Holpainen and Toivonen, 2012):

> ... first symptoms of strategic discontinuities, ie symptoms of possible change in the future, acting as warning signs or signs of new possibilities.

The possibility of training for visionary competency is something that has recently been taken seriously by the England Rugby Union team under the guidance of Vision Coach Sherylle Calder, where the focus is on picking up information early and acting on it (Kitson, 2019).

Whilst the idea of 'signals' might also suggest listening out for things, ultimately it is the picture that someone forms from the signals that indicates visionary competency. As Regina, VP marketing, telecom and IT services emphasized to us, you have to listen and see to create a vision:

> Our role is to listen, listen, listen to people within our company whether it's sales or engineers or service delivery managers or solution architects or executives, or industry analysts. We need to understand what they hear when they talk to customers. We have to take different pieces of input, distill it down to get to that nugget, and connect the dots so we can stand out.

From a sales perspective, seeing where to go plays a critical role in B2B sales effectiveness. Kirk, senior vice president in technology product management, told us:

> Being forward thinking is critical. From time to time when I go into a client meeting, I'll actually bring a press release from one of their competitors to understand who their suppliers are today and who their suppliers are going to be. Having conversations with your customer about their current and potential suppliers and how you can help them by meeting their future expectations – I'm a big believer in that.

Saying we should be good at forward thinking is one thing and doing it is of course another. When we asked Robson, US telco president, to tell us how good he thinks marketing and sales people are at spotting emerging trends and potential opportunities out into the future, he responded with:

> Not very good, I think it's something to do with the amount of time invested in understanding that future space. This time allocation issue slows people down. It's easier to talk about what happened in last month's results and what's going to happen in the next 90 days' results. It's a lot harder to talk about the trends.

In the famous words of Kaplan and Norton (1992), 'what you measure is what you get'. Seeing where to go will only be an organizational reality if an indicator for seeing where you are going exists on the management dashboard. Bob, chief commercial officer, building supplies, observed the lack of such indicators with some dismay:

> From a sales perspective, I'm just totally amazed that I can talk to salespeople, and they're not interested in their clients or the industries that they operate in. They would not think to read something, or think, that's an interesting concept, I'm going to find out more about that. They need to have that level of curiosity. They're not really spotting those trends because they're very close to it.

It is worth pointing out that implicit in all of these observations lies the idea of discernment. Herbert, consultancy managing partner, offers sage advice about going too far the other way and becoming fixated with what he calls 'shiny objects' or the next new thing. What is clear is that sensible judgement needs to be made about what is noticed and how it should be responded to:

> I'm very comfortable at spotting new things we're very good at. The counter of that is that people in our world do get very easily attracted to shiny objects, and the grunt and grind of that everyday sometimes gets lost in the pursuit of the new.

Imagining

Using our imagination is commonly associated with artistic creativity and origination, or with pejorative descriptions such as 'childlike fantasy' and 'idle daydreaming' (Warnock, 1976; Brann, 1990). Having the imagination to come up with novel and effective B2B sales and marketing solutions, recognizing trends and customer need implications, is an ability considered by visionary competent people as something that sets them apart from their peers. John, business investor and strategic marketer, told us:

> Someone with vision says we've done some thinking and this is conceptually what we think might be of interest to you. If somebody gives you a product specification you don't just make that product exactly to specification, you add in other things and you would offer a number of other possibilities, not just take the order. The person with vision will be thinking of future possibilities and probabilities.

Aaron, senior sales professional and business funding and growth advisor, gave this example of the use of imagination:

> I'll probably have seen something which I can say, well, that either worked for that customer or it didn't. So things you see in pharmaceuticals are equally relevant to paints and coatings or recycling. You never really know, but it all goes into one big melting pot.

The imagination described as a mental melting pot in which ingredients are transformed to produce new insights seems to be a highly apt metaphor to describe the function of vision in this context. Blackburn (1994) offers this definition of Aaron's 'melting pot' as:

> the faculty of reviving or especially creating mental images in the mind's eye. But more generally the ability to create and rehearse possible situations and combine knowledge in unusual ways, or to invent thought experiments'

Herbert, consultancy managing partner, sees this type of creative imagination as critical for effective B2B selling:

> Sales is about the kind of creativity being more of a businessperson than a transactional salesperson. I think in order to break away from just operating with the stuff that you get, which means that you are repeating the same mantra as everybody else, I think you do need that level of creativity in selling.

In that sense visionary competency can be understood as an ability to position the firm's offer in the mind of the customer. It is all about outcome-based thinking, or supposing what might be possible. As William, Director of a training and development company, put it, you help the customer see what is possible 'by painting a picture in the mind's eye of what needs to be done'.

In his training business William would invite people to visualize a situation that needed a training solution he could provide. Visionary competency is therefore a central ability in the communication of a value proposition. Gronroos and Ravald (2011) say value propositions are suggestions and projections of impact, promises of potential future value creation. Visionary competency is also important for creating scenarios relating to wanted and unwanted possibilities, such as Aaron asking his customer what the cash tied up in the business might be, what the return on the investment might be, and how it could look.

It is with the idea of scenarios that visionary competency comes into its own. Peter Senge (1993) defines them as:

> A series of imaginative but plausible and well-focused stories on the future.

And in that definition sits a crucial point. Having a vision about possible business solutions has to be grounded in reality, otherwise the vision simply falls into the category of unbounded creativity and musing.

Ultimately our sense-making, trend projections, scenarios and value propositions all rely on our imaginative ability to join the dots between different things and recombine them in ways our competitors haven't.

Visionary competency assessment

Let's return to Victor the Visionary. How do you and your team stack up against his ideal ability? Victor is of course excellent at everything.

For each element that has been scored spend some time thinking about the 'so what' of this situation. What are the implications for you, your team, your organization and your customer?

TABLE 5.1 Visionary competency scale

	Poor	Quite Poor	Neutral	Quite Good	Excellent
Outside-in					
Farsight					
Zooming					
Predicting					
Imagining					

Now what? What actions could you take to move your visionary competency in the direction you want? Here are some ideas to get you going:

1 read the science and technology pages of quality news websites;
2 read a popular science magazine like *New Scientist* or *Scientific American*;
3 subscribe to TED Talks.

Vision is nothing without action

Sales and marketing professionals with visionary competency are conceptual thinkers who create images of markets and customer worlds. In that sense they have vision. Not in the grand sense of vision given in corporate strategy statements but in the more everyday sense of seeing possibilities and connections; showing the customer and the rest of the organization how things might be.

We mentioned at the beginning of this chapter that visionary competency is about noticing things; however, this is only part of the challenge of transforming your business and changing its direction in the light of new information. You might notice the growth of Smart Cities or the Space Tourism sector and recognize there is a need to change and adapt, but if you fail to take action, the knowledge is wasted. A telling take on the impact of not taking action is given here by VP of marketing Christine:

> Many visionaries have no interest or ability to actually ground out a real solution that could be sold. Without a straight line between vision and action, then you've got vision for vision's sake. We must have the ability to influence the design and development of products and services so they are relevant to the customer's world.

Chapter 6 considers the competency of Activation as a necessary ability that complements Visionary competency.

References and further reading

Beaney, M (2005) *Imagination and Creativity*, The Open University

Blackburn, S (1994) *The Oxford Dictionary of Philosophy*, Oxford University Press

Brann, E T H (1990) *Imagination: Sum and substance*, Rowman & Littlefield

Brett, M (2004) Using the imagination: consumer evoking and thematizing of the fantastic imaginary, *Journal of Consumer Research*, **31**

Clark, B (2013) *Relevance Theory*, Cambridge

Day, G and Shoemaker, P J H (2005) Scanning the periphery, *Harvard Business Review*, November

Driscoll, J (2000) *Practising Clinical Supervision*, Balliere Tindall, Edinburgh

Garratt, B (1990) *Creating a Learning Organization: A guide to leadership, learning and development*, Director Books

Garratt, B (1992) Creating a learning organization, *Industrial Management & Data Systems*, **92** (1), p 28

Gronroos, C and Ravald, A (2011) Service as business logic: implications for value creation and marketing, *Journal of Service Management*, **22** (1), pp 5–22

Gummesson, E (2003) All research is interpretive, *Journal of Business & Industrial Marketing*, **18**, pp 6–7

Hamel, G (2000) *Leading the Revolution*, HBR Press.

Hamel, G and Prahalad, C K (1996) *Competing for the Future*, Harvard Business Press

Holpainen, M and Toivonen, M (2012) Weak signals: Ansoff today, *Futures*, **44** (3)

Kaplan, R S and Norton, D P (1992) The Balanced Scorecard: measures that drive performance, *Harvard Business Review*, Jan/Feb

Kitson, R (2019) England's vision coach Dr Sherylle Calder, 'Jones is a rugby mastermind', *Guardian* [online] https://www.theguardian.com/sport/2019/oct/30/england-vision-coach-dr-sherylle-calder-eddie-jones-rugby-mastermind-world-cup-interview (archived at https://perma.cc/RQB9-FXLU)

Leroy, J, Cova, B and Salle, R (2013) Zooming in vs zooming out on value co-creation: consequences for BtoB research, *Industrial Marketing Management* (42) pp 1102–11

Levitt, T (1960) Marketing Myopia, *Harvard Business Review*

Piaget, J and Inhelder, B (1948/1956) *The Child's Conception of Space*, Routledge & Kegan Paul, London

Raynor, M E (1998) That vision thing: do we need it? *Long Range Planning*, **31** (3), pp 368–76

Rigby, D K, Gruver, K and Allen, J (2009) Innovation in turbulent times, *Harvard Business Review*, **79**

Rivera, L (2012) Hiring as cultural matching: the case of elite professional service firms, *American Sociological Review*, 77 (6), pp 999–1022

Ryan, L (2017) Five reasons to hire someone with no 'industry experience', *Forbes* [online] https://www.forbes.com/sites/lizryan/2017/09/24/five-reasons-to-hire-someone-with-no-industry-experience/#7a6ec38c6de3 (archived at https://perma.cc/35W9-63QM)

Senge, P (1993) *The Fifth Discipline: The art and practice of the learning organization*, Random House

Senge, P (2000) *The Dance of Change*, Nicholas Brearley Publishing

Sheffield Star (2018) How police caught Yorkshire Ripper Peter Sutcliffe in Sheffield 37 years ago this week [online] https://www.thestar.co.uk/news/how-police-caught-yorkshire-ripper-peter-sutcliffe-sheffield-37-years-ago-week-50913 (archived at https://perma.cc/2JL8-4G3N)

Stanko, M A and Bonner, J M (2013) Projective customer competence: projecting future customer needs that drive innovation performance, *Industrial Marketing Management*, **42** pp 1255–65

Van Mele, P (2006) Zooming-in zooming-out: a novel method to scale up local innovations and sustainable technologies, *International Journal of Agricultural Sustainability*, **4** (2), pp 131–42

Warnock, M (1976) *Imagination*, Faber, London

Weick, K (1995) *Sensemaking in Organisations*, Sage

Westrum, R (1982) Social intelligence about hidden events, *Knowledge*, **3** (3), pp 381–400

06

The activator – competencies for getting things done

In this chapter we will:

- share our competency research – focusing on what sales and marketing leaders said about activation competencies;
- explain what activator competencies are and why they are important;
- discuss what 'getting activation done' looks like;
- provide a checklist of the key activation competencies.

What do we mean by activation competencies?

In Chapter 3 we described 'Activation' as competencies needed to get buy-in to initiatives that are being developed to provide differentiation in the market and to drive growth in the business.

The definition of activation we like best is 'to put (an individual) or unit on active duty' (Merriam-Webster dictionary).

To put an individual or unit on active duty gets right to the heart of what we mean by activation competencies. In order to successfully activate you need a bunch of competent activators. To get anything done in organizations large or small, you need to sell your ideas, create buy-in internally and mobilize the team.

So, who would you think of as a role model 'Activator'? Take a few minutes to write down who your role model is, what they did, and how they managed to put people on active duty to work towards achieving their cause or organizational objectives.

In 2020 it's difficult to overlook the young Swedish climate change campaigner, Greta Thunberg, as the ultimate 'activator'. In seven months, she went from standing outside the Swedish Parliament with a hand-drawn 'School strikes for climate change' banner to a point where 1.6 million students went on strike in many towns and cities across the globe (BBC News, 2019). She has succeeded in bringing a sense of urgency to a problem that many of us thought may occur sometime whenever, making it a 'burning platform' issue that now has the attention of global political leaders. Not least because she now gets invited to speak at United Nations conferences.

Creating Fear, Uncertainty, and Doubt (FUD) is one way to mobilize action; highlighting the urgency for change as a first step to 'putting people on active duty' is something you may have also recognized in your own role models. The opposite to causing FUD can be creating a vision by painting a picture of a brighter future.

In Chapter 5 we talked about how John F. Kennedy in his 'We choose to go to the moon' speech painted a vision of things that did not seem possible in 1962. Another iconic historical example is the 'I Have a Dream' speech given by American civil rights activist Martin Luther King Jr during the March on Washington for Jobs and Freedom on 28 August 1963, in which he called for civil and economic rights and an end to racism in the United States. His 250,000 supporters present on the day were treated to his vision of a brighter future depicted in his dream (Oppenheim, 2016).

Did your Activator role model have the ability to paint a picture of a brighter future? What other competencies did they have that led you to choose them as your role model? Hold onto your notes until the end of the chapter and see what we found through our in-depth research interviews with business, marketing, and sales leaders.

Why are activation competencies so important?

Vision without action is merely a dream. Action without vision just passes the time. Vision with action can change the world

JOEL A BARKER, 1992

You may have seen this Joel A Barker quote or something similar. Without doubt, a challenge in organizations of all sizes is getting great ideas executed both internally and externally.

Terry, chief executive of a telecoms company with experience in both sales and marketing, usefully highlighted the importance of activation in the organization as an essential precursor to effective customer activation:

> I think activation is incredibly important; success has a thousand fathers and failure only one. But you need people to be invested in a solution because it's the only way you can be successful. If you can't inspire seeing these possibilities, the market is going to struggle too, so it's a very important part of what we do.

Here Terry was specifically referring to taking a new solution to market and the need to have activators in his organization who can create a vision for where this can take the customer. In order to do this effectively people need to buy into it internally; if they don't then the solution is not going to fly.

From a sales standpoint, it's long been acknowledged that you need to activate a whole range of people in the customer buying centre before you even consider potential users of the service you are looking to sell. We know that organizations are becoming more conservative in their buying behaviour and that the number of people involved in the B2B buying process is now 6.8 (Toman, Adamson and Gomez, 2017).

There are lots of books that have sold in big numbers that try to deal with the skills required by salespeople to activate customer buy-in leading to a sale. What seems to have had much less coverage is the competencies required by sales and marketing people to activate their own organization to create and develop solutions for their customers. We aim to put that right in this chapter.

So, are your marketing and salespeople good activators? Can they get people to buy into their ideas? Are they able to put individuals or units on active duty to help deliver their ideas? Can they put themselves in their customer's shoes to activate and mobilize the rest of the organization towards giving the customer superior value to your competitors? How did your role model do this?

> In our survey, 89 per cent of respondents said that the ability to execute was a very important competence, and 70 per cent said the ability to create buy-in was very important.

What does good look like?

The end result of effective activation can be measured by an uplift in revenue, a positive change of perception, or more satisfied customers. Getting to that point, depending on the size of your organization, may involve thousands of people marketing and selling your solution effectively in a way that customers find compelling. The customer will need to be convinced it's worth changing from what they've got now because what you can offer is better than your competitors.

Activation doesn't just involve getting the marketing and sales teams onside, which is hard enough; it can mean getting buy-in from senior executives, manufacturing, logistics, and customer service to name a few. Having worked in and with organizations that vary in size between 3 and 250,000 people we know that activation is difficult in different ways for organizations of all sizes.

Combining the research interviews with our experience working in and with organizations of all sizes let's walk in the shoes of our own role model, Alison the Activator. We'll begin with what we call the 'Enabling Factors' – things that need to be put in place by Alison, to give her a platform for success.

Enabling conditions for successful activation

To begin the journey towards successful activation, there are a number of things that need to be put in place when the baton has been handed over from Victor the Visionary. These enabling conditions provide a strong bedrock for activation.

Focus

Practitioners see having a clear focus as a platform for effective activation. In big organizations with diverse sets of customers and thousands of product lines, the task is all the more complex. Being clear about which customers you are trying to provide value to, with which value propositions that are relevant to the customer, is what we call providing focus. It's no surprise that in Chapter 4, segmentation, targeting and positioning (STP) was seen by salespeople as one of the most important things they were looking for from marketing.

Kirk, a veteran sales leader with experience in several large organizations looking to take market share from competitors, highlighted the need for marketing to provide sales with focus:

> So, first and foremost in my mind is segmenting, targeting and positioning. You can't take a 'spray and pray' approach. That is something I think you just need to get fundamentally correct.

Kirk is saying that without the focus that STP provides, the organization would be 'spraying and praying'. By this he means just randomly communicating (spraying) to a whole universe of companies in the hope (praying) that some of them will think that what you have said is meaningful to them. Without this focus, lots of calories, time, and money can be burnt that could have been focused on the customers your organization could really help.

Purpose and outcome

Being clear about what you are trying to achieve for your customer and your own organization was seen by practitioners as an enabling competence for Alison the Activator.

Where positive role models were cited, often the start point was the clarity about why programmes and initiatives were being rolled out, what the organization hoped to achieve, and the WIIFM (what's in it for me) for the salespeople.

Herbert, a former sales leader in a global technology organization, with experience in different sectors, emphasized the importance of a purpose and outcome focus:

> One global technology company I worked in was particularly good at activation. Most of the marketing programmes had to have a clear outcome. There was a rationale for why they were being invested in and the same went for investment in sales programmes. Everything had to have some attempt to build a return on investment (ROI).

This clarity of purpose helps the sales team see what the organization is striving to do and the part sales need to play which helps get buy-in, especially when this includes a strong case for how the idea benefits the customer. The need to be able to demonstrate predicted ROI links to the final enabling factor, a *strong business case.*

Strong business case

To get any initiative off the ground, Alison the Activator will have to develop a case that motivates the organization to want to take the initiative forward, that is likely to be compelling for customers too. The business case will have to include a forecast of the potential benefits for customers and the organization alike, the resources required to make the initiative work, along with timing and prioritization. Crucially, if your intent is to stand out, the business case needs to specify how what you are proposing is better than the competitors in the eyes of the customer.

We recommend that all business cases contain a value proposition for the organization that shows how the potential benefits of an initiative outweigh the likely costs. Here's an example for X-Wire, a fictitious telecommunications organization:

> X-Wire PLC will be able to improve customer retention by 10 per cent or £500,000 annually by implementing our 'white-glove' service programme for £100,000.
>
> In one year (insert actual date) X-Wire will be able to demonstrate the delivery of value by improved customer retention and revenue growth through the 'white glove' programme.

The business case should also contain a value proposition for how the proposed solution will help the customer, in this case the fictitious Money Bank:

> Money Bank will be able to improve customer satisfaction by 10 per cent and revenue by £1m due to improved service up time as a result of implementing X-Wire 'white glove' service for £75k pa.
>
> In 12 months (insert actual date) X-Wire will be able demonstrate the delivery of value to Money Bank by improved customer retention and revenue growth.

Research undertaken by Professor Malcolm McDonald, Emeritus Professor, Cranfield University, has shown that only 5 per cent of salespeople present numeric value propositions to their customers. This despite the fact that CFOs demand to see financial return (Kelly, Johnston and Danheiser 2017).

From a marketing standpoint, to get an internal business case over the line it needs to benefit both the customer and your own organization. Where customer needs coincide with company needs is what Barta and Barwise (2017) call the Value Creation or V-Zone.

Derailers – what can prevent effective activation?

What we heard most often both in our formal research interviews and in informal discussions with practitioners is that effective activation is effortful. Once a business case has been approved to take an initiative forward, the fun begins – trying to get people across the organization to buy in to the idea. Before we go on to discuss the competencies needed to be recognized as an ace activator let's consider the things that can get in the way of effective activation, what we like to call derailers.

The battle against other priorities

Robson, president of a global company, highlighted competing priorities as a big potential derailer:

> Activation is hard work, it's a lot of effort. You may get initial buy-in then along come initiatives 2, 3, 4, and 5, in successive weeks. All of a sudden, the buy-in you had has been diluted and lost through the organization, who forgot about your sales and marketing initiative.

While Alison can plan to prevent this potential derailer by providing focus, and developing thematic programmes, not all the initiatives that demand the time of marketers and salespeople relate to initiatives you are trying to take out to market. It could be the roll-out of some new technology, an HR management initiative, all these on top of yet another product launch.

For salespeople this prioritization issue is amplified when they are dealing with the customer. What may be getting traction today may get stalled because priorities change. So, both inside the organization and in the customer's world, initiatives have to be continually reinforced after initial buy-in. Of course, it's in your own gift to head this issue off at the pass by cutting down on the number of initiatives you are trying to get buy-in for, either from the customer or internally.

Is the battle against other priorities an issue for you?

CHALLENGE

Write down all the initiatives you are working on that need buy-in from other people in the organization or from customers. After this write down initiatives that are coming from other parts of the organization that demand time from the same people you are hoping to mobilize.

How many of your own initiatives could you cut or delay? How many of the initiatives coming from the rest of the organization could you try to influence to be delayed or ditched?

Fully baked answers – marketing with no sales input

In Chapter 3 we saw how marketing initiatives which were developed with clear input from sales were far more likely to succeed. We recall that Saskia, a Marketing Director with cross-industry experience, said that sales usage of collateral skyrocketed to 100 per cent compared with a 20 per cent usage if marketing had put together the collateral without sales input. The same principle applies to working with customers. If you go in with a fully baked answer without involving the customer in a dialogue to help shape the answer, you are heading for failure.

Some marketers we spoke with openly acknowledged that they needed to get better at asking key stakeholders for input. When asked how good her team was at getting input from others, Siobhan, a university marketing leader, said:

> We are rubbish. This is something we absolutely need to get better at. As a marketing department, I'd say we probably did marketing to the university, rather than bringing the university with us on the thought process behind it. And that's something that we are massively changing.

Identifying the lack of engagement of people outside marketing to be a problem means Siobhan has taken a giant stride towards solving it. We particularly like the way she expresses the problem as 'marketing to rather than marketing with'.

From a sales standpoint there is, of course, a filter. If you try to drive salespeople towards taking fully baked answers to customers in a tightly prescribed way it is unlikely to reach the customer.

> CHALLENGE
>
> Think about how you and your team currently work: do you market *with* or *to* internal stakeholders and external customers? Write down the last three things you worked on that you could have got input from others on and score yourself. How did you fare? How could you improve?

Executive buy-in and beyond

An ace activator like Alison would be unlikely to skip the step of getting executive-level buy-in. If you don't have executive buy-in it could become more of a train wreck than a mere derailing.

Many of the methodologies used by sales organizations around the world emphasize the need to get executive buy-in. Internally, some executives are happy to give sign-off at a strategy level, for example the overall marketing plan or an account plan for a major customer. Others might want to be involved in more tactical programmes, so it's good to know the preference of your executive team.

Bob, an executive steeped in the building supplies industry, pointed at the need for a big improvement from marketers:

> Marketers are quite good at getting buy-in to short-term executional activity; I don't see many driving coherent, medium-term programmes or initiatives through an organization. They don't engage the people elements across the organization, and are not particularly savvy at the boardroom level, where they need to get sponsorship for their programmes.

Here Bob emphasizes that it's not just tactical activity that needs buy-in and that support or 'sponsorship' for more strategic activities has to come from the executive team. Bob went on to say that this inability to get executive sponsorship was compounded by problems getting buy-in from the wider organization. The underlying theme here is that getting buy-in requires good people engagement, beyond the technical marketing knowledge required to develop a marketing plan.

While the need to get buy-in from executives and across the broader organization is well recognized in sales, the frustration is that marketing training and education tends to focus on the technical aspects of marketing rather than softer skills.

> CHALLENGE
>
> How good are you and your team at getting executive level and cross-organizational buy-in? Think about the last five initiatives you needed organizational support for internally, or in the customer organization. What does this tell you about how good you currently are at getting buy-in?

Plethora of product programmes

Of all the potential derailers we had to reserve a special place for something that gets mentioned by all customer-focused marketing and sales practitioners – the plethora of product 'marketing' programmes.

While marketing and sales leaders seek to develop competitive advantage by developing solutions that resonate with customers, they are often battling against product managers and product 'marketing' people who are trying to push their own product without setting it in the context of what the customer is trying to achieve, and with no input from marketing and sales.

Herbert, amongst others, highlighted these types of inside-out product programmes when thinking back to his time as a sales leader in a global technology organization:

> There were lots of products created that just sort of fizzled out because people couldn't articulate the proposition well enough, and just didn't sell anything.

Alison the Activator may have made attempts to head this issue off by developing customer themes like 'agility' or 'productivity' under which any new products have to fit. Unfortunately, it is a constant battle fighting off product launches. We did some work with a medium-sized technology company who developed two really clear go-to-market themes that we know through research resonated with customers. They had problems implementing the theme-based approach because their time was consumed with numerous product launches that took their focus away from customers.

> CHALLENGE
>
> So, here's the challenge: how many individual products does your organization have? How many launches of new products and changes to existing products were pushed out to customers in the last 12 months? How much time was consumed in marketing and selling these products? How much did you sell?

Mobilizers for activation

Having discussed the enabling factors and derailers for effective activation let's turn to what Alison the Activator has to be good at to mobilize the organization to work on the marketing and sales programmes she is driving. We will then reveal how these translate into personal competencies.

Sales and marketing alignment

Activation 101 is getting alignment between sales and marketing. In our last book *Value-ology: aligning sales and marketing to shape and deliver profitable value propositions* (Kelly, Johnston and Danheiser, 2017) we made it clear that this is not just alignment between the marketing and sales functions but crucially, with the customer.

Robson, president of a global telco, while stressing the need for a strong alignment and partnership between sales and marketing, made it clear that this had to begin at the leadership level:

> First of all, you need your marketing leader and sales leader to be arm in arm in making differentiation happen. If there is a fractured relationship it's not going to happen, it's not going to be good for the company in the long run but you're not going to get buy-in through the organization. Because people will see the left arm and the right arm not working together.

TABLE 6.1 GRRIPS Alignment Framework

Theme	Action
Goals	Set common 'strategic goals' for marketing and sales. Integrate tactical goals that complement strategic goals.
Roles	Understand that roles are interlocking and must work in harmony to achieve success.
Resources	Ensure resources required to 'get the job done' are understood. Develop clear mechanisms for budget requests and allocation.
Information and conversation flow	To be aligned to the customer there needs to be a constant flow back from the market. Agree information flow and process for coordination.
Processes	Agree key processes for moving towards goals.
Success measures	Agree what success looks like. Measure against the strategic goals. Make sure score cards are all the same colour!

Adapted from Kelly, Johnston, Danheiser (2017), p 175

So, if you are a sales or marketing leader, how well aligned are you with each other? How well aligned are you on what's important to the customer? If you are in a marketing or sales organization, how well aligned do you think leadership is?

In *Value-ology* we spent a lot of time talking about what needed to be aligned in order to help organizations stand out. Our GRRIPS model provides a checklist for alignment, which you may find useful to test yourself against.

The elephant in the room is how you go about getting this alignment, how you demonstrate this and become a competent practitioner of alignment.

Getting buy-in

We know that if you are a salesperson then going into the customer with a fully baked solution before you've got their input is setting you up for failure. We've already talked about the downsides of not getting input from salespeople before you fully bake anything, from a marketing plan to a piece of collateral. So, you have to be good at getting buy-in as an early step in achieving activation.

Caroline, CMO of a financial services company, spoke about some good practice in her world:

> Marketing comes up with the idea, thinks of all the good and bad ramifications, then writes up the plan. Once we have something written, we do a brainstorming session with the relevant team (sales, executives, etc) to get their input and buy-in. Usually, something comes up during the process that provides us with a different perspective or something that we didn't think about. We then tweak the plan based on that input.

So, going in with an idea that's reasonably well-formed and based on customer research is seen by Caroline, and others, as a good start point for getting buy-in. The willingness to change the plan based on input will be taken positively by the 'relevant team' as they now have a stake in it. At this point, marketing and sales can agree on programme goals that help towards achievement of annual targets.

In identifying more than one 'relevant team' Caroline also recognizes that alignment and buy-in needs to go beyond sales and marketing, something more akin to stakeholder management.

Stakeholder management

Stakeholder management is about understanding who it is you need to mobilize to effectively take forward a marketing and sales initiative, when and how. Depending on the nature of your organization there could be a large number of functions that need to be brought into your idea or to sign elements as you develop the programme.

Christine, marketing leader in a large telecoms company, gave an insight into what stakeholder management entails in her world:

> There's a place in the campaign development process that says, okay, where are we against stakeholder management? Who's going to go manage which stakeholders? Some of it is evangelizing what we're doing and why it's exciting. Some of it is very procedural – legal wants to make sure that we've checked little boxes so we don't get sued.

Here, Christine is talking specifically about a marketing campaign and distinguishes between stakeholders who she needs to mobilize to take the campaign forward, and those who have to give technical approval, like the legal department.

Increasingly, in order to 'stand out' from competitors, organizations will work with other companies together to create solutions that offer more to customers than they can in isolation. The activation task here starts with getting the partner on board, making it clear what you need from them to help deliver the solution you're taking to market together, and keeping in lock step with external partners throughout the campaign. This element of stakeholder management is a non-trivial task.

From a sales standpoint stakeholder management has become more important as the number of executives it takes to sign off a deal has grown. Managing these stakeholders involves developing value propositions to different functional executives because they may all want different outcomes

> CHALLENGE
>
> So, here's a challenge: think about your last marketing or sales campaign. Who were the stakeholders? What buy-in or help did you need from them? Who needed to sign off elements of the campaign? What executive engagement did you need? How well did you manage the stakeholders? What can you learn from this for your next campaign?

from the same solution. As if that wasn't difficult enough, if a deal involves a solution that brings together partners from outside the organization they will need to be kept on board. For major deals this may involve lining up senior executives from each organization, which is never easy.

Competencies for activation

So far in exploring enabling conditions, derailers, and mobilizers for activation we have focused largely on the what. Hopefully you have had a chance to reflect on what you are doing well and what you need to do better. We hope that this got you thinking about your own ability to get these things done, and those of your team. Competence is all about how people go about doing the right things right. Based on what you need to get done, we think key activation competences are:

- balanced advocacy;
- listening;
- negotiation;
- tenacity;
- people-centricity;
- contextualization.

The rest of this chapter will focus on these competencies. We will round off with a checklist and activities to help you consider whether you and your team have these competencies.

Balanced advocacy

We hear a lot about the role of the salesperson as the customer advocate. Customer advocacy is knowing what the customer wants and championing it across the business, which usually includes taking responsibility for customer satisfaction.

The customer satisfaction element was something that Christine, a marketing vice president at a global telco with a sales pedigree, called out:

> You can't be a successful salesperson and ignore customer satisfaction. You've got to sell them something that's working and meets the customer's needs. If something is not working, you will often be the point person for helping

> the customer figure it out. What I've seen over and over again – your best salespeople are great customer advocates too.

Christine recognizes that the salesperson does run the risk of 'getting in too deep' and moving the line between advocacy and 'wasting too much time' away from the sales numbers. In an environment where organizations are increasingly trying to gain advantage by superior customer service this can be a burden on salespeople who will have to balance the advocacy role with selling.

On the broader point of being the customer champion for all their needs it was interesting to see a sales leader like Kirk, vice president for a product line in a global telco, with a long sales career background, stressing *Balanced Advocacy* as a key competence for a sales role:

> So, first and foremost there should be balanced advocacy for your company. I definitely see sales organizations and sales professionals who forget that they do get a cheque from the current company.

The implication for sales competencies would seem to be the ability to achieve this balanced advocacy. While sales and marketing have to be the voice of the customer then to prevent inside-out product obsession this has to be tempered with commercial realism.

So how balanced is your advocacy? Ask yourself for the last three marketing or sales campaigns you worked on: did you take sufficient time and effort to think about how your idea benefited your own organization as well as the customer?

Listening

> *Most people do not listen with the intent to understand; they listen with the intent to reply.*
>
> STEPHEN R COVEY (2013)

LISTENING TO UNDERSTAND

Habit 5 In Steven Covey's *The 7 Habits of Highly Effective People* was 'Seek first to understand, then to be understood'.

We are sure if we are honest with ourselves that most of us are guilty of faux listening, with the intent to reply, not to understand the point of view of the other person. Covey described empathic listening as reflecting back what someone says and feels in your own words to their satisfaction; in doing this they will feel listened to and understood, but do you really do this?

From a sales standpoint listening to understand the customer rather than just to reply can be the key to unlock the door to what's important and urgent for them or losing them by pushing your products too early on. Jill Konrath (2015) in 'Agile Selling' said that buyers keep sellers out because they are 'Product-pushing peddlers who don't bring value to the decision-making process.'

William, a training and development company owner, explained the contrast between good and poor practice in customer conversations:

> If two training providers were meeting the same managing director (MD), and I was talking to that MD, I would wager that within five minutes in I'm still listening to their stories and becoming super interested, showing empathy, enjoying the conversation. Whereas salesperson number two would be telling them about their products already, talking about themselves.

He portrays how to model good listening by really taking time and showing an interest in what's important to the customer from both a business and personal point of view. He goes on to say that while the aim is to probe and question until the customer has 'expelled everything', the salesperson needs to be able to adapt to individuals who may have different time constraints and preferences for these need-gathering conversations.

LISTENING TO PERSUADE

Herbert cited listening and observing as the essential start point for persuading customers and getting their buy-in:

> In terms of the competencies required to get buy-in, I think you've got to listen and observe. You really need to understand what motivates people and how they work and how they think. And what it is you've got that can influence that to get their overall buy-in. I think a lot of marketing teams fall down because somebody designs it, throws it over the wall to sales and says 'we're doing this'.

Building on William's observation, Herbert also emphasized the need to connect with what motivates individuals, on top of understanding what the business needs are. Only then should you talk about what it is you can do for the customer.

Here Herbert highlights a recurring theme that often the product-push discussion comes because someone designs an offer that is 'thrown over the wall' to sales, which reflects back on the need for marketers to improve on their own willingness to listen, and to not go into conversations with sales with a fully baked idea without sales input.

Regina, VP of marketing for an IT company, drew this out starkly:

> I let a marketer go for this very reason; they couldn't get buy-in. They didn't want to listen to other people's input. They didn't believe in the 'better together'. They needed to be the smartest person in the room.

In order to successfully activate marketing programmes and campaigns marketers have to actively listen to a broad range of internal stakeholders to mobilize them towards shared goals: salespeople, senior executives, product managers, operations to name a few. Taking valuable input on board at the early stages of programme and campaign development requires a lot of effort. Importantly, it can help reshape ideas by taking on board fresh insight from others and getting their buy-in.

Regina laid bare the stark consequences for marketers who can't embrace this element of the job, because in her view, it's tantamount to not being able to effectively perform in the role. From her perspective marketers:

> need to be curious. They need to put their egos aside; you have to know how to take input and to ensure people feel heard. No matter how cynical they are. Put whatever your personal beliefs are aside and try to see their perspective.

CHALLENGE

Do you listen to understand? Are you a faux-listener or an empathic listener? How often does listening to others reshape your ideas? Do you recognize that listening is a platform for persuasion?

Here's a drill that can help you test how good you are at listening; try it with a friend and then with your team at work, then next time you are with a customer.

Talk to a friend or colleague for three minutes. Try to retain five pieces of information that are important to your colleague. Try to move beyond 'faux-listening' or 'listening within your own frame'. You can be attentive by summarizing what you think has been said or repeating back what you think you have heard. Did you really listen with empathy by understanding what really was important? Did you really listen 'within the other's frame of reference'? Play back the five things you retained – what did your colleague think?

FIGURE 6.1 Do you really listen?

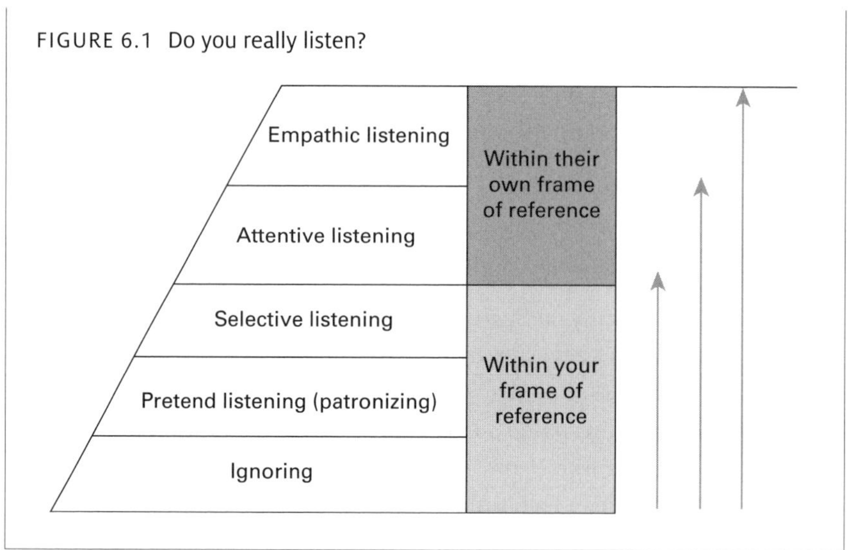

Negotiation

Negotiation has long been seen as a core element of the sales process and something that features heavily in sales training.

There are lots of slightly different variations of what negotiation is – our own definition is:

> Negotiation takes place when organizations or people, with differing views, come together to attempt to reach agreement on some issue.

Most significant B2B sales deals will require some form of negotiation, formal or informal. For this reason, the most widely taught sales methodologies have negotiation embedded in them, which stress that salespeople have, by necessity, got to be competent negotiators. For example, if a salesperson offers a 5 per cent discount to a customer on a £1m deal then if the gross margin is £400k the discount takes 12.5 per cent from the gross margin. If the profitability was initially £100k then the discount has just accounted for 50 per cent of the profit.

So, where salespeople are involved in multimillion-pound deals that can seriously affect their company's bottom line there is no wonder that they have to have powerful negotiating skills.

Surprisingly, negotiation skills are largely absent from university marketing courses, and get little consideration in the training of marketing practitioners and leaders. Surprising because the CMO usually holds one of the biggest non-capital budgets in any company and, with the rise of marketing technology, an increasing influence on IT spend. On any given day a marketer will be involved in negotiating deals of all sizes ranging from small deals with the likes of graphic designers to big contracts with advertising agencies. From our experience we contend that marketers have to negotiate more often than salespeople with external organizations, so the need to be a competent negotiator is paramount.

For effective activation the need for a marketer to be an ace negotiator is heightened because every new programme or campaign is up for discussion, because the interested parties you need to mobilize will not start from the same position as you. So, negotiation 101 is to not go into discussions with sales, senior executives or product managers with a fully baked idea... your own.

Marketers, like salespeople, need to embrace the key principles of negotiation found in seminal texts like *Getting to Yes* (Fisher and Ury, 1992) used by salespeople the world over. The start point is considering a range of possible outcomes, otherwise there are no conditions for negotiation, as we can see from Figure 6.2.

We can see that there are conditions for negotiation because each side is viewing a range of possibilities from 'must haves' to 'would likes' and these two bands of possibilities overlap.

If you haven't had any form of negotiation training or coaching, we'd suggest you get some, or negotiate to get some! Thankfully we do it a lot in our daily lives: with our children about screen time on mobile phones, with friends about whether you go to see a movie or go to the pub, with our bosses about when we can take a holiday. So, we do get practise with negotiation,

FIGURE 6.2 Conditions for negotiation

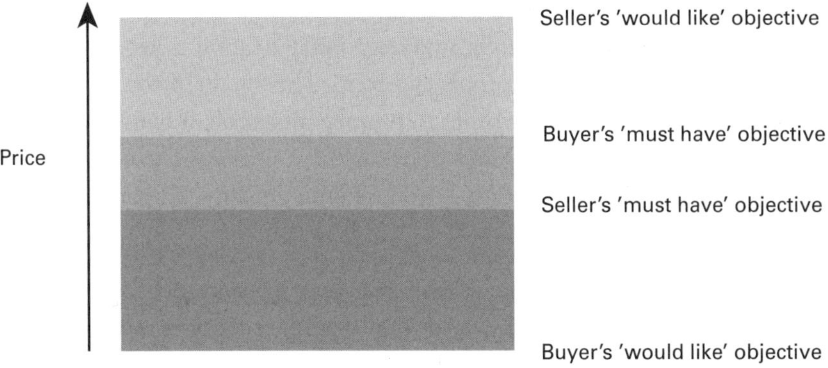

Adapted from Winkler (1996)

whether we like it or not. We can't pretend to give you what it takes to be an excellent negotiator but here's a challenge to start you off.

NEGOTIATION DRILL

Next time you go into a discussion where you think your sole objective is to sell your fully baked idea, think about the other party and ask yourself what they may want to get from your proposal. Complete the table below by setting out your objectives, thinking about what you would like to get versus what you must have. After this, think about what you are prepared to concede or trade. Concessions oil the wheels for negotiation so think about what you can give, and what you'd like to get back. Don't forget to think about what the other side may want. Now take it into the discussion – how did it go for you?

TABLE 6.2 Negotiation drill

What are your objectives?		
What are your 'must haves' and 'would likes'?	Must haves:	Would likes:
What are you prepared to concede or trade?		
What might the other person want?		

Tenacity

If we were to set this chapter aside to just one competence that gets lots of emphasis when we talk to executives, sales, and marketing leaders it would be tenacity, the determination to continue what you are doing.

By now it should be painfully apparent that activation is not easy. While we can give you some advice, tools and frameworks to help you improve in the confines of this book, learning to become an excellent activator is lifelong... because it takes a lot of effort.

Robson, president of a global technology company, emphasized how much effort activation can take:

> The buy-in part takes more time than people generally invest. So, for thousands of people to buy in it takes a lot of effort and a lot of time to get there from bottom-up involvement in the journey to the answer, ownership at the leadership level, cascading it effectively down through the organization,

> reinforcing on a daily basis why we're doing this and what the benefits are. And then continue to reinforce it with examples of success.

While Robson is giving a large organization perspective here starting with a view of how effortful getting initial buy-in is through to the need for continual reinforcement, the principles apply to companies of all shapes and sizes. We would acknowledge that the larger the organization the greater the complexity, the more the need for tenacity.

We've already seen that getting and keeping buy-in is often set in the context of lots of other initiatives competing for the time and headspace of the people we need to have working with us. If you are asking a customer to change from what they have now to something new, or your own organization to take a different approach to marketing or selling, then to quote Katie, CEO of a small software company and former large company CMO:

> It's like changing the car tyres while trying to keep the car moving.

Katie paints a picture where everybody is busy and focused on the near term, presenting a challenge for marketers:

> It seems like everybody is running trying to post the numbers up on the board. In order to build a marketing or sales programme you've got to be able to take a step back and change the tyres on the car. But you know you've got to keep the car moving so that profits come in today. People are just busy, and they only see the near-term value – they don't see the long-term value that you are trying to build if it doesn't help them this quarter.

While the enablers such as sales buy-in have to be in place, for Katie there is no escaping the fact that driving programmes through the organization can be down to the tenacity of one individual to just keep ploughing through to make it happen.

Jerry, a marketing consultancy owner, combines the need for tenacity in the context of activating the whole organization, a recurring theme in this chapter:

> Activation is a tough job. It's hard to really understand a market and it's hard to align the forces in the organization – it's a very political job. In the best organizations good marketers are activating the whole organization towards a goal of doing something for customers. But in a lot of organizations marketers don't have that confidence or capability so they become the packagers of things that the organization produces.

Jerry acknowledges the political nature of activation, which requires competence in understanding the preferences, motivations and personal values of the wide variety of people that need to be 'put to work'. A stark consequence of not being able to activate the big marketing and sales change programmes that Jerry referred to is being reduced to tactical packaging and lead generation. What does your team do?

For salespeople the need for tenacity and resilience, combined with political nous, has always been to the fore. Having to bounce back from customer rejection is an enduring feature of a good salesperson's character. Operating in an environment where now 6.8 people in the customer organization have to sign off a deal (Toman, Adamson and Gomez, 2017) and potentially hundreds have to be mobilized in favour of your proposal takes tenacity and nous. The principles that Katie used to describe the tenacity required by marketers internally manifests itself in the customer environment for sales. In addition, if the customer requires something slightly bespoke or new then the salesperson will have to convince a number of internal stakeholders that it's something worth doing, which can take a lot of tenacity.

If you don't have the tenacity to take on the big deals you could just be reduced to the small quick wins – is this you?

> CHALLENGE
>
> So how tenacious are you? Does your team have tenacity? Do you hire sales and marketing people for tenacity? Can you think of a time when you succeeded in the face of adversity?

People-centricity

For marketers and salespeople alike the need to be customer-centric, interested in what the customer needs and how you can help them, goes largely uncontested. What came out of our interviews is the need to be people-centric, generally wanting to interact and have the competence to deal with people, and work in teams, effectively.

When we asked Kirk about the competencies he looked for in good salespeople, orientation was his first port of call:

> I look for people who like working with people. I've seen people moving to sales because they think it's a good financial opportunity. But then sometimes you look and say, do you even enjoy people? You can't be a lone wolf.

Here Kirk brings to the fore the necessary trait required by salespeople of enjoying working with people. He seems to caution against the extrinsic financial motivation some people may have in wanting to join sales. In characterizing the wrong type of person as the 'lone wolf' Kirk points to the need for salespeople to operate in a team environment as it's rare for one person to be able to start and finish a sale on their own.

Changing his focus to marketers, Kirk, emphasized that marketers had to have team orientation in their DNA and behaviour. Kirk saw team orientation as an enabler for getting marketing and sales alignment, a necessity for activation as we've discussed. Given how fragmented marketing organizations can be, this team orientation is a must to get buy-in from fellow marketers, senior executives, and other stakeholders. This is having the 'better together' mindset Regina spoke about earlier in this chapter.

Bob, the chief commercial officer from a building supply company background, was sceptical about the ability of marketers when it comes to dealing with people:

> I don't think a lot of marketers have made the connection on that people piece; I don't think they've connected that marketing orientation works across the entire organization.

Bob emphasized that marketers are in the fortunate position of having a job that requires interaction and mobilization of all sorts of people across the whole organization. The problem Bob sees is that marketers don't seem to realize that they have a people-centric job. He re-emphasized the need to be able to engage with sales to get buy-in and fiscal support from finance to fund programmes in the first place. We will deal with the finance relationship more in Chapter 9 when we look at evaluator competencies.

This people-centricity has to bring with it a level of social ability and agility which comes from understanding that you have to deal with people from a broad spectrum of roles, often from different backgrounds, and certainly with different personality traits, as Bill, serial entrepreneur pointed out:

> You have social ability and agility as you need to work with a range of different types: the binary thinker, the empath, communicating well between these types is vital. I know from taking different personality tests that other people aren't like me, so I have to account for that.

Building on this, Norman, a head of marketing for a gaming company, stressed how useful being able to communicate both inside and outside the organization was as a relevant competence for sales and marketing people:

> Social abilities are relevant outside and inside the organization. Friendliness is a great trait, to be able to interact at all levels, because that enables you to do your job more effectively, because it doesn't matter who you are talking to, you can interact with anyone.

The ability to interact at all levels, across all job roles, is underpinned by the final competence, contextualization.

> So, are you and your team people-centric? Do you hire for people-centricity and social agility? Does people-centricity get trumped by looking for more technical skills?

Contextualization

Context is a word that comes from the Latin *contextus*, where *con* is 'together' and *texere* is 'to weave'. To help your organization stand out, sales and marketing need to 'come together' to 'weave' value propositions, ideally based on customer needs, in ways that you can meet uniquely.

Context is defined in the *Oxford English Dictionary* as meaning 'The circumstances that form the setting for an event, statement, or idea, in terms of which it can be fully understood'. What this means practically is that sales and marketing need to understand the precise circumstances of the person they are dealing with in order to shape value propositions that resonate with them, be it external customer, or internal executive.

Theology literature is a good place to make sense of contextualization. Strong parallels can be drawn to the theological concerns of setting the gospel in the context and culture of recipients of the gospel, as defined here by Luzbetak (1988, p 69):

> Contextualization is various processes by which a local church integrates the Gospel message (the 'text') with its local culture (the 'context'). The text and context must be blended.

Putting this back into the context of marketing and sales, marketers have to be able to rise to the challenge of moving from 40,000-foot brand messaging level (the text) and themes that work across their whole customer base, into context for specific industries, for example financial services. They then need to help sales by contextualizing for individual customers, eg HSBC. They then have to focus on the decision makers in the HSBC customer buying unit. We call this the value stack, which we introduced earlier in Chapter 2.

At the end of the day, if a salesperson cannot create a value proposition that resonates with the individuals in a buying centre then he has not contextualized the offer for the customer. Without being able to set customer value in context you will likely just be pushing products, and the customer will resist.

Kirk, explaining his move from sales leadership to running a product group, gave an everyday example of what we call contextualization:

> Part of my responsibility today is product management. We are responsible for working hand in hand with our sales force. When I took this role on, the first thing I asked was, 'do you have a very simple battle card?' This says for a particular market, here's the competitive landscape, here's what their strengths are, here's what their weaknesses are. Then, based on all of that, here is how you differentiate our current company. People looked at me like I had two heads.

What Kirk has encountered in his move to product management is a group of people that have been used to pushing out generic product 'brochure-ware' and expecting those further downstream towards the customer to do all the hard work of contextualizing. The chances of mobilizing the sales team towards selling the product would be greatly improved by working with them to set the product offer in context.

CONTEXTUALIZATION DRILL

So: how good are you and your team at contextualizing? Do you hire for this competence?

Here's a simple drill to test yourself.

TABLE 6.3 Contextualization drill

Context	Biggest customer challenges	How do you stand out
Generic across all customer level eg website messages		
Industry vertical eg airlines		
Customer level eg British Airways		
Individual level eg CFO at British Airways		

Begin by thinking about challenges that are common across a broad range of customers. If you were trying to stand out on your website what could you say and do?

Move down the table to see if you can adapt how you stand out in the different contexts, keeping true to the overarching messages you developed to stand out at the generic cross-customer level. Did you find this hard or easy?

Now do the same but looking from the perspective of implementing a marketing or sales programme internally. Change the headings in the 'context' column to match your organization and programme, eg pan-organization, executive board level, marketing people, salespeople. Were you able to set your programme in context for the different types of people?

Chapter summary

In this chapter we have given you a view of the enabling conditions that need to be in place for a strong basis for activation. We have drawn your attention to a few things that can derail successful activation if you're not careful. There are some key steps that need to be taken in order to mobilize the people and teams you need to put on 'active duty' for the customer, and inside your own organization.

There is no escaping that activation is effortful. Activation competencies are, without doubt, core competencies for marketing and salespeople, as 'vision without action is a dream'. We identified a set of competencies that are needed for successful activation that should help your organization stand out in ways that are meaningful to customers. Developing these competencies to a high level is a non-trivial task, and to help you on your

TABLE 6.4 Activation conditions and competencies

Enabling conditions	Derailers	Mobilizers	Competencies
Focus	Other priorities	Sales and marketing alignment Getting buy-in	Balanced advocacy Listening
Purpose and outcome	Fully baked answers	Stakeholder management	Negotiation Tenacity
Business case	Executive buy-in Plethora of product programmes		People-centricity Contextualization

TABLE 6.5 Visionary and Activator Competencies

V Visionary	A Activator	L Learner	U Usefulness	E Evaluator
Victor the Visionary	Alison the Activator	Laura the Learner	Ulysses the Usefulness	Erica the Evaluator
Outside-in	Balanced advocacy			
Farsight	Listening			
Zooming	Negotiation			
Predicting	Tenacity			
Imagining	People-centricity contextualization			

way we gave you a few drills to test where you are at now. You probably need to put a plan in place that puts you on a path to learn to be better at these competencies. Which takes us nicely onto the next competence we will turn to in Chapter 7, Learning.

Before we do, Table 6.5 shows a summary of the competencies we have seen so far for Victor the Visionary and Alison the Activator:

References and further reading

Barker, J A (1992) *Discovering the Future: The power of vision*, Winter Park, Florida

Barta, T and Barwise, P (2017) *The 12 Powers of a Marketing Leader: How to succeed by building customer and company value*, McGraw-Hill Education, New York

BBC News (2019) School strike for climate: Protests staged around the world, [online] https://www.bbc.co.uk/news/world-48392551 (archived at https://perma.cc/Z4HL-BMBM)

Covey, S (2013) *The 7 Habits of Highly Effective People: Powerful lessons in personal change* (25th anniversary edition), Simon & Schuster, London

Dixon, M and Adamson, B (2013) *The Challenger Sale: How to take control of the customer conversation*, Portfolio Penguin, London

Fisher, R and Ury, W (1992) *Getting to Yes: Negotiating agreement without giving in*, 2nd ed, Business Books, London

Kelly, S, Johnston, P and Danheiser, S (2017) *Value-ology: Aligning sales and marketing to shape and deliver profitable customer value propositions*, Palgrave Macmillan, Basingstoke

Konrath, J (2015) *Agile Selling*, Portfolio/Penguin, New York

Luzbetak, L J (1988) *The Church and Cultures: New perspectives in missiological anthropology*, Orbis, New York

Miller, R D, Heiman, S E and Tuleja, T (2011) *The New Strategic Selling* (Rev 3rd ed), Kogan Page, London

Oppenheim, M (2016) Martin Luther King Day: Read civil rights leader's 'I have a dream' speech in full: One of the most definitive iconic moments of the 20th century, *Independent*, 18 January [online] https://www.independent.co.uk/news/people/martin-luther-king-jr-day-read-civil-rights-leaders-i-have-a-dream-speech-in-full-a6819481.html (archived at https://perma.cc/U445-URA7)

Toman, N, Adamson, B and Gomez, C (2017) The new sales imperative, *Harvard Business Review*, March/April

Winkler, J (1996), *Bargaining for Results*, Heinemann, Oxford

07

The learner – competencies for staying in tune with your customers

In this chapter we will:

- share what learning competencies are and why they are critical to develop;
- explain what it means to be a good learner;
- provide ideas to develop yourself as a learner;
- discuss common pitfalls to learning in the context of B2B sales and marketing.

Learning is continuous

> *I have not failed. I have just found 10,000 ways that won't work.*
>
> THOMAS EDISON (CITED IN ELKHORNE, 1967)

In 1859, at the age of 12, Thomas Edison dropped out of primary school. His teachers deemed him 'slow' and unsuccessful in the classroom, so his mother kept him home and taught him herself. He had a laboratory in the basement to experiment and test out his ideas. Like all good inventors, Edison had a knack for building on previous inventions and making them better. You may think of him as the inventor of the light bulb, but in fact, his design was based on the work of several inventors that came before him. What made his discovery different is that he figured out a way to make a commercially viable light bulb that could be produced inexpensively and burn for several hours/days. Thus, the 'first' incandescent light bulb was born in 1879.

Edison didn't stop learning and inventing after his very successful invention. He worked well into his 80s and held a record 1,093 patents at the time of his death.

Edison's story perfectly illustrates the concept of learning as a continuous process. In other words, the learning journey is never-ending. While we may not all be famous inventors, we have a vast amount of information, knowledge and tools at our disposal to constantly be learning and growing... and that's an important mindset to accept.

What is a learner?

Learning is not compulsory... it's voluntary.

W EDWARDS DEMING (CITED IN VOEHL, 1995)

When we talk about 'learning', you may immediately think of being a student in a traditional classroom setting. However, the majority of us only spend about 25 per cent of our lives receiving formal training and education. The rest of our learning takes place outside the classroom in the 'real world'.

As we outlined in Chapter 3, we define 'learner' as someone who 'acquires knowledge or skills or modifies a behavioural tendency' (Merriam-Webster.com). These skills or knowledge may be gained in a variety of ways – through personal experience, self-study, formal or informal education and training.

There is much research on the topic of learning, and it would be helpful to paint a picture about what a good learner looks like. Adult learning expert Malcolm Knowles (1990) notes some important characteristics of adult learners that apply to sales and marketing professionals:

- they know why they need to learn about markets and customers;
- they take responsibility and are motivated to learn what is necessary to do their job;
- they draw from experience.

We define the top characteristics of a *good learner* as being:

1. Open to new ideas – constantly seeking out new information.
2. Critical thinker – testing their assumptions.
3. Self-directed – don't wait to be told what to do.

4 Deliberate about learning (informally and formally).
5 Collaborative – asking questions and seeking input from others.
6 Reflective – making meaning out of what was learned.
7 Flexible – adapts and doesn't get stuck.

Good learners also practise double-loop learning, a learning model created by Argyris and Schön (1978) which helps identify the underlying causes of problems, not just the symptoms.

For example, let's say an organization keeps losing deals they bid for in the manufacturing sector. On the surface, they may blame their 'high prices' for the reason they lose. But in double-loop learning, they would dig deeper, looking for patterns. If they keep asking themselves why certain things are happening, they will uncover the root cause of the issue.

- Why do we keep losing deals in manufacturing?

  We submit RFPs but get the same response, 'your price is too high'.
- Why do prospects think our prices are too high?

  We are a new entrant to the market and customers thought we would be cheaper.
- Why would they think we'd be cheaper?

  Because we told them we can help them cut costs.
- Why did we tell them that?

  Most of our messaging and marketing/sales content is all about how we can help control your costs and save you money.
- Why are we still going to market with a cost savings message?

  Because we haven't updated our value proposition since the 2008 recession.

The value of learning

Greek philosopher Heraclitus once said, 'change is the only constant'. Just look at the marketing technology landscape for proof of this famous quote. For example, in 2011 there were just 150 marketing technologies available; by 2108 marketers had more than 7,000 technology solutions at their disposal (Brinker, 2018). With so many options available, marketers must understand and ultimately choose which technologies will best suit their needs. This is no small task.

As Regina, VP of marketing for an IT firm, told us:

> We've introduced seven new technologies and programmes this year that everybody had to learn. We have to outsmart our competition. And that requires a lot of new tools and capabilities, a lot of new systems.

What Regina points out is that things are moving fast, and everyone on the team must learn and adapt. The goal isn't to just implement new technology for the sake of having something new. Regina rightly views technology as a platform to learn more about their customers so that they can go to market in a distinctive way, and operate a more efficient and effective marketing team.

So why are we devoting a whole chapter to describing the importance of being a learner?

Quite simply, it boils down to what Christine, VP of marketing, shared:

> I think learning is hugely important in global business. Everything is constantly changing. So you really have to be in that learning mindset.

Christine describes the need to 'keep up' with changing times. Whether that's changing customer demands, industry shifts or internal organizational changes – your job and company success is dependent on your ability to adapt and go with the flow.

In other words, if you are not dedicated to constantly learning and trying new things, you will find yourself disconnected from what your customers really want and expect. This disconnect can lead to creating:

- products that nobody wants;
- marketing content that nobody uses;
- sales conversations that waste everyone's time.

Further, more so than anything else in your career, learning is something you have complete control over.

You get to own your own growth and invest in learning new skills and knowledge. This can be a highly rewarding process. In fact, workers surveyed by LinkedIn (2019) found that 89 per cent agreed that acquiring skills is more important than job titles.

But we question why today's organizations and individuals aren't putting more emphasis on continuously learning. When we asked survey participants to rate the importance of various marketing and sales competencies, we found that:

> Only 52.5 per cent stated that 'A dedication to learning new things' was 'very important'. On the flipside, 90 per cent stated that 'the ability to connect the dots from customer needs to company solutions' is very important.

This indicates a significant gap between 'what' is important (connecting the dots) and 'how' this actually gets done (learning about your customers).

Similarly, Hays, a top marketing recruiting firm located in the UK, surveyed 300 marketers to understand what skills are most important in the digital world (see Figure 7.1). They found that the top five most essential in-demand skills amongst today's 'generalist' marketers are strategic thinking, campaign/project management, creativity, commercial awareness, and customer-centricity.

Again, what's interesting is that the ability to learn and adapt is a common thread throughout many of these competencies (Figure 7.2). For example, how can one claim to be 'customer-centric' without first learning about one's customers? And it would be impossible to come up with creative solutions without first having an understanding of the problems your customers are trying to solve.

As buying preferences evolve and change, so must you.

B2B buying preferences have dramatically evolved over the last several years. Buyers are demanding more personalized solutions and communications

FIGURE 7.1 Top core marketing generalist skills

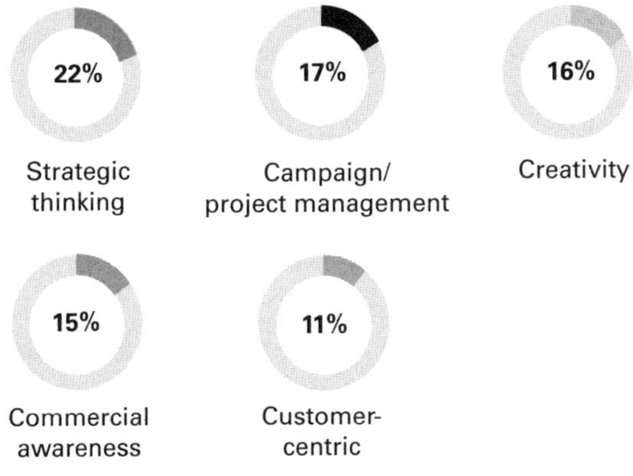

SOURCE Hays (2019)

FIGURE 7.2 It starts with a learning mindset

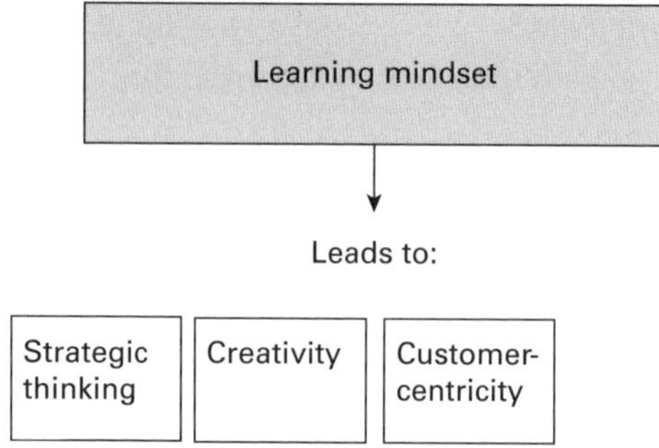

and they are tired of wasting their time with vendors that don't learn about their business.

In a 2019 Aberdeen study, 97 per cent of respondents found that B2B buyers want sales reps that can 'demonstrate a stronger knowledge of their company and needs' (Aberdeen, 2019).

Think about that for a second. Only 3 per cent of sales reps are spending enough time to learn about their prospects and show that they understand their world. Most are just showing up to meet with prospects unprepared. This leads to buyer frustration and is why 65 per cent of buyers believe that 'vendors and sales reps are more interested in selling their products/services than listening to my needs' (Merkle, 2017).

One of the best ways to get out of this 'product pushing' mode is to adopt an 'always be learning' mindset. Malcom Knowles (1990) talks of people in the context of learning as either dogmatic (pushy) – this is how it is and I'm going to tell you what you must know – or reconciliatory (build bridges) – let's try and understand how to work together. So it could be that your instinctive attitude to learning drives how you interact with customers!

Instead of thinking about what you want to sell, start thinking about why your customer would buy your solution and what problem it will solve. This requires you to get curious!

> In a survey, 62.5 per cent of respondents stated that 'curiosity' was a 'very important' competency for today's marketing and sales professionals.

Children are intensely eager to learn how everything works in the world. Research has shown that mothers are asked nearly 300 questions a day by their children, amounting to roughly 105,000 questions a year (news.com.au, 2013)! If you're a parent of a small child, you know how relentless their questioning can be. But when we reach middle school we stop asking questions – losing our sense of wonder and interest.

Yet curiosity gets to the heart of what B2B buyers want from today's vendors – insights, value-added resources and a partner that is interested in helping them. Marketing and sales professionals that develop their sense of curiosity are able to build better relationships, uncover more insights and solve problems faster. How? By demonstrating a desire to genuinely know more about the customer and asking better questions.

We'd encourage you to look beyond your industry or your customer's industry for inspiration. Some of the best ideas could come from sources that aren't immediately connected to your world. For example, Hollywood screenwriting techniques can be applied to storytelling in business and advertising.

The key takeaway is that organizations that value learning more about their customers will be in a position to innovate faster and stay ahead of the competition.

So now that you understand why it's important to learn, your first question may be – *what should I learn to help my company stand out?*

Remember, the premise of this book is to help you stand out amongst a Sea of Sameness. Building on the fact that your customers want and expect you to bring them value in the form of unique insights, guidance and solutions, we suggest that you have a full understanding of the dimensions shared in Chapter 5 (Visionary).

FIGURE 7.3 Building your unique value proposition

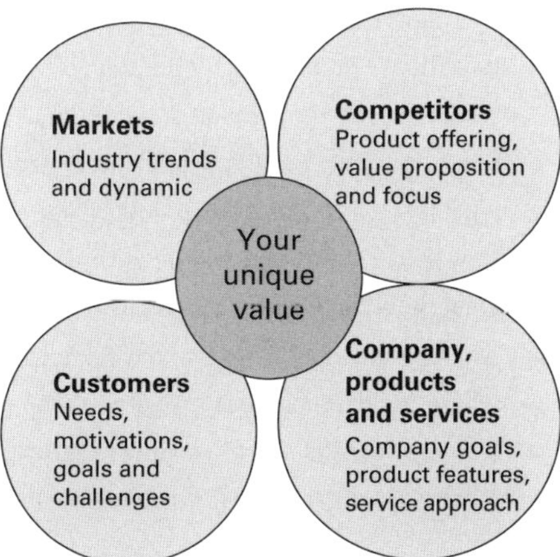

Many of the B2B companies that we work with admit to not being fully knowledgeable about one or more of these areas. What's worse, most companies just skip the customer and competitor research (or conduct it once and assume the information stays the same year over year).

But we argue that it's *everyone's* job in the company to help deliver customer value – not just the sales, product or customer service team.

Stand-out organizations understand where they are going, how they are unique and why customers should follow. So take some time to reflect on these questions (Table 7.1) and see how many you can answer with confidence.

Which questions did you find difficult to answer? How does this relate to where you spend most of your time on the job? Can you commit to learning something new in these areas?

Let this be the starting point in your learning journey.

TABLE 7.1 Reflection questions

Category	Questions to Ask Yourself
The market	• How much do I understand about the market we operate in? • What are the market trends for the next 5 years? • How much do I understand about the market my customers operate in?
Your customers	• Who is our ideal customer? • What are the customer's top needs and pain points? • What are our customers trying to gain or achieve in their business? • Why do customers work with us?
Your competitors	• Who are our top competitors? • How does our company compare to the competition? • What do we do different/better than the competition? • What does the competition do better than us?
Your company and product-service solutions	• What are our revenue targets this year and next? • What is the mission of our company? ie why are we in business? • How do we measure the value we provide to customers? • What problem do we solve for customers?
Your role	• What are my top strengths and weaknesses? • Where could I improve in my current job? • Where do I wish I had more knowledge/expertise? • What skills do I need to develop to take my career to the next level?

Developing as a learner

First and foremost, a *good* learner isn't someone passively sitting on the sidelines waiting for knowledge to be dumped in their lap, but rather, someone who actively seeks out new and improved information and ways of doing things. At the core, this requires you to step outside of your comfort zone.

Kristen, CMO at a financial services firm, described this as 'being fearless':

> You could be taking on a new project like data analysis or data mining, and really not have a whole lot of experience in that area. But you have to have this willingness to try and to see what comes of it or try to figure it out and problem solve. There's an element of not being scared to try new approaches and being open to learning new things.

While learning is deemed fundamental by the business leaders we spoke to, we've found that many people are not taking the time to do it. In fact, the #1 reason employees say they are not engaging in workplace learning is because they don't have the time (LinkedIn, 2019).

Summed up by Jeff, a business unit president at a global professional services firm: 'I think learning is important... it just gets deprioritized'.

You've probably experienced firsthand what Jeff is saying. You may have several projects to juggle at once, a growing list of 'to-do's' and internal demands from your peers that get in the way of learning. But the reality is, you have to take personal responsibility for your learning and growth.

Let's follow our next fictitious character, Laura the Learner, to illustrate how this may look inside a company. Laura always wants to learn more about her customers, new technologies, business approaches and market trends. She spends at least an hour every day reading LinkedIn updates, news, Google and business alerts about her industry and her customers. She knows that customer and competitor research is a daily practice – especially in the fast-paced world of tech, where she works.

Like most things in life, learning is a competency that can be developed and practised. The more you carve out time to do it, the easier it will become, and the more enjoyable and rewarding it will be!

Here we share a few ways to develop your inner learner.

Get introspective

It's helpful to first understand a little bit about yourself – like your motivation for learning and your preferred learning style. When it comes to motivation for learning, you may find that you're driven by various reasons.

INTERNAL MOTIVATION

Do you have a natural desire and drive to get better? For example, Tom, VP of sales, said that he often examines his performance after failing at something:

> I studied negotiation skills early in my sales career because I lost a big deal. I always want to know – am I putting enough time in to stay relevant? I only do this out of necessity or if I'm being self-critical.

Psychologists Ryan and Deci (2000) call this intrinsic motivation 'self-determination theory'. Rather than relying on external factors to become motivated, individuals pursue learning and growth for the enjoyment of experiencing competence (mastery), autonomy (control over one's life) and relatedness (connection with others).

Thomas Edison and Stephen Hawking are two examples of people who dedicated their lives to learning for the thrill of discovering something new.

This way of thinking doesn't just apply to scientists and inventors. In a business context, imagine that *you* are the one to share your revelation about what your customers are thinking and expecting from your company. Or that you are the one to uncover a strength that your competitors don't have.

EXTERNAL MOTIVATION

Acquiring new skills or taking on new projects may also help you earn additional compensation or a promotion at work. Indeed, our research found that many leaders recognize employees who put in the extra effort to round out their skills for the betterment of the company.

As Regina told us:

> Not everybody can have a promotion in a company of our size. But what we can do is teach our employees new things that increase their value and give them more compensation because they've demonstrated a new skill.

Kristen, CMO of a financial services company, shared that she's open to having her team decide what they want to learn and improve, as long as it positively impacts the company:

> If my team has an interest in something, I tell them to 'raise your hand'.

So think about what you are personally interested in learning – a new skill, like SEO, perhaps – and how that may contribute to both your personal growth and the advancement of your team and company.

This may be more feasible if you work in a smaller company where people must wear many hats. But the point is – are you taking the initiative on what you want to learn and asking your manager to help support your growth?

It also helps to learn with a goal in mind. What do you want or need to know? What are you trying to achieve? What do you want to be able to put on your resume?

Learning preference

We each have a preferred way that we like to learn. You may be familiar with the VARK® model (Fleming and Mills, 1992), which suggests there are four main learning styles:

- visual;
- auditory;
- reading/writing;
- kinesthetic (hands on).

You may favour looking at charts, images and graphs vs reading a report or listening to a podcast, for example. Most of us possess a combination of these methods depending on what we're learning.

It's helpful to understand what your learning preferences are so that you can seek out opportunities to learn that are consistent with your style. For example, sitting and listening to a tutorial about how to use a new software may seem extremely boring and ineffective to you. Instead, you may desire to just 'dig in' and start discovering what the software can do.

Keep in mind that your customers also have a preferred learning style. Are you creating content in only one format? Or are you producing materials that cover all the various learning styles? For example videos, podcasts, whitepapers, and hands-on exhibits or trials.

Be the teacher and the student

At any given time, you are a master or 'expert' at certain things and an amateur at others. You may have been working in marketing for the last 15 years, but just recently started to work at a new company, for example.

In daily life, you constantly have the opportunity to be both the teacher – passing your knowledge onto others – and the student – being willing to be taught.

The first step is to recognize when you need to play each role. If you are a leader in your organization, you may feel like you have to have all the answers. But this is an unrealistic expectation; you can't possibly know everything there is to know. This mindset of pretending to know everything can stifle creativity and shut down good ideas.

Some organizations may value the opinion of an executive or business leader more than anyone else's input. But when only one person's voice matters, employees and co-workers may just stop sharing their ideas. As Robson, former President of a US telco pointed out, 'If somebody's already got all the answers to everything, then why would they need to learn from other experiences?' This is a dangerous place to be, as it leads to herd mentality and groupthink as discussed in Chapter 1 – where everyone blindly follows along with the leader.

If you've ever been a mentor, you know that you can learn just as much from the mentee as they can learn from you. Kirk, SVP product management for a technology company explains it this way:

> Every mentor has come to realize it's been more bi-directional than they ever thought it would be. Especially with Millennials and being able to bounce things off them. It actually helps the mentors from an emotional intelligence standpoint – how to better relate with this next generation of employees.

The second step is to be open to learn from others and demonstrate humility. This will go a long way to create trust and an open environment for learning. In the age of social media, where everyone can widely share their opinion, however, humility has become an endangered competency.

So what can you do to combat this?

- **Encourage a culture of questioning things** – get in the habit of inviting feedback and being open and receptive to what you hear. One of the best questions to ask in business is 'why?' Agency owner Jerry works with a lot of B2B clients in the UK and sees that many organizations get stuck when creating new content because they fail to ask, 'why are we creating this?' As customer needs change, it's imperative to keep questioning whether or not your marketing content and programmes are still relevant.

- **Constantly ask 'do we have all the information?'** Whether you're trying to learn more about your customers, or simply trying to make your internal initiatives better, someone has to step up and shine the light that there is more than one way of doing things. Tom, CMO for a US-based agency shared that they've made questioning part of their culture: 'We have a culture of encouraging contrarians and questioning things. We are brutally honest with each other. This takes humility to constantly question what you know.'
- **Be present** – if there's something important you'd like people to learn, be there and take part yourself. For example, we've worked with clients who have invested in important cross-department initiatives, like revising their value proposition. On the day of the training, the executive will send junior-level delegates or participate half-heartedly in the workshop. As a result, they miss out on key information being shared that ultimately impacts how their company communicates and delivers value to customers. Our advice – don't skip critical learning opportunities, especially if you are a leader within your organization!
- **Actively listen** – perhaps an underutilized skill in business today, actively listening requires you to focus on what's being said. Put down your device and pay attention to the speaker. What are they saying? What is their body language communicating? You will be surprised what you can learn when you really tune into the words, tone of voice and gestures being used.

MISSED LEARNING OPPORTUNITY

Jessica, a product marketing director for a mid-sized technology firm, received an email from a software vendor that she didn't not know, and whose products she'd never heard of. Like most typical cold emails that Jessica receives, the sender didn't ask her any questions or demonstrate that he even knew what her company did before launching into his product pitch and 'free trial' offer.

She wanted to see how this salesperson would respond if she provided a little more information. Would he be curious enough (or smart enough) to recognize the input she was giving him to better position his solution?

So she fired back a note and told him that she was currently not interested as she has 'other top priorities', and that she was gearing up for 'a new product launch in Q3' which should lead to changes in their business.

The salesperson's response was typical – 'Great, I will follow-up with you in Q4!'

Jessica thought – *why didn't he ask for more information about my 'top priorities' or what my 'new product launch' was all about?*

This example points to a common mistake that salespeople make every day – ignoring the opportunity to learn more about their customers. Some simple questions would have opened the door and ultimately helped this salesperson better position their solution.

Set aside time for formal and informal learning

Not everything you learn needs to be in a traditional or formal setting. We'd encourage you to find a mix of both formal and informal learning opportunities.

FORMAL LEARNING

This type of learning is more structured and can include classes, conferences and seminars at your local university, online or through professional associations. Look at joining associations for your job function (sales or marketing), the industry your organization operates in and your customer's industry (manufacturing, for example).

The majority of survey respondents attend conferences or seminars once a year (14 per cent) or twice a year (43 per cent).

Several people we spoke to mentioned that their company has a semi-formalized approach to help keep all employees informed. Whether that's an internal e-newsletter, webinar, weekly conference call or internal website or chat group, the expectation is that employees are making the time to consume the information being shared.

Kirk, SVP of product management for a technology firm, said that his company hosts regular internal webinars:

> We host two types of webinars: one to share updates on products and marketing campaigns, and one for interesting and trending topics – like the immersion of Bitcoin and e-commerce and social media best practices.

Think about how beneficial it is to have the entire sales and marketing team hearing the same information.

Another approach is to make your department or team meetings more valuable and actionable. Regina, VP of marketing for an IT company, said that she's implemented an approach with her team that makes them more invested in their growth:

> We started having marketing all-hands meetings every two weeks. But they're not a readout. Everybody is expected to show up to teach each other something they think will be of value.

We love this idea of meeting to learn vs meeting to update!

Whether or not your organization has a formal internal training department or programme in place, it's crucial that you seek out opportunities to learn outside of your company.

Katie, Managing Director of a US software company, observed that:

> a lot of companies get rid of training and knowledge management systems when they are trying to cut costs. And therefore they depend on the individual employees in key positions to learn and keep up to date themselves.

Indeed, it's up to you to create your own learning plan.

INFORMAL LEARNING

There are infinite ad-hoc opportunities to grow your knowledge when you're 'in the moment'. For example, let's say you are putting together a new marketing campaign targeting healthcare. In preparation for developing your campaign plan, you may seek out a variety of different types of information:

- an article or research report outlining healthcare trends;
- internal data/stats about how your content/tactics have performed with healthcare customers in the past;
- picking up the phone to ask your sales colleague what roadblocks they are running into in customer meetings;
- talking 1:1 with customers on the phone or at an industry event;
- watching an online video or webinar about content trends in B2B/healthcare.

While the learning in this case isn't structured, you still need to start with a goal or objective in mind to stay focused and avoid slipping down the internet rabbit hole! Start with identifying what it is that you want to know that will help make your programmes and content stronger.

And we will point out something that is often missed by marketers – taking advantage of meeting face to face with your customers. Marketers are responsible for planning customer-facing events, trade show sponsorships and participation at local industry gatherings. Yet, in our experience, most fail to engage with customers in a meaningful way when they are face to face at the event. This is a huge missed opportunity to learn directly from your customers.

How much time you invest in each learning method is up to you. The important thing is that you set aside time to learn!

Let's go back to our role model Laura the Learner. Laura is a member of both a national and a local B2B marketing association as well as a cross-industry professional women's organization. She sets a goal for herself to attend one event (in person or online) per quarter. She recently started tracking her top competitors to become more knowledgeable about how they are communicating, what products they are pushing and which marketing channels they are heavily using. While she doesn't have a fancy tool or technology to use, she's starting with a simple spreadsheet to see what sort of insights she can uncover.

Common pitfalls that impede learning

Besides the obvious pitfall of not taking the time to learn, there are three common stumbling blocks that we want to call attention to as you embark on your learning journey.

Not reflecting on what you learned

> *We do not learn from experience... we learn from reflecting on experience.*
>
> JOHN DEWEY (1933)

Reflecting on what you've learned – that is, to think deeply about it – allows you to take something theoretical and see how it could apply in your world. Learning and education expert Patricia Alexander defined reflection as 'the deliberation, pondering, or rumination over ideas, circumstances, or experiences'.

Donald Schön, MIT professor and founder of the reflective practice concept, believed that executives who reflect on their practice are more successful than those who don't. The aim is to understand what works and what doesn't and how you can improve things.

Asking yourself reflection questions during and after reading, listening, watching or executing something helps make it 'stick' in your brain. This could be done informally, sitting alone at your desk with a notepad or laptop, or you could host a formal 'debrief' meeting with a larger project team.

The questions you ask yourself will vary from situation to situation but should cover both the process of learning and the specifics you've learned. This can be neatly summed as considering:

- what;
- so what;
- now what.

For example, at the end of a marketing or sales initiative, you may reflect on the following:

- What:
  - Did we achieve the results we wanted?
  - What went well in the project? What didn't go well?
- So what:
  - What is the most important thing we learned about our customers?
  - What is the most important thing we learned about ourselves?
  - What is the impact to our organization?
- Now what:
  - How can we apply this information to future campaigns?
  - How might this apply to other areas/segments of our business?
  - Who else needs to know what we learned?
  - What are some barriers that might get in the way of applying what we learned?

Besides project debriefs and reflective questioning, our earlier research found that the most successful organizations – those exceeding revenue targets – conduct formal win-loss analysis after every deal. This is a great tool to help understand why you are winning or losing business. Collect this data over time and you can start to see areas in your business that you may need to work on to help differentiate yourself from the competition – ie product enhancements, better sales and quoting process, more engagement from your leadership team, etc.

Not sharing what you learned

How many trade shows, seminars or webinars have you attended in the last year? How much of your new knowledge did you pass along to your team? We all have good intentions to share what we've learned, but we come back to our day jobs and our new knowledge disappears.

Have you heard of the Ebbinghaus forgetting curve? First established in 1885, German psychologist Hermann Ebbinghaus found that the brain starts losing knowledge over time (Ebbinghaus, 1885). See Figure 7.4 to see just how quickly we let slip new knowledge. Within the first month, our brains forget 90 per cent of what we've learned!

This is why it's important to immediately summarize and share what you've learned. That new technology trend you just read about? Share it with your product team. That B2B sales questioning technique you just successfully used with a prospect? Share it with the rest of your sales team. That crucial piece of information your customer mentioned about why they work with your organization? Share it with your marketing team!

Additionally, how many departments are 'hoarding' information they're collecting about customers or competitors? We found that most organiza-

FIGURE 7.4 The forgetting curve

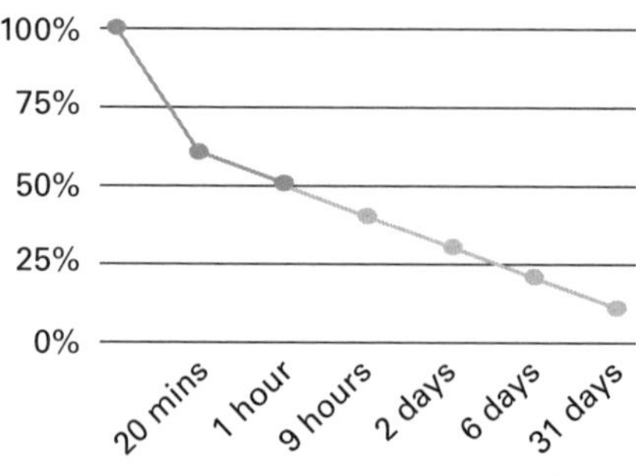

Learners will forget about 90% of what they've learned within the first month

tions lack a formal process to gather customer and competitor intelligence and share this information throughout the organization.

Think of all the interactions your company has with customers – from sales to product to service delivery, to onboarding, customer service and billing. When knowledge and expertise are trapped within one department, it prevents collaboration and the development of innovative ideas.

In our book, *Value-ology*, we concluded that 'Cohesion is the new differentiator'. What we meant was that organizations who have a feedback loop from customers into the rest of the organization will set themselves apart.

Setting up a feedback loop isn't easy. But it's a crucial step to help your company make sense of what is coming out of the daily sales and service calls then re-shaping value propositions in line with what customers want.

Use the idea of the Kolb learning cycle, which breaks down the learning process into four steps. Figure 7.5 shows an example for evaluating your value proposition after winning or losing a deal.

In business, we continuously go around this loop and for it to work, it depends entirely on feedback at each stage.

In this regard, it's worth doing a 'feedback health check' with your colleagues to ensure what's working and what's not so the whole organization is continuously sharing and learning.

Not applying what you learned

Perhaps the most detrimental thing you can do after investing the time to learn something new is to simply not apply it.

Imagine that you are learning to play the guitar. You've invested in an online course and diligently watched 10 hours of training videos to learn the fundamentals. Maybe you've even picked up a few tips from online forums and friends. But what if you never pick up the guitar and actually practise what you've learned?

This may seem ludicrous, but many marketing and sales professionals fall into this trap. They read articles, attend conferences, talk to peers about 'best practices', then... do nothing. It's not enough to acquire new knowledge, you have to put it into action.

At the heart of this, leaders need to empower their teams to take action on what they've learned. VP of marketing Caroline's take on it:

> I'm a big fan of 'fail fast'. If you fail, figure out what the failure point was, fix it and move on and use that to learn. I think failing is fine. Not learning from it is not.

FIGURE 7.5 Applying the Kolb Learning Cycle

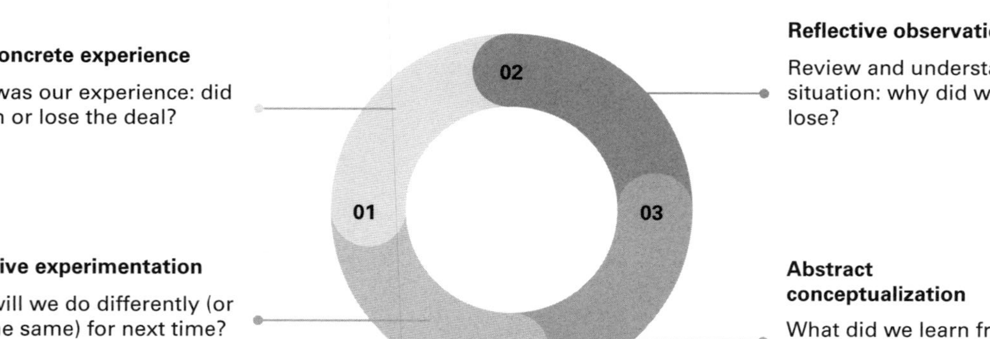

Concrete experience

What was our experience: did we win or lose the deal?

Reflective observation

Review and understand the situation: why did we win or lose?

Abstract conceptualization

What did we learn from this experience? Do we need to better define customer benefits?

Active experimentation

What will we do differently (or keep the same) for next time?

Embrace the fact that the first time you apply your new knowledge, things may not go as planned. In other words, you're going to make mistakes. You may be eager to test out a new customer-facing message in your email campaign based on some information or data you collected. But what if nobody opens your emails? Should you scrap the whole thing and write it off as a 'bad idea'? Maybe. But before you can answer that, you have to reflect on what happened, adjust your message and try again.

As Regina told us:

> If you really want learning to stick or become impactful, you've got to empower people to go and act on what they learned, and then let them do it in an environment, in a culture where if it fails fully or partially then that's okay.

Thus, adopting a mindset of experimentation is key, as shown in the Kolb model above. If you are a leader in your organization, it's your job to encourage your team to implement what they've learned. Otherwise, the team will continue to get stuck in a rut. On the flipside, as an individual contributor, your job is to take the initiative to practise and act upon what you've uncovered.

Looking once again at Laura, our avid learner, she both challenges and encourages her team to seek out new information and knowledge. When her employee Jack presented a new approach that he learned about how to improve their email open rates, she told him to go implement it and test it that same week. And do you think she forgot to check in with him to see how the initial test went? Of course not!

Final thoughts

It's easy to get stuck in your current routine and bad habits, especially when things are going well enough. As we've pointed out, though, your organization will continue to get stuck in the Sea of Sameness unless you make the commitment to be a learner.

If you're still on the fence about how seriously you should be taking learning, consider these stats from LinkedIn's 2019 Workplace Learning Report. They found that heavy learners – those spending over five hours per week learning – are:

- 74 per cent more likely to know where they want to go in their career;
- 48 per cent more likely to have found purpose in their work;
- 47 per cent less likely to be stressed at work.

So start by setting some boundaries around what you need to learn. Refer back to Table 7.1 at the beginning of the chapter for help in deciding what to focus on first.

Next, take the following assessment (Table 7.2) to see how you may need to develop yourself as a learner. Score yourself for each area on a scale of 1–5 (strongly disagree–strongly agree). If you are a people manager or business leader, score yourself personally as well as in your role as a manager.

TABLE 7.2 Learning assessment

Question	Individual	Team leader
I know my preferred learning style (Visual, Auditory, Reading/Writing, Kinesthetic)		
I create an environment for learning in my team		
I am curious and always have lots of questions		
I make time to seek out opportunities to attend new classes/conferences/webinars		
I don't take things for granted. I question why we are doing things		
When I learn new information, I reflect on how it will impact our organization and customers		
I share what I learn with others across the organization		
I experiment with new and improved ways to do my job		
I encourage others to try something new, even if that means making a mistake		

In Chapter 8, we will build on your learning competencies and look at what today's organizations need to do to stay relevant and useful to customers. Here's a summary of the competencies we have seen so far:

TABLE 7.3 Learner value competencies

V Visionary	A Activator	L Learner	U Usefulness	E Evaluator
Victor the Visionary	Alison the Activator	Laura the Learner	Ulysses the Useful	Erica the Evaluator
Outside-in	Balanced advocacy	Curiosity		
Farsight	Listening	Proactive and engaged		
Zooming	Negotiation	Reflective		
Predicting	Tenacity	'Fearless' experimentation		
Imagining	People centricity contextualization	Receptive		

References and further reading

Aberdeen (2019) Why do B2B Buyers Struggle? The answer is in the data [online] https://www.aberdeen.com/old-resources/b2b-buyers-survey/ (archived at https://perma.cc/3DWP-9KQP)

Alexander, P (2017) Reflection and reflexivity in practice versus in theory: challenges of conceptualization, complexity, and competence, *Educational Psychologist*, **52** (4), pp 307–14

Argyris, C and Schön, D (1978) *Organizational Learning: A theory of action perspective*, Addison-Wesley

Biography.com (2019) Thomas Edison [online] https://www.biography.com/inventor/thomas-edison (archived at https://perma.cc/58HK-C5NG)

Brinker, S (2018) Marketing Technology Landscape Supergraphic (2018): Martech 5000 [online] https://chiefmartec.com/2018/04/marketing-technology-landscape-supergraphic-2018/ (archived at https://perma.cc/J9EE-B9QA)

Burgoyne, J and Reynolds, M (1997) *Management Learning*, Sage

Dewey, J (1933) *How we Think*, Heath & Co, Boston, DC, p 78

Ebbinghaus, H (1885) *Über das Gedächtnis*, Dunker, Leipzig

Elkhorne, J L (1967) Edison – The fabulous Drone, *73 Magazine*, **XLVI** (3) [online] http://www.arimi.it/wp-content/73/03_March_1967.pdf (archived at https://perma.cc/2EQD-5K9B)

Fleming, N D and Mills, C (1992) Not another inventory, rather a catalyst for reflection, *To Improve the Academy*, **11**, p 137

Gibbs, G (1988) *Learning by Doing: A guide to teaching and learning methods*, Further Education Unit, Oxford Polytechnic, Oxford

The Indian Express (2013) Mothers asked nearly 300 questions a day by kids [online] http://archive.indianexpress.com/news/mothers-asked-nearly-300-questions-a-day-by-kids/1094922/ (archived at https://perma.cc/5JHW-J7HN)

Hays (2019) Elements of a Marketer: Skills for a digital world. Available from: www.hays.co.uk/job/marketing-jobs/marketing-skills-report (archived at https://perma.cc/Q6MX-QREX)

Knowles, M (1990) *The Adult Learner: A neglected species*, 4th ed, Gulf Publishing, Houston

Kolb, D (1984) *Experiential Learning*, Prentice Hall, Englewood Cliffs

LinkedIn (2019) Workplace Learning Report [online] https://www.news.com.au/lifestyle/parenting/littlewoods-retailer-survey-finds-mothers-asked-228-questions-a-day/news-story/9cca3e25f5981147d1e0bff293f6e3f2 (archived at https://perma.cc/VQN6-JBMF)

Merkle (2017) Programs That Connect: B-to-B loyalty programs that create pathways to new opportunities and business growth [online] https://www.merkleinc.com/thought-leadership/white-papers/programs-connect (archived at https://perma.cc/EPE6-ZSA6)

Murre, J M and Dros, J (2015) Replication and Analysis of Ebbinghaus' Forgetting Curve. *PloS one*, **10** (7), e0120644 [online] https://doi.org/10.1371/journal.pone.0120644 (archived at https://perma.cc/C6K4-YWYC)

news.com.au (2013) Littlewoods Retailer survey finds mothers asked 228 questions a day. Available from: www.news.com.au/lifestyle/parenting/littlewoods-retailer-survey-finds-mothers-asked-228-questions-a-day/news-story/9cca3e25f5981147d1e0bff293f6e3f2 (archived at https://perma.cc/DSZ2-8KBJ)

Ryan, R and Deci, E (2000) Self-determination theory and the facilitation of intrinsic motivation, social development, and well-being, *American Psychologist*, **55** (1), pp 68–78

Voehl, F (1995) *Deming: The way we knew him*, CRC Press LLC

08

Usefulness – competencies for becoming indispensable to your customers

In this chapter we will:

- explain what usefulness means and why it's important;
- discuss your role in connecting the dots for customers;
- cover the competencies needed to be useful;
- provide an exercise for you to test the usefulness of your own marketing and sales content.

What does it mean to be useful?

Have you ever had a friend that always seems to have a perfect recommendation no matter what problem you're facing? If you're looking for a new house, they can introduce you to the ideal real estate agent. Trying to decide where to take your next holiday? They just got back from a blissful trip to Italy. Struggling to motivate your sales team? They have the ultimate performance playbook.

These friends are extremely *useful*. They seem to be well-read, well-travelled, and well-rounded. The key is that they don't share everything they know all at once. They wait until their knowledge and experience is relevant and appropriate to you. Similarly, websites that contain hotel, product or restaurant reviews and ratings are contextually useful as they tell you what you need to know at the precise moment you need the information. The benefit? It simplifies your choices and makes your decision easier.

FIGURE 8.1 The Usefulness Triangle

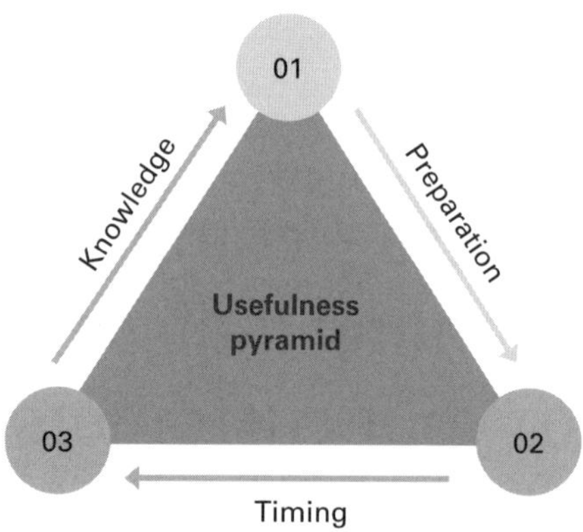

This same principle applies in business. The more relevant, or in other words, connected, you are to your customers, the more likely it is that they will keep returning to you for advice and solutions.

Usefulness is where everything we've covered in previous chapters comes together. Crucially, it means that your business is on the right track. When you're being useful to your customers, you have successfully identified the right set of customers, studied their pain points and challenges thoroughly and can now offer them something so fitting and perfect that they are inclined to say 'yes'.

In Chapter 3, we summarized that being useful was about being practical, applicable and serviceable to others. At the heart of being useful is to understand that it's not about you, but about what your customers will find valuable and helpful.

Being useful means you have to deeply understand your customers – what motivates them, what frustrates them, and what they would find beneficial as they make decisions about their business.

To be *useful*, you need to have all three of the key characteristics shown in the Usefulness Triangle, Figure 8.1.

Knowledge

First, you have to possess relevant knowledge, skills and experience that others would find helpful. Just as you wouldn't take your car to be fixed by an untrained mechanic, your customer isn't going to buy something from you if you don't demonstrate mastery and understanding. Of course, this knowledge accumulates over time and it's not something you can 'fake'.

If you don't have the knowledge that your customers are seeking, you can be sure that they will go elsewhere to find what they need (probably to one of your competitors).

B2B buyers, in particular, want and expect to work with sellers that understand their business. It's why many customers will follow their favourite salesperson when they switch jobs. For example, Joe, a seasoned B2B buyer within the IT industry, explained to us that the primary reason he chose to work with a particular telecom company was that they 'understood what we were looking for, took time to understand our business and give us the attention we needed to find a solution'.

As a marketing or sales professional, your level of understanding and knowledge is extremely valuable to customers. But your customers aren't the only ones who will benefit from your expertise. Your internal organization also finds value when you share what you've learned about your customers. The information you collect may help influence the launch of new products, new strategies and new marketing and sales programmes.

According to Deloitte's Redefining the CMO report (O'Brien, Veenstra and Murphy, 2018), the top factor driving CMO success is 'being the voice of the customer at the leadership table'. In other words, CMOs who develop and share useful information and insights about their customers earn a right to influence the strategic direction of their organization.

Preparation

Another element of being useful is to make sure you are ready and willing to be helpful. This requires you to anticipate what your customers may need. You've likely heard of the phrase 'putting yourself in the customers' shoes'. The idea is that you need to think like your customer if you really want to understand their point of view and be able to offer value. As a marketing and sales professional, part of your job is to constantly remember to be the voice of the customer internally.

But we see that most companies miss the mark here, trying to go with a 'one-size-fits-all' approach.

Why? Because not only is it really difficult and time-consuming to put yourself in one customer's shoes, but apply that to the whole decision-making unit, and you're likely to give up! As Katie, former senior vice president of marketing, told us, 'understanding how our customers evaluate their options, and the financial modelling they use, is arguably the hardest thing to do'. You may be thinking – well, I'm getting paid to promote or sell something on behalf of my company, so of course I'm motivated and disciplined! But we see many marketing and salespeople stop trying because it's too hard or tedious to create something useful for their customers.

For example, imagine that you are preparing a proposal for a prospective client. You may be tempted to just use an old proposal, replace the company name and logo and send it over to your prospective customer. But you have a much higher success rate in the acceptance of your proposal if it's tailored to your customer's situation and needs.

This level of thinking requires you to accept that your customers are not just one big homogeneous group. They each have their individual needs, preferences and decision-making criteria that may be different from one customer to the next.

Research shows that the extra effort is worth it, however, as 65 per cent of business buyers say they'd switch brands if a company didn't make efforts to personalize their communications (Salesforce, 2017).

Timing

You've likely heard the phrase 'timing is everything'. And understanding this principle is especially critical in business and how useful you are perceived to be by your customers.

While B2B buyers are doing more research online to get educated, according to the CSO Insights 2018 Buyer Preferences study, the vast majority of B2B buyers (90 per cent) are open to engaging with a sales rep earlier in the buying process. The report found that buyers are more willing to engage when the business problem they are trying to solve is:

- new for the buyer;
- particularly risky for the organization;
- perceived as risky for the buyer (as an individual);
- difficult and complex (eg involving many departments).

This presents a huge opportunity to the seller who can get in early while the customer is still defining their needs and shaping their decision criteria.

Xant (2014) research also shows that 35 to 50 per cent of sales go to the vendor that responds first to a customer inquiry.

For example, imagine that you need to get an electrician out to your house to fix a broken light in your kitchen. You do a quick search online or ask a few neighbours if they know any good electricians. Then you text the first three people on your list. If John was highly recommended by your neighbour, but he isn't available to come to your house until next week, you won't choose him. You may have to go to the third or fourth option on your list because your timing is 'now'.

On the other hand, many customers sit complacently at their jobs waiting for some catastrophe to strike before they make a major change like switching vendors or implementing a new solution. In these situations, you likely have to help your customers see a connection with something larger, such as how their declining stock price is tied to their inefficiencies in the area for which your company provides solutions.

Take action

Of course, all of this is meaningless unless you take action. We talked extensively about the importance of becoming an activator in Chapter 6. So think of usefulness as a formula:

Knowledge + Preparation + Timing + ACTION = Useful

Why is being useful so important?

Today's B2B buyers are stretched. With access to more information and an ever-increasing list of options and solutions at their fingertips, buyers simply don't have time to waste with vendors that don't add value. In other words, when your customers don't find what you have to share useful, they'll just switch vendors.

According to Accenture's 2019 'Service is the New Sales' report, 44 per cent of B2B buyers surveyed have switched sellers in the last year. The top-cited reasons fall into two basic categories:

1. Functional:
   - uncompetitive pricing (25 per cent);
   - long lead times for delivery/fulfilment (25 per cent);
   - missed delivery dates (25 per cent).
2. Usefulness:
   - poor website (15 per cent);
   - insistence on using a sales rep for all purchases (15 per cent);
   - being offered irrelevant products and services (14 per cent).

The *functional* reasons for switching seem pretty obvious. If your customer buys a product and it doesn't work properly, chances are that you will know all about it. Your customer will complain about their bill, the ill-functioning product and their disappointment with the installation and onboarding process. They likely won't stick around while you make improvements.

The *usefulness* reasons, however, are a bit less obvious, as your customer may not complain directly to you. Instead, they may just start searching online for other solutions and alternatives or explore talking to sales reps from your competitors. You will feel blindsided when they announce that they are not renewing their contract.

As a salesperson, your job is to help the customer learn more about their problem and explain how your solution will help solve it. While that sounds simple enough, B2B buyers complain that sellers are 'more interested in selling their products and services than listening to my needs' (Merkle, 2017). Imagine the frustration your customer feels when they expect to learn something from you as the seller, but they end up sitting through another product pitch.

Sometimes this is a lesson best learned the hard way, as Jeff, a business unit leader for a large IT conglomerate, shared about his early days as a sales rep:

> Early in my career I had a whole presentation prepared and the customer flips to the last page and says, 'that seems expensive'. I stumbled and told him I wanted to go through the entire pitch and he said, 'dude we're not going through the slides'. I was kicked out of his office for 'wasting his time' and was very embarrassed.

Sadly, experiences like these are typical, as RAIN research found that 58 per cent of sales meetings are not valuable to buyers! If you want to stand out as a salesperson, stop focusing on your products and consider how to help your customers – as 63 per cent of buyers will connect with a seller that offers to share something of value (Schultz, Murray and Smith, nd).

Now think about how many opportunities your customers have to interact with your company. There's your website, social media pages, emails, content downloads, inbound or cold calls, sales meetings, events, etc. Each interaction represents an opportunity for your customer to find value from what you're sharing, or not.

As Kirk, senior vice president of product management, shared:

> Every interaction with the customer is an opportunity. Maybe I'm completely old-school. I don't just pick up the phone and call the customer. I've thought through the fact that I'm taking up 30 seconds of their time. What's the seed I want to plant? What's the message I want to reinforce? What is the question I want to get answered? I want to be respectful of their time.

This way of thinking puts your customer at the centre of your decisions and helps you to remember that their needs are different than your own.

SHOW YOUR CUSTOMER THE VALUE OF YOUR SOLUTION

Mark, a small business owner, needed a new website for his growing business. Like all savvy consumers, he did some research online to understand what his options were. On one end of the spectrum, he could design and build the website himself. On the other end of the spectrum, he could hire an expensive web design agency. He had limited technical and design skills, so the DIY route wasn't for him. He asked some of his colleagues for a recommendation on a local web designer, and decided to interview two agencies to see which one was the best fit.

The introductory meetings couldn't have been more different.

Tom, a seasoned web developer, started his presentation by talking about himself, how long he'd been in business, how many web redesign projects he'd completed and how long the process usually takes. He then proceeded to share a lot of technical and security details that left Mark feeling overwhelmed and confused as to how Tom could help him. He didn't pause to explain the terms he used and assumed that Mark had the same level of training and understanding of the acronyms as he did.

Jason, also a talented and seasoned web developer, walked Mark through his sales presentation. He started with 'why a website is important' and shared results and customer testimonials from past projects. He then proceeded to put Mark at ease by describing the process step by step and explained the benefits of why each step was necessary. Mark left the meeting feeling smarter and more confident that making an investment in his new website would help achieve the results he sought for his business.

In the end, Mark chose to work with Jason instead of Tom.

As you can see from this example, sales presentations and marketing content that is all about yourself, your company and your products leave your customer feeling tuned out and overwhelmed.

Connecting the dots

Professional interpreters are hired because they have mastery in multiple languages and can decipher what each person is saying. Without their help, both parties would be staring blankly at each other, leading to a very unproductive meeting and conversation.

Likewise, one of the primary roles of marketing and sales professionals is to translate product features (what you sell) into benefits (why your customer would buy it). Think about this as the concept of 'connecting the dots'. On one side is your customer, and on the other side is what you offer. Your success lies in your ability to build a bridge between both parties and patiently walk with your customer across the bridge.

> Ninety-three per cent of survey respondents believe that 'connecting the dots' from customer needs to company solutions is a 'very important' competency for today's marketing and salespeople to develop.

It's a simple concept, but it's not easy to implement.

One reason for this is that it's not always clear whose responsibility it is to ensure that something is deemed 'useful' to customers. Whether it's a new piece of content or a new product that's being created, the reality is that it needs to be a collaborative process throughout the organization due to the fact that one cohesive view of the customer rarely exists.

Leaders we spoke to agreed that information about the customer exists throughout multiple departments and that it's a shared responsibility between product, marketing and sales to 'get it out there in a digestible way for a complicated product' as Caroline, CMO for a real estate firm put it.

Another reason may lie in the imbalance of internal training. From our experience working with numerous B2B organizations, we've seen that salespeople are expected to attend weekly or monthly internal training to learn about the products they sell. On the other hand, they rarely (or never) attend training to learn about the customer, what's happening in their industry, and their changing needs and expectations. As a result, when salespeople get in front of prospective customers, they revert to what they feel most comfortable talking about – product facts and features.

So ask yourself – how well do you and your salespeople translate facts about your products or services into the value they bring to customers?

When your customer agrees to meet with you, it's not because they are interested in hearing you recite a product brochure. They agree to meet with you because they are genuinely interested in learning how you can help them solve their problem.

Every single one of your customers thinks the same thing when they receive an email or a phone call or take an in-person interaction with you and your company – *is this worth my time?* Robson, former president of a US-based telco, told us that his interactions with salespeople must provide value and be relevant to a problem he's facing: 'What I really want to know is – *how will this make my life as a customer better?*'

Consider that 73 per cent of B2B buyers in a 2019 Demand Gen report stated that although they consume between three and seven pieces of content before contacting a salesperson, they have less time to devote to reading and researching solutions. Imagine that your organization could stand out by ensuring that your sales and marketing interactions make it easier and faster for your customers to become educated.

Finally, we've noticed a trend that too many companies don't know how to explain what they do, in terms that are relevant to the customer. We've seen too many marketing and sales communications that are filled with industry jargon, company acronyms and deep technical language that assume the reader has the same level of knowledge and interest on the subject. Jerry, a marketing consultancy owner who works with numerous B2B organizations in the UK, brings up the fact that the closer you are to your product, the harder it is to imagine that not everyone has the same level of familiarity and depth that you do: 'It's very difficult to write about the benefit for the customer rather than the features of your product. I can't do it for my own business easily.'

To get out of this cycle, let's see what competencies you can develop to make yourself and your interactions with customers more useful.

What does good look like? Usefulness competencies

Going back to our usefulness triangle (Figure 8.1), you need Knowledge, Preparation and Timing to be successful. We've identified three key competencies that support your journey to become more valuable and indispensable to your customers.

Let's see what our role model, Ulysses the Useful, does to ensure that he's producing materials that would only be deemed as extremely helpful and practical by his customers.

Build Knowledge by being a learner

It all starts with... knowing your customer

First – it's probably obvious to point this out, but your ability to be useful lies in how well you understand your customers and what they need. You can't begin to offer up solutions if you don't have this knowledge and foundation first.

In Chapter 7 we covered how to become more in tune with your customers, which really starts with having a learning mindset. At the heart of being a learner is understanding that your customer's circumstances and priorities are constantly changing. Some patterns are easy to recognize but other changes may not be as obvious. Crucially, if you want to stay ahead, you have to be responsive to your customer's needs.

This can be challenging, as many organizations are not set up to have a constant pulse on the customer or their competitors.

If your organization is one of these, don't worry. You can still take personal responsibility in your quest to become more useful by having an understanding of which customers you serve and why your customer is in business.

To start, consider what the World Economic Forum issued in their 2020 Davos Manifesto, 'The Universal Purpose of a Company in the Fourth Industrial Revolution':

> The purpose of a company is to engage all its stakeholders in shared and sustained value creation. In creating such value, a company serves not only its shareholders, but all its stakeholders – employees, customers, suppliers, local communities and society at large (World Economic Forum, 2020).

What this manifesto outlines is that a company can no longer just be in existence for the sole benefit of profiting its investors. The new generation calls for businesses to represent something greater – integrity instead of corruption, helping the planet and the community instead of hurting it, respect and diversity instead of disdain and intolerance.

So how does this relate to demonstrating relevance and usefulness to your customers? If you understand the purpose of *why* your customer is in business, you can more strongly link to how your solution will help them achieve their goals.

Since the intent is to learn more about what your customers are trying to achieve, here are some questions you will want to answer:

- Who does your customer serve?
- What problem does your customer solve for their customers?
- What's their value proposition?
- How do they make money?
- What challenges/issues do they face when trying to deliver on their value proposition?
- How does your customer serve society at large?
- What's their employer value proposition? ie why do people work there?
- Who else does the customer rely on to be successful? ie partners, suppliers, vendors.

Kirk, SVP of product management, insightfully points out that most companies are trying to solve four things:

1. Grow top-line revenue.
2. Grow bottom-line revenue or profitability and even it up.
3. Differentiate themselves.
4. Mitigate risk.

In some companies it's all four. Sometimes it's a combination of a few. In other words, kickstart your customer conversations by trying to understand which of these four problem areas are most important to your customer. You don't have to recreate the wheel every time. And you certainly shouldn't treat every customer conversation like a brand new affair. Your customers expect you to have baseline information about their industry, their company, their department and so on. Build upon your knowledge base and continue to dive deeper to understand what your customers want to achieve.

As a marketer, the more you know about your customers, the more likely it is that you can create interesting and practical content and tools for them. This means you have to meet with customers too. You can't just rely on the sales team to pass along information to you. But far too many marketers sit behind their computers and don't interact with customers! It's a pain point and observation that Kevin Tolson, former SVP of marketing for a US-based software company noticed on his team: 'I see too many marketers not really engaging with customers or going with the sales team into a customer's premises.' This is a missed opportunity for marketers, as it's very difficult to learn about your customers when you're sitting behind a desk.

The bottom line is that if you want to be more useful, you have to constantly have your finger on the pulse of your customers – and one of the best ways to do this is to get out and talk to them!

Ulysses the Useful is extremely resourceful, gathering customer information on his own using publicly available data on the internet (in the annual report, for example). Other bits of information are collected through 1:1 conversations with his customers. Even though Ulysses is in the marketing department, he actively participates in customer events, tradeshows, and networking events put on by the industry associations that his customers are a part of. He regularly reads trade publications and news to keep up with trends and changes happening in the industry – which makes him an excellent source of information.

Discipline drives preparation

There are many philosophers and business gurus that talk about the importance of preparation. Success doesn't happen by accident, after all; it comes from hard work, training and preparation. Vocabulary.com explains preparation as 'the act of preparing – getting ready, planning, training or studying with a goal in mind.' For example, culinary school is preparation for chefs just as boot camp is preparation for soldiers. How does this relate to being 'useful'? It's all of the activities that must take place before you can become useful.

First you need the discipline to recognize that providing value to your customers is all about what the other person wants, not about what you or your company are trying to achieve. One of the reasons that companies struggle to produce relevant and practical content and programmes is because they are too internally focused. When you are worried about hitting your sales number instead of helping your customers, you miss out on the clues your customers are giving to make yourself and your solution invaluable.

Think about the last time you bought something for your personal or business life. Was it because you wanted to help the vendor achieve their revenue goals for the year? Or because you needed something to improve your own life? Most companies forget that a customer only ever buys a product or service if it solves their problem. Yet when creating marketing and sales content, Tanya, an account director for a B2B digital marketing agency, has found that many companies 'are too focused on their own goals, such as producing more video or promoting certain messaging'.

Indeed, it's important to know what your organization is trying to achieve before you just start creating content for your customers. Certainly, if your effort and resources aren't directly tied to a business objective, you will waste your time and money. But also consider that your reputation is on the line. If you are known as the organization with unhelpful content and product-pushing sales interactions, how many customers will want to work with you?

Get into the buyer's mindset

Fifty-seven per cent of B2B buyers surveyed by Forrester said they find much of the content they receive from vendors useless (Ramos and Camuso, 2018).

To combat this it's helpful to understand what the decision-making process looks like for your customers. There are many buying journey frameworks out there. In our book, *Value-ology*, we showed five basic decisions that customers go through: Awareness, Education, Comparison, Purchase and Confirmation. This can be a complicated process once multiple decision-makers get involved, as it leads to the customer getting stuck at one phase or flipping back and forth between the steps.

The buyer's journey can be a great tool to use before creating a piece of content, as it forces you to figure out how it will be helpful to your customer. When only 41 per cent of marketers always/frequently craft content based on specific points of the buyer's journey (Content Marketing Institute, 2018), demonstrating that you understand the buyer – no matter what stage of the buying process they are in – is certainly one way you can differentiate your content.

It's also interesting to note that B2B buyers are referring to an average of 5.2 information sources when making a decision (TrustRadius, 2019). At the top of the list is:

- product demos;
- user reviews;

- vendor/product website;
- free trial/account;
- vendor sales rep.

When asked which sources were the least trustworthy, buyers ranked vendor-produced resources such as case studies, sales/support reps, blogs, marketing collateral and websites in the bottom five. In other words, buyers need the resources and information that vendors produce, but they don't necessarily trust what they are reading or hearing.

We think a massive opportunity exists for organizations to uplevel their marketing and sales content by partnering with reputable sources such as researchers, academics and other experts in their industry. Rather than internally produced marketing content and product brochures, a layer of transparency and credibility is needed to help present the whole story.

At your next internal meeting to discuss a new customer initiative or campaign, we'd encourage you to remind your peers to be as disciplined as Terry, CEO of a European telco is with his team:

> We only communicate something when we've got something compelling to say. We go out of our way to make sure we don't put news out for the sake of it. And when it comes to language, we aim to use stronger verbs, short sentences and not use the same jargon as everyone else.

With this approach, Terry ensures that their company is always adding value to their customers and readers. After all, if your customer had to choose between reading an article that will help them become smarter about their business problem, or a self-promotional article about a vendor – which one do you think they would find more practical?

To be timely... you must be flexible

Lastly, your ability to be useful to customers is highly dependent on your timely involvement and response to their needs. One of the most critical competencies to enable this is flexibility and adaptability. Why? Because as Greek philosopher Heraclitus put it, 'The only constant in life is change' (Mark, 2010).

You may have clearly thought out marketing and sales plans that get derailed by circumstances beyond your control.

As an example, in 2008, the global economy was in a state of uncertainty and turmoil. The financial crisis left consumers and businesses alike hunkering down and saving their money. Companies that previously had their eye towards growth and investment were now suddenly more concerned about cost savings to keep afloat. If you were in marketing during this time, you will remember that your campaigns and messaging promising 'business growth' became ineffective. The message was no longer the most important or practical thing on everyone's mind. Companies that were able to adapt their message to reflect the times were more likely to connect with their customers and stay in business.

One of the ways to create flexibility in your marketing programmes is to go with the idea of content themes. Rather than developing all of your communications at the product level, you communicate based on what your customer is trying to achieve. In our book, *Value-ology,* we provided in-depth details on how to implement a theme-based approach. The gist is that through your customer research, you identify two or three universal themes that are *most* relevant to your customers.

We advocate that a theme should:

- be grounded in business issues;
- resonate with your customers;
- lead to solutions that you can sell to help with the issues;
- be enduring;
- be able to accommodate topics and products to maximize the theme impact.

Looking again at our role model, Ulysses the Useful, he understands that to create helpful and worthwhile content and programmes, he must have his pulse on what his customers care about. He recently learned through customer conversations that 'reducing risk' is a big area of concern for their business owner clients. As a result, he challenges his product team to clearly show how their products help business owners reduce risk and create peace of mind. Now, rather than creating 25 standalone product marketing brochures, his team has a consistent customer-focused storyline to implement throughout all of their communications.

Besides freeing up marketing bandwidth, a theme-based approach ensures that you aren't churning out loads of product marketing content with no connection to customer benefits. Regina, VP of marketing for an IT firm, shared that her team is trying to create more useful content by focusing on three different areas: 'use-cases, trends, and equipping our buyers to sell internally – *how to position your security strategy to the board of directors*, for example.'

Marketo found in their State of Engagement report that the #1 reason customers don't engage more often is due to 'irrelevant content' (Marketo, 2017). Making the shift from product-only content to a customer theme-based approach takes time, but it also gives you and your team a flexible platform to ensure that what you're putting out there is always pertinent to customers.

EXERCISE

Is your content relevant and useful?

Have you ever published a piece of content or sent something to a prospect that you knew wasn't 100 per cent relevant?

This is strongly linked to Chapter 6 about activation. Some companies become so focused on execution that they lose sight of WHY they are executing in the first place.

We've found that many marketers especially like to 'feel busy' by generating a lot of activity. As Christine, VP of marketing, put it, 'I've seen plenty of marketers that execute programmes for programmes' sake.' Plenty of salespeople are also guilty of sending blanket messages to prospects in hopes that someone responds to their generic claims.

One of the ways to combat this is to score yourself on a usefulness matrix, as shown in Table 8.1.

Take a look at your website, social media channels, marketing and sales collateral to assess the effectiveness and customer-centricity of your messaging. Then fill out the assessment below.

Score yourself on a 1–4 scale:

1 = Strongly disagree

2 = Disagree

3 = Agree

4 = Strongly Agree

TABLE 8.1 Usefulness Matrix

Category	Your score (1–4)
It is clear who our company aims to serve.	
We communicate and articulate the customer's business problem and pain points.	
We aim to help the customer understand their own problem.	
Our content is customer-focused instead of product-focused.	
We use the right balance of 'we' vs. 'you' language in our content.	
Each piece of content has a clear purpose in the buyer's journey.	
We understand how our company story is different.	
We demonstrate how our product uniquely solves the customers' problem.	
We showcase benefits, not just product features.	
We quantify the value our solutions provide to customers.	
Proof points are used to support our message.	
We avoid industry jargon and acronyms.	
Overall, our customers find our content helpful and useful.	

How well did you score? Check out your results below and review our recommendations.

If you scored under 20 points: It's likely that your content is internally focused and filled with 'jargon' and that your message doesn't clearly show a prospect how you can help solve their problem:

- Define your ideal customer, then develop buyer personas based on real customer conversations. More than just a profile of your buyer, a persona should help you understand how your prospect thinks, their pain points, goals, desires, how and why they buy and what information/sources are important to them in the decision-making process.
- Replace any jargon and acronyms in your marketing content with straightforward explanations.
- Identify the themes that are most important to your customer base – what are they trying to achieve?

If you scored between 20 and 35 points: You have taken some steps to understand and communicate with the customer on their terms. But are you consistently producing content that helps your prospect along their decision journey?

- Get sales involved in brainstorming content themes/topics that will help move a buyer along. What objections does the sales team frequently receive? How does your firm consistently respond to these concerns?
- Show your prospect what it will be like to work with your firm. Paint a picture (use visuals, videos, graphs, etc) so that your prospect can visualize themselves using your solution and achieving their desired results.
- Conduct an audit to determine if your messaging is consistent across all channels. For example, do your website, sales literature, product brochures, etc all tell the same story about your customer and how you help them achieve their goals?

If you scored over 36 points: Congratulations! Your organization is doing an excellent job connecting with potential buyers and demonstrating why they should choose your solution. Keep up the momentum by:

- Investing in cross-functional programmes and processes to harvest customer insights. Every touchpoint with your customer – from your sales team to your customer service team – represents a learning opportunity.
- Share best practices and key learnings across the marketing and sales organization to continue to increase the value provided through all customer interactions.
- Ensure your sales team is adept at creating and delivering 1:1 customer value propositions. For high-value accounts and opportunities, account-based marketing (ABM) programmes, whereby sales and marketing jointly strategize, research and execute against a customer-specific plan, can be highly effective.

Chapter summary

You have likely unsubscribed from email newsletters that you found were no longer relevant, unfollowed social media pages because their content wasn't helpful or useful, or ignored a salesperson trying to set up a meeting with you. Your customers are faced with the same daily dilemma: too much information and not enough value.

As we've shared in this chapter, usefulness is about tuning in to what your customers value so that you can present relevant content and solutions to their problems. When in doubt, make sure you can answer the one critical question shared by Christine, VP of marketing:

> It gets back to what's the big problem we are solving or what's the big gain we are enabling for our customers?

If you can't answer that, it's time to go back to the drawing board before pushing out something that is irrelevant and useless.

In the next chapter we will share why being able to evaluate your marketing and sales programmes is the final competency that will help your organization stand out.

Table 8.2 gives a summary of the competencies we've covered so far

TABLE 8.2 Value competency summary

V Visionary	A Activator	L Learner	U Usefulness	E Evaluator
Victor the Visionary	Alison the Activator	Laura the Learner	Ulysses the Useful	Erica the Evaluator
Outside-in	Balanced advocacy	Curiosity	Connecting the dots	
Farsight	Listening	Proactive and engaged	Learner	
Zooming	Negotiation	Reflective	Customer-centricity	
Predicting	Tenacity	'Fearless' experimentation	Discipline	
Imagining	People centricity contextualization	Receptive	Flexibility and adaptability	

References and further reading

Accenture Interactive (2019) Service is the New Sales: The Through line for B2B growth [online] https://www.accenture.com/ca-en/insights/digital/service-new-sales (archived at https://perma.cc/E6RK-KELU)

Content Marketing Institute (2018) B2B Content Marketing 2018: Benchmarks, Budgets, and Trends – North America 2018 [online] https://contentmarketinginstitute.com/2017/09/research-habits-content-marketers/ (archived at https://perma.cc/GDZ3-RDUP)

CSO Insights (2018) The growing buyer–seller gap: results of the 2018 buyer preferences study. Miller Heiman Group

Demand Gen (2019) Content Preferences Survey Report [online] https://www.demandgenreport.com/resources/reports/2019-content-preferences-survey-report (archived at https://perma.cc/42RZ-FXNZ)

Kelly, S, Johnston, P and Danheiser (2017) *Value-ology: Aligning sales and marketing to shape and deliver profitable customer value propositions*, Palgrave Macmillan, p 77

Mark, J J (2010) Heraclitus of Ephesus, *Ancient History Encyclopedia* [online] https://www.ancient.eu/Heraclitus_of_Ephesos/ (archived at https://perma.cc/5HR4-8NMK)

Merkle (2017) Programs That Connect: B-to-B loyalty programs that create pathways to new opportunities and business growth [online] https://www.merkleinc.com/thought-leadership/white-papers/programs-connect (archived at https://perma.cc/RLY2-GYNV)

Marketo (2017) The State of Engagement: Insights on engagement from 2,000 global consumers and marketers [online] https://www.marketo.com/analyst-and-other-reports/the-state-of-engagement/ (archived at https://perma.cc/L6SQ-9M8X)

O'Brien, D, Veenstra, J and Murphy, T (2018) *Redefining the CMO*, Deloitte Insights

Quelch, J and Jocz, K (2009) How to market in a downturn, *Harvard Business Review*, April

Ramos, L and Camuso, M (2018) 'Crap' content continues to describe B2B marketing – don't let it describe yours, Forrester Research [online] https://go.forrester.com/blogs/crap-content-continues-to-describe-b2b-marketing-dont-let-it-describe-yours/ (archived at https://perma.cc/42BA-P2CE)

Salesforce Research (2017) Fourth Annual State of Marketing Report

Schultz, M, Murray, J and Smith, G (nd) 5 sales prospecting myths debunked: 488 buyers sound off about how sellers get through and win their business, Rain Group Center for Sales Research [online] https://www.rainsalestraining.com/resources/sales-white-papers/5-sales-prospecting-myths-debunked (archived at https://perma.cc/GTN3-BWJV)

TrustRadius (2019) The 2019 B2B Buying Disconnect: An in-depth study on buying preferences, vendor impact, and the persistent trust gap in b2b technology

World Economic Forum (2020) Davos Manifesto 2020: The universal purpose of a company in the fourth industrial revolution [online] www.weforum.org/agenda/2019/12/davos-manifesto-2020-the-universal-purpose-of-a-company-in-the-fourth-industrial-revolution/ (archived at https://perma.cc/Y6YM-L9ZX)

Xant (2014) Lead Response Report [online] https://www.xant.ai/resources/2014-lead-response-report/ (archived at https://perma.cc/H9XA-3F9S)

09

The evaluator – competencies for making good decisions

In this chapter we will:

- share our competency research – focusing on what sales and marketing leaders said about evaluator competencies;
- outline why evaluator competencies are important for standing out;
- explain what evaluator competencies are and why they matter;
- provide a checklist of the key evaluator competencies.

What do we mean by evaluator competencies?

The Merriam-Webster dictionary defines evaluation as 'the act or result of evaluating a situation that requires careful evaluation. Here evaluation means: determination of the worth, nature, character, or quality of something or someone.'

In Chapter 3 we said that evaluator competencies are needed to make informed choices about the bets your company needs to take on strategies that will help them perform better, based on insights about the future, or on interpretation of performance to date

Whilst we would go along with the mantra 'If you can't measure it, you can't manage it', we firmly believe that you don't measure to report, you measure *and* evaluate to get better: for your customers, for your organization, and to be better than your competitors. Evaluator competencies are great enablers for standing out; done well they can facilitate greater credibility, trust, and business impact.

We see evaluation competencies as paramount at different ends of the marketing and sales cycle. The starting point for evaluation is linked very much to visionary competencies. How do you make sense of what value a potential opportunity might be in the future? So, while a visionary would have to be the kind of person who can come up with an original view of where the future might take the customer this has to be blended with more left-brain analytical competencies to be able to assess the potential value of a future opportunity.

We heard Christine, a VP of marketing, talk about the relationship between visionary and evaluator competencies in Chapter 4:

> Marketers also need to be businesspeople. They need to understand what the profit profile is of what we're trying to do here. So really beyond just marketing tactics, how does the business work? How do these things make money?

We have all seen the hype about 'big data', which runs to over 5 million articles if you run a search on Google Scholar. Simply put, big data refers to the potential ability to collect and analyse the vast amounts of data now being generated in the world, from supermarket transactions to the photographs we put on Facebook and Instagram. With all the data that's supposedly available to marketing and sales teams do you and your team have the evaluator competencies to make sense of what the data is saying? Can your people provide unique interpretations of the data that competitors might not see?

At the other end of the cycle is analysing the results of marketing and sales programmes. The advent of social media and internet technologies has made a number of things easier to measure such as page views, click-through rates etc... but these can be divorced from real sales and profitability numbers.

So, can you or your people really demonstrate ROI (return on investment)? The role of the CMO is traditionally not highly perceived by the CEO or CFO because of the difficulty they seem to have measuring return. It's not as if the disconnect with the CEO or CFO is a new problem for marketers. Way back in 2005, Shaw and Merrick pointed out that quantifying the impacts of marketing spending in terms that the non-marketing community could appreciate was not just a fad, or an optional extra (Shaw and Merrick, 2005). So, why does measurement and evaluation still appear to be seen as an 'optional extra' in spite of the damage this does to the perception of CMOs. Do you have the competencies to evaluate potential new opportunities, marketing and sales programmes? Or are you just guessing – if you are doing it at all?

Our evaluation model, Figure 9.1, depicts where evaluation takes place in the marketing and sales cycle. At the start of the cycle, the evaluator takes input from the visionary and through market insights to assess potential future revenue growth and profitability. This evaluation is the start point for driving decision making; if the visionary 'insight' looks potentially viable a business case is made to be presented for funding and resource, which moves into the activation phase as a marketing and sales programme. Evaluator competencies then come into play to review the programme to decide whether to enhance and continue or to kill the programme off. The review should lead to a better programme going forward or provide an opportunity to re-invest budget into a more successful campaign.

FIGURE 9.1 Evaluation in the marketing and sales process

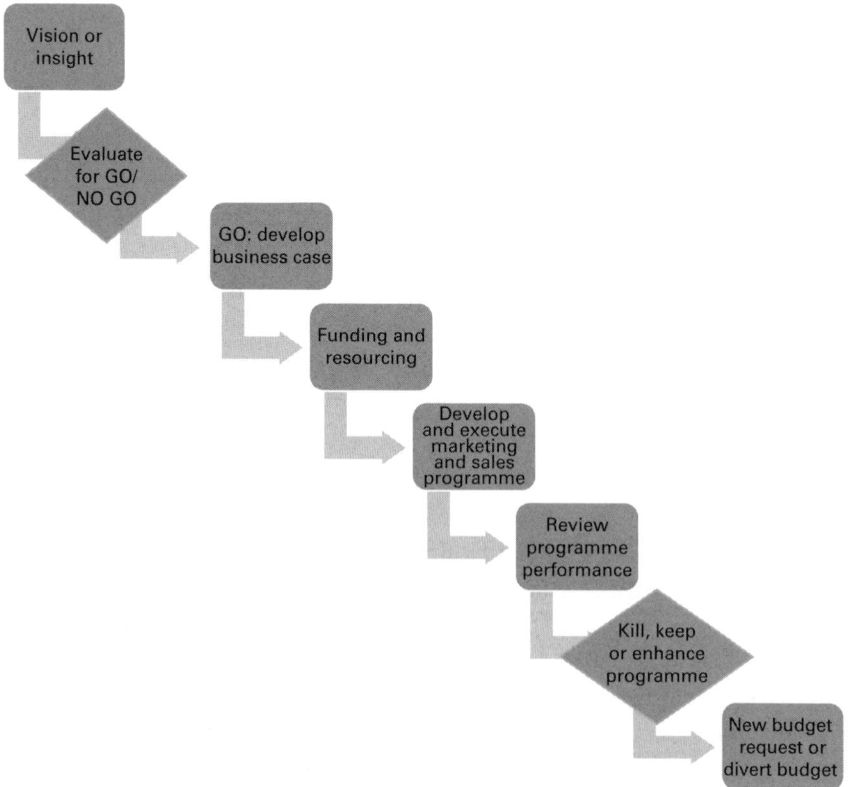

Key to this evaluation process is to assess whether the revenue and profit goals of your organization have been delivered against. In line with the return on marketing investment (ROMI) put forward by McDonald and Mouncey (Woodburn, 2006) we believe that an assessment of competitive advantage is a key criterion in the evaluation process: does the idea give you a stand-out competitive advantage? Does it help you deliver against 'qualifying factors' that customers now expect? Or does it increase productivity by increasing sales or reducing costs?

Why is evaluation so important?

Performance evaluation is not particularly a problem for salespeople, as generally if they hit their sales and revenue numbers, life is good. That said, we do know that at any one time only 54.3 per cent of sales people are on target (CSO Insights, 2018). For marketers, evaluation is a burning platform; the relationship between the CMO and the CEO is a troubled one in some part explained by the CMO's lack of ability to prove commercial impact. Research by Korn Ferry (2017) showed that the average CMO tenure was just 4.1 years, the lowest in the C-suite, in contrast to the average eight-year tenure of CEOs. A recent CMO survey by Deloitte and Touche (2019) found that when asking what the top three success factors are for the CMO role the use of customer data came top, with proving quantitative impact coming in fourth, behind taking an enterprise-wide view and being the voice of the customer. In recent research performed by Hays (2020) exploring the DNA of a marketing leader, 69 per cent of marketers felt that effectively reporting ROI was going to become more important. It's no surprise that CMOs have the shortest tenure of any C-level executive as they are increasingly being expected to deliver numbers. If they can't speak the language of shareholder value and operating margin they will not resonate with the CFO and CEO, which can only hasten their departure.

According to Gartner (2019) only one-third of CMOs say that ROMI is a key performance indicator (KPI), while a Forrester study found that 77 per cent of B2B CMOs cited use of data to guide marketing decisions as one of their department's top five weaknesses (Snow, 2018). Without the ability to measure and evaluate performance, marketing can be seen as an arts and crafts function that throws parties – the colouring-in department, a cost centre that provides mouse mats. This perception is a long way removed from being seen as a part of the company revenue-generating machine that uses metrics and evaluation that matter to the CEO and CFO.

According to a Forbes marketing accountability study (Forbes, 2019), marketers who measure and manage marketing performance get a 5 per cent uplift in ROMI and 7 per cent better growth. At the same time 78 per cent of CMOs feel that the inability to measure marketing performance hurts them both personally and professionally. So, without the ability to communicate, quantify and evaluate marketing value, not only does CMO credibility suffer, so does growth.

The bottom line is that evaluation is a problem specifically for marketers, affecting personal reputation, career prospects, relationships with other key players they need on their side, and the ability to make coherent cases to ask for more money.

How can you swim away from the Sea of Sameness if you can't prove what's worked with customers or course correct if things aren't working? Do you have people in your team who are effective evaluators?

> The fact that only 35 per cent of our survey respondents viewed 'data analytics' as a 'very important' competency is a reflection of this as an emerging competence that we believe will come to the fore in the future. The 81 per cent who saw 'ability to execute' as very important can only prove effective execution with robust evaluation.

How well are you evaluating right now?

So, how well do the marketing and sales leaders we spoke with think their organizations are evaluating performance, to help improve it? Let's begin by taking a look at the front-end evaluation of insights.

Kirk, currently vice president of product management at a large IT company, drew on his many years of sales experience to contrast how two different organizations he worked for used credible third-party data to help build intelligence and insight, placing them at opposite ends of a 10-point scale. Kirk saw using data from credible third parties such as Gartner and Forrester as a signal of intent to develop and evaluate insight and to provide it to sales, once marketing had made sense of the data:

> The marketing team collected all this data, aggregated, sliced and diced it and handed it to sales to help develop more powerful sales conversations.

By 'all this data' Kirk meant the third-party intelligence combined with other information relating to the market. The contrast between the two organizations he cited was stark and demonstrated how gathering and evaluating data could help one competitor stand out from the other.

> Does your company draw on credible third-party research and data? Do you have someone who aggregates data and evaluates it for potential profitable insights?

Data mining – still in its infancy?

Data mining is all about looking for interesting and useful patterns from large volumes of data, to help develop programmes that improve performance. There is huge potential for its use in B2B organizations, especially given the large number of sales and service calls made to customers every day. Big data can only measure and describe behaviours so there is still a need to evaluate why these behaviours happen and what that might mean for the business.

Robson, a company president with sales and senior management experience in several large technology companies, said he had not experienced data mining used in the companies he had worked in:

> Maybe it's just too early in the journey and people are finding their feet with data mining. Everybody knows the concepts and has heard about it but I've not seen anybody operationalize it and say we've improved customer experience by 10 points.

He went on to say that he had seen examples in adverts but to him it still seemed like 'a big science experiment', as if it were taking place in a laboratory divorced from reality.

Christine stressed the need to have the capability to mine data in the first place to facilitate evaluation:

> Mining for customer insights is a key capability. You've got to have somebody in there doing that. You can imagine at Global Telco, we've got tens of thousands of customers who generate millions of data points so there's a plethora of stuff to be mined there.

There does need be to someone in the marketing team who can actually mine the data and look for patterns and trends. Christine also spoke of the plethora of tools that are out there to help organizations do data mining, going on to say that it's critical that organizations have people who can work these tools to mine the data. Part of the evaluator role is to seek out data mining technologies to apply to your world, and to learn from applications in other industries that are more advanced in its use. For example, if you work in a highly regulated industry such as insurance, healthcare or financial services, you can look to see how others may be creatively solving similar problems to the ones you're facing.

Based on opinions – not fact

Despite the proliferation of data, a number of our interviewees said that evaluating potential new marketing and sales programmes was largely based on opinions, not facts. For example, Katie, CEO of a software company and former marketing leader at a global technology company questioned:

> Do organizations have people evaluating the future profitability of potential programmes? Not really. You're really depending on people's opinions rather than an evaluation process that says this is going to work.

Here Katie is hitting on a key point, that in the absence of data there is opinion, and in the presence of data there is still opinion, because people make their own interpretation. She is suggesting that companies should have some sort of a framework or process to take a more objective view on what may or may not work. Perhaps it's the job of the evaluator to develop the process and bring more objective analysis, such that it exists, to the decision-making table.

Data is used to justify its own end – it is politicized

Evaluation that takes place in organizations is often a highly politicized world and is tainted by self-interest which heightens the need for evaluator competencies. How can your organization perform better, and stand out from competitors in a positive way for customers, if lots of calories are being spent taking 'dead donkeys' to market? This is difficult because at the stage where approval is being sought to move an insight to a marketing programme or product launch, assumptions and forecasts need to be made about potential profitability.

Herbert, former sales VP at a large mobile company, was among a number of leaders who thought that data was often used just to further someone's own ends. He spoke about a particular product that a former company took to market for which there clearly wasn't a market, given the results:

> When I think of Global Product X, if they'd properly evaluated the data, they would have worked out it was a dead donkey as there was insufficient demand for it. People didn't actually need it so why spend ages developing this service?

In the case cited by Herbert, the global product manager was the person driving the case for the product, which meant the 'evaluation' that was performed necessarily supported the case for Product X to further their own ends.

Herbert, like many others, did not see Global Product X as an isolated case; in his experience people were protecting their jobs rather than accepting the reality of what the numbers said: '"I'm making this look shinier than it actually is because my boss said I need to do it." I see a lot of that going on.'

Part of the evaluator role should be to challenge these assumptions and draw on different data points to test the efficacy of forecasts to try and ensure the right products get developed and projects taken forward.

How good are organizations at evaluating ROMI?

Now that we've looked at how well organizations evaluate potential opportunities, how about the other end of the sales cycle – how good are you at evaluating ROMI (return on marketing investment)?

In Chapter 3 we drew on some interviews from research for our previous book *Value-ology*, in which we were looking at how well marketing and sales were aligned in developing customer value.

We saw that marketers often measure things in different ways to sales and we know this can cause tensions. Kyle, president in a global data centre company, when talking about a previous role as a sales leader said:

> I can remember all the marketing scorecard being green while all mine was red; that just cannot be right.

Feeling the need to have to prove that marketing deliver value in order to have credibility conferred upon them can often lead to tension with sales.

Davina, vice president of marketing of a global fintech company and veteran of five blue chip companies in different sectors, said:

> I think it's a very delicate balance between proving the value and the ROI of what we're doing. And that I find is a tension point.

What Davina is hinting at here is that the pressure to prove value to sales and the broader organization can lead marketing to over-claim the role they may have played in bringing in business that might already have been in-flight.

In the research for this book we were keen to understand how effectively sales and marketing leaders felt ROMI was being measured from the point of view of helping organizations make decisions, to help them perform better, based on an evaluation of results.

Do you measure the things that matter?

We did discover that some of our respondents were measuring various things. The question is: are they measuring things that really matter? Most organizations are probably measuring at least one aspect of marketing programmes, but it's usually done in a silo.

Kristen, CMO of a financial services company, said that they did use ROI data to help make future decisions:

> We use the data to make decisions – definitely events because that's the one where we really track ROI. It will influence the number of events we have. Our approach, who we invite.

It's good to know that Kristen tries to base decisions on some calculation of ROI. In our experience, too often B2B events can be measured on customer 'happy sheets', about whether they enjoyed the event rather than if it delivered something for the company. The task for the CMO is to make decisions as to whether Event A trumps Tactic B in future decisions, so it would be interesting to know if Kirsten was applying the ROI approach to all marketing activity. Customers don't just interact with your company once – they are going to your website, subscribing to your emails, attending your events, talking to salespeople, etc. Someone needs to be able to evaluate which tactics seem to be working the best for that particular audience.

Then there is the difficult question of quite how much can be attributed to a customer attending the event, as Davina has already alluded to.

How do you evaluate attribution?

In our experience, how much can be attributed to a particular marketing programme or campaign is a very contested area. While Robson, among others, accepted that correlating dollars spent to dollars won was not scientific, he thought that there needed to be more rigour around assessing ROMI, starting with more thorough reviews:

> The look back is light for many organizations, which is why marketing always seems to get a black eye. You spent five million and what did you get? ROMI is grey; it's hard to do but you have to do it to start valuing those investments.

So, Robson is saying that it's difficult to say just how much a marketing dollar spent impacted on a final sale. He went on to say that despite the grey areas, companies do need to have some sort of framework to evaluate investments and campaigns. Like Davina, Robson recognized that a judgment call has to be made about how much a marketing campaign has impacted on an end result. If you cannot make a serious attempt to evaluate marketing and sales programme performance how can decisions on future investment be made?

ROMI helps make the case for future investment

In the context of standing out, the whole idea of ROMI is to help your organization decide which programmes to expand because they are resonating with customers, and to re-invest dollars from programmes that aren't working.

Kirk again compared two organizations he has worked with to give a stark contrast between Company A, where people don't understand ROMI, and Company B, where it was used to help guide future investment decisions.

Talking of his good practice company example, Company B, he said:

> I would say that was an eight or nine once again and I hammered it home. If we have the right ROMI, instead of asking for $10,000 this year, we're going to ask for $15,000 next year. When they say wait, that's a little audacious, 50 per cent increase, I can say we'll go back and look at the ROMI we had on the programmes.

In this simple example Kirk is demonstrating that Company B can invest more into a programme that has worked and that more investment can help them perform better or stand out. Meanwhile, Company A may be wasting money running programmes that may be nice to do but fail to give any return.

The definition of success can be open to interpretation, and as politicized at the front-end programme evaluation.

Measuring ROMI – politicized

Earlier in the chapter we saw that evaluating potential future opportunities was seen as very political. This also came through at the other end of the cycle when we asked how marketing and sales programmes that were in progress were measured and evaluated for ROMI.

Herbert, after saying the global mobile company he used to work at was good at programme measurement, once again turned to the political nature of evaluation. While he accepted that there was tons of data and tons of analysis, he said the main consideration was 'Who is interpreting the results and for what purpose?' He felt that in the big organizations he had worked in it was unlikely that anyone would 'shoot themselves in the foot' and report an underperforming programme or product.

Here Herbert is pointing out that an individual's personal reputation could be at stake, which may well impair the honest reporting of results. This view starts to point towards the traits of a good evaluator as someone who can make the case to enhance and continue a programme, or kill it, from a standpoint where their personal success is not at stake. Often behaviour is driven by the need to get your pet programme funded again, while enhancing your image, at the expense of developing something that could help you stand out in the market.

What does good look like?

For an organization to be doing evaluation well it has to be able to demonstrate that it's enabling better performance for customers and itself, standing out from the competition. This means evaluating performance based on what's working for the customer, what generates cash and not spend (Ambler, 2000). Ultimately if you are doing evaluation well then you are measuring the effect on revenue and making trade-offs about what to invest in going forward based on likely success. This suggests being discerning about what to measure and evaluate, concentrating on things that will guide decisions you need to make to drive more revenue and profit. The evaluation should take into account the standpoints of key players such as the CEO and CFO.

What do our sales and marketing leaders think that good looks like? And did they have any examples of good practice?

Be accountable

Marketing leaders seem happy to accept the need to be accountable; some of our respondents must be part of the 78 per cent of B2B marketing leaders that measure revenue impact, according to a 2020 Marketo study.

Regina, VP of marketing at a large IT company, focused on the need for accountability for everyone on the marketing and sales team:

> Everybody needs to have the accountability to understand, when I spend a dollar, what am getting out of it?

In Regina's organization sales and marketing report to their board alongside each other, so there has to be a coherent flow from marketing activity into the sales numbers. Even if marketers cannot currently measure ROMI they have to have a mindset about driving revenue.

Caroline, CMO of a financial services and real estate company, reflects a similar level of accountability in her own organization:

> We have a quarterly meeting where we sit down with the head of sales and we talk through the enablement pipeline. This is how many leads we've delivered; how many into actual dollars in the door. They see everything.

Here Caroline reviews performance at a more tactical level with the sales leadership team. It's good to see that the review includes 'actual dollars in the door', as all too often marketers measure lead volumes and sales moan about lead quality.

Link marketing activity to business performance

While tactical reviews of leads are important to execute against the key demand generation role assigned to marketing in Chapter 4, more strategic reviews are required if marketers are to assess for impact on overall business performance.

Kristen waxed lyrical about how much her CEO loved the quarterly performance review, labelling it his 'favourite meeting in the company' because the marketing team 'tracked everything' from website traffic and downloads through to account retention rates. What is instructive here is that Kristen is making a link from marketing activity through to business impact, beyond the usual marketing vanity metrics of website visits and click-through rates.

It's about making trade-offs

Christine, VP of marketing at a global technology company, makes the essential point that evaluation is to support decisions about 'trade-offs':

> Somebody has got to tie our programmes back to real-world results. At the end of the day, this is all trade-offs of both time and money. Is my time and my money better spent here or over there? And without measuring and somebody presenting those insights in an organized way, you just end up going by gut feel.

The role of the evaluator is to look across all marketing programmes and provide insight that informs decisions on trade-offs for future investment. As we said earlier, there's no point in measuring just the ROMI of events if you don't have a similar measurement and evaluation process across all marketing and sales activity.

In the end it's all about the sales numbers

Katie observed that there has been a lot of focus in the last 10 years on better tools to help marketing more easily make decisions about future investments:

> But at the end of the day the way I look at it is the sales numbers justify the marketing investments, not whatever data gets kicked out about the campaign, the Tier 2 metrics that a marketing team would have: website visits, SEO conversions and all that other stuff that's interesting and helpful. But in terms of return on investment for the company it's: Do my sales numbers justify my marketing expense?

Here, once again, Katie is advocating the primacy of the 'sales numbers' above marketing vanity metrics. In line with Ambler (2000) she judges the success of a marketing programme based on programme profitability (sales minus marketing expense).

Sales numbers roll up to CFO and CEO metrics

When Katie talks about 'sales numbers' she means revenue or new sales dollars. Making these numbers a key focus of your evaluation puts you on a good path to addressing the concerns of the CFO and CEO in turn.

Bruce, a seasoned VP of marketing spanning a number of global technology companies, put it very succinctly:

> The language of success with a CFO is revenue, margin, profitability. So, when you think about marketers and the way they often talk to CFOs, they get what they deserve because they talk about the vanity metrics: event attendees, clicks, etc. You then become the guy who gets 15 minutes on the agenda.

Having an evaluation system that focuses on measures that are important to the CFO is likely to get him on your side when it comes to investing in future programmes. Bruce explained how his approach to articulating performance extended to the CEO too:

> I always try to pivot the conversation to talk about things in a way that's important for the person I'm talking with, eg CFO – margin, CEO – business success, capability, big deals won.

So, what good looks like means using measures and evaluation that tune into the key stakeholders: revenue, margin, new sales, customer satisfaction supported by stories of new business successes. Not a vanity metric in sight!

Evaluation cuts both ways

Jeff, a VP of business development at a global IT company, said that some of his large customers actually asked him what doing business with them was like:

> Some of our customers survey us and ask us to give them a score about what it's like to work with them. How responsive they are, how easy they are to work with, how we would rate their process, etc. This is interesting and something I haven't seen before.

We agree that this is an interesting approach. If evaluation is all about becoming better then why not task some of the people that are trying to sell to you and help you implement IT systems? If this approach can help unlock improvements and make your company become easier to do business with, and more agile, it can help you stand out from those afraid to ask in the Sea of Sameness.

It's about being in the numbers – everyday

Bob, commercial director of a building services company, felt that B2B marketers needed to do more to be in the 'heartbeat of the business' every day:

> I don't think marketers take enough time to understand on a weekly basis or daily basis what's actually going on. I don't think marketers typically will look at a dashboard of numbers at the start of the day.

What Bob is suggesting here is that even marketers who may be trying to measure and evaluate performance of their marketing programmes don't keep in touch with overall company performance or change their campaigns accordingly:

> How many marketers have changed their plan, that campaign, can I call it, as a result of trading performance? They don't. They may within retail environments or different sectors, but certainly within a lot of the B2B stuff that I've been involved in, I haven't really seen that.

Bob is hinting that what good looks like is course correcting and adjusting plans informed by trading performance. While business cycles might be different, Bob hints that B2B marketers may be able to learn something from other sectors, like retail, about tuning plans in to trading performance.

Evaluator competencies – so what are they?

By now you will appreciate that in this book we have been putting forward a set of higher-order human competencies that can help organizations 'stand out'. Evaluator competencies are needed to make informed choices about the bets your company needs to take on strategies that will help them perform better going forward, based on insights about the future, or on interpretation of performance to date. For us the focus is not on the technical skills required to 'work the machine', keeping score, but the competencies to make informed choices based on evaluation.

Before we get to the higher-order competencies let's try to address a question that may be on your mind: just how many evaluators do you need?

How many evaluators do you need?

It's important to keep making the distinction between keeping the score and making judgements based on evaluating data that's come from score-keeping or from patterns coming from data mining.

Caroline made the point that she doesn't need a whole heap of evaluators on her team:

> The evaluator role to me is mission critical to everything we do. But I don't need everyone on my team doing that. That would be inefficient and a waste of time. Generally speaking, my data person is not my collaborator and I don't need them to be. But if I don't have a data person, then all of the marketing in and of itself is useless.

It's interesting to note that while Caroline sees the evaluator role as 'mission critical' she appears to view the evaluator as 'the data person', someone who doesn't have to collaborate with other people in the organization. This seems to suggest the Caroline sees the 'evaluator' as the scorekeeper who passes the results on to someone else in the marketing team to do something with.

On the other hand, while she concurs that not everyone has to be an evaluator, Christine appears to see the evaluator role as more far reaching:

> Well, I don't know whether everybody has to have the evaluator, but somebody does and they actually have to fill a fairly powerful role. They've got to have a loud voice and a big influence either by title or competency because it absolutely has to be a data-driven decision process.

We concur with Christine that the evaluator has to have a loud voice, both by competency and title, it goes much beyond the score-keeping 'data person' view of the role, which is why some of the higher-order competencies making up the evaluator may surprise some people. So, what are they?

Competencies for stand-out evaluators

INTEGRITY

Two dictionary definitions help explain what we mean by integrity in the context of the evaluator competence:

Integrity – the quality of being honest and having strong moral principles (Cambridge English Dictionary).

Integrity – the state of being whole and undivided (Merriam-Webster Dictionary).

The evaluator has to have the bravery to honestly report programme results alongside each and make recommendations about whether programme A should continue to go forward, or be replaced by programme B. They need to be able to do this from a holistic perspective that takes into account the overall goal of evaluation, which is to help the organization perform better and stand out. They need to rise above the tendency of marketers to be seen as 'selective or manipulative'. Senior business leaders need to be able to look the evaluator in the eye and say, 'I trust that you are giving me balanced recommendations because you are a person of integrity'. The marketing and sales leadership team need to have confidence that the evaluator is suggesting that programme A trumps B and C because they can take a complete and undivided view across the gamut of potential programmes that could be run.

Do you hire evaluators for integrity, on because they can count?

BALANCED ADVOCACY

In Chapter 6 we talked about the need for the activator to be a balanced advocate, and this is definitely a competence you need in your evaluator, a competence that good marketers and salespeople need in equal measure. In Chapter 6 we heard Kirk talk about balanced advocacy as a key competence in a sales role, requiring people to advocate for the interests of the customer and the people they get a pay cheque from, their own company.

In the context of evaluator competencies, the salesperson needs to be able to demonstrate that a customer need they may be advocating for is actually in the best interests of their own company too. We have all sat in rooms hearing some salespeople put forward ideas on behalf of their customer that we know would not make a dime for our own company.

The evaluator has to role model balanced advocacy, looking for the overlap between customer needs and company interests, and to approve ideas that can help your company stand out from competitors, which at the same time demonstrates integrity. In Figure 9.2 we see that the evaluator is looking for programmes that fall in the 'C-Zone', deriving value for the customer and company at the expense of the competitor.

While the start point for an idea should be what can we do better for the customer, and can we walk in their shoes to truly understand this, to get through the evaluator's go-no-go gate the idea needs to land in the C-Zone, where customer and company interests are served, at the expense of the competitor.

Do you hire for balanced advocacy? Think about the last three sales or marketing programmes that got approval in your company – did they land in the C-Zone?

FIGURE 9.2 C-Zone for stand-out marketing and sales programmes

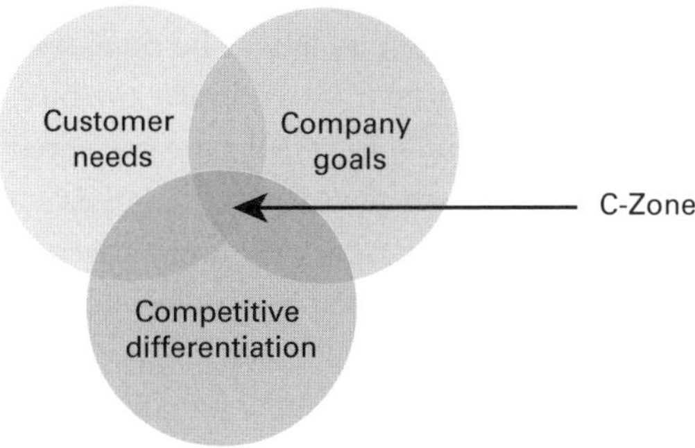

CONNECTING THE DOTS

We saw in Chapter 4 that connecting the dots meant painting a picture for customers from providing an insight into possible changes ahead to bringing potential partners to bear in developing solutions (see Figure 4.1).

In the context of evaluator competencies, 'connecting the dots' means making the link from overall company goals through to programme performance and driving a learning loop to help continually enhance performance improvement.

From this perspective the evaluator will be able to root out business cases that appear to be based on vanity metrics in favour of those that support revenue growth with attractive margins. This would also be one test to help decide whether an existing programme should continue to run.

Transcending the numeric analysis, the evaluator should be able to develop a keen eye for why a potential idea is likely to work, and why a programme has worked or not from a qualitative point of view. Over time, an evaluator should be able to provide advice to marketing and sales programme leaders that helps them improve proposals and methods for executing new programmes.

Persuasion and political nous

To put forward a future world view where all decisions are based purely on 'facts' presented by an all-seeing, totally objective evaluator would be naïve in the extreme. Whilst we have provided you with some ideas for making more considered decisions with better data these decisions will always be political in nature, as many of the sales and marketing leaders we interviewed pointed out.

Even if the evaluator has credibly sourced data to show that programme A has not been successful or new idea B looks more favourable than new idea C, the presentation of the results has to be done with sensitivity. The CMO may well think they've been 'thrown under the bus' if a programme is presented as being unsuccessful if the results are presented to the executive team before the CMO has seen them.

From experience we know that some new imperatives that really need to move forward may require the approval of people who may not see the new idea initially as in their best interest. We remember a time at the beginning of the millennium when many technology companies sold mainly through their direct sales force. Common sense pointed towards moving to a multi-channel model involving more desk-based salespeople, and indirect channels. We recall that presenting this idea to a room full of sales VPs was a political misfire as it looked like asking turkeys to vote for thanksgiving and Christmas all at the same time. The evaluator needs to have the political nous to know when to present recommendations and in what way. Or, if the evaluator is developing presentation material for an executive to make the case for one programme over another, they need to take account of the need to persuade people 'beyond the numbers' and be aware of the political climate the decision is taking place in.

What we do know is that sales and marketing people are being asked to provide stronger justification for new ideas, and to continue existing programmes. Which brings the competence of evaluating why things should or should not be done to the fore.

Chapter summary

In this chapter we have given you a view of the importance of evaluator competencies to help your organization to perform better and stand out. We have given you a view of what marketing and sales leaders think is not currently working, and some examples of good practice. In providing a set of competencies drawn from our analysis we intended to paint a clear picture of the strength we attach to the evaluator competencies and how they play out in marketing and sales roles. We believe that the evaluator should be given a loud voice, which demands a highly credible operator in terms of both title and competence levels.

Evaluator competencies go way beyond keeping score, to providing intelligence and insight on which potential initiatives to go forward with because they can help your company stand out. Erica the Evaluator has to be someone who practises balanced advocacy, seeking out programmes that land in the C-Zone where customer and company interests help you stand out from competitors. Someone who can connect the dots from a potential new initiative and a successful ongoing campaign. In doing this Erica needs to be seen to have integrity combined with political nous. Table 9.1 summarizes the high-level competencies required by the evaluator, and their components.

TABLE 9.1 Evaluator competencies and components

Evaluator Competencies	Components
Integrity	• Honest evaluation of potential new programmes based on credible data • Honest reporting of programme results • Bravery to kill under-performing programmes and re-invest in highly performing programmes • Seen to evaluate performance consistently and fairly
Balanced advocacy	• Can evaluate programmes based on positive impact on customer, own company, and competitive differentiation
Connecting the dots	• Can link from overall company goals through to programme performance • Drives a learning loop to help continually enhance performance improvement • Gives advice that helps improve proposals and methods for developing and executing new programmes
Persuasion and political nous	• Political skill and sensitivity to handle executives when taking fact-based decisions to kill, keep, or develop programmes

In the next chapter we will consider the conditions that have to exist in organizations for the stand-out competencies we have covered in Chapters 5–9 to flourish.

Before we do, here's a summary of the competencies from Victor the Visionary to Erica the Evaluator.

TABLE 9.2 V.A.L.U.E. competencies

V Visionary	A Activator	L Learner	U Usefulness	E Evaluator
Victor the Visionary	Alison the Activator	Laura the Learner	Ulysses the Useful	Erica the Evaluator
Outside-in	Balanced advocacy	Curiosity	Connecting the dots	Integrity
Farsight	Listening	Proactive and engaged	Learner	Balanced advocacy
Zooming	Negotiation	Reflective	Customer-centricity	Connecting the dots
Predicting	Tenacity	'Fearless' experimentation	Discipline	Persuasion and political nous
Imagining	People-centricity contextualization	Receptive	Flexibility and adaptability	

References and further reading

Ambler, T (2000) Marketing Metrics, *Business Strategy Review*, **11** (2), pp 59–66

CSO Insights (2018) Selling in the Age of Ceaseless Change: The 2018–2019 Sales Performance Report [online] https://www.csoinsights.com/wp-content/uploads/sites/5/2018/12/2018-2019-Sales-Performance-Report.pdf (archived at https://perma.cc/A28C-MMLS)

Deloitte and Touche (2019) CMO Survey Fall 2019: What insights can we gain from marketing leaders? [online] https://www2.deloitte.com/us/en/pages/chief-marketing-officer/articles/cmo-survey.html (archived at https://perma.cc/N8R8-R9M9)

Farris, P *et al* (2017) *Key Marketing Metrics: The 50+ metrics every manager needs to know* (2nd ed), Pearson, Harlow, England

Forbes (2019) Marketing accountability report [online] https://www.forbes.com/cmo-practice/marketing-accountability-report/ (archived at https://perma.cc/W2C6-9PTT)

Gartner (2019) Gartner CMO spend survey 2018–19 [online] https://www.gartner.com/marketing/research/the-2018-2019-cmo-spend-survey-spotlight.html (archived at https://perma.cc/ZDR6-PKGM)

Hays (2020) The DNA of a marketing leader [online] https://www.hays.co.uk/job/marketing-jobs/dna-of-a-marketing-leader (archived at https://perma.cc/2XZH-D2D3)

Kelly, S, Johnston, P and Danheiser, S (2017) *Value-ology: Aligning sales and marketing to shape and deliver profitable customer value propositions*, Palgrave Macmillan, Basingstoke

Korn Ferry (2017) Age and tenure in the C-suite: Korn Ferry Institute study reveals trends by title and industry [online] https://www.kornferry.com/press/age-and-tenure-in-the-c-suite-korn-ferry-institute-study-reveals-trends-by-title-and-industry (archived at https://perma.cc/6SXB-H3XM)

Marketo (2020) The Definitive Guide to Marketing and Sales Analytics [online] https://www.marketo.com/definitive-guides/marketing-metrics-and-marketing-analytics/ (archived at https://perma.cc/TQ3Z-8SQ2)

Shaw, R and Merrick, D (2005) *Marketing Payback: Is your marketing profitable?* Pearson Education

Snow, A (2018) Anchor sales and marketing alignment with revenue growth analytics best practices to collaborate on analytics that supports growth, *Forrester* [online] https://www.forrester.com/report/Anchor+Sales+And+Marketing+Alignment+With+Revenue+Growth+Analytics/-/E-RES136061 (archived at https://perma.cc/LH2H-F5UX)

Whitler, K A and Morgan, N (2017) Why CMOs never last and what to do about it, *Harvard Business Review*, **95** (4)

Woodburn, D (2006) Marketing measurement action research model, *Measuring Business Excellence*, **10** (2), pp 50–64

10

Building a V.A.L.U.E. competency culture

In this chapter we will:

- look at what sales and marketing leaders said about the way company culture and leadership affects the firm's ability to differentiate in the market;
- explain why the right company culture is essential for V.A.L.U.E. competency to thrive;
- discuss the professional attitudes and behaviours that are needed to produce differentiated B2B value propositions;
- provide you with a V.A.L.U.E. competency culture self-assessment inventory.

Differentiation is a whole company initiative

What goes on inside the organization directly affects what happens outside the organization. Culture and leadership profoundly shape the way value propositions are designed, delivered and communicated, and how feedback from markets and customers is used to create real differentiation. When US telco president Robson talked to us about culture and leadership and how it affects competency and the pursuit of differentiation he raised a vital issue about a firm's overall ability to differentiate. Here's what he said:

> Does the organization truly value what you've got to do to separate you from the sea of sameness? Does the chief exec actually get it, value it understand it, and sign off on this? You could try all day long to persuade the CEO that the sea of sameness is a serious issue and tell him that the customer isn't interested in hearing

'about' his company and his thousands of route miles of network. You're not going to win unless you've got a top-down thirst for committing to this.

Three things stand out in what Robson says:

1. In addition to the five individual elements of V.A.L.U.E. competency we introduced in the previous chapters we can see they are bound together by an overarching organizational ability and attitude towards customer value creation and this can have a positive or negative effect on achieving differentiation.
2. The attitude and focus of the CEO plays a critical role in setting the right conditions for V.A.L.U.E. competency to operate.
3. Feature-based, about us and vanity claims do not create customer-relevant value proposition differentiation.

These factors are about the 'feel' of the organization. Establishing the right culture that values the importance of the task of differentiation is essential. This is very different to efficiently undertaking everyday sales and marketing tasks and processes and is all about what strategic management researchers and authors Johnson *et al* (2017) describe as 'the way we do things around here'. Robson went on to capture the idea like this:

> It's a culture issue. It's a senior leadership issue too because you can have the best sales and marketing execs and they can be completely on message, but sameness will get worse if the culture is wrong and they haven't got organizational buy-in.

So what do we mean by organizational culture?

As readers will appreciate, the idea of culture is rather abstract, so it's helpful to bear in mind some general principles when considering how culture works in a B2B sales and marketing context. Culture in B2B businesses can be thought of as:

> the patterns of shared values and beliefs that help individuals understand organizational functioning and thus provide them norms for behaviour in the organization (Deshpande, Farley and Webster, 1989).

Former professor of the Sloan Management School Ed Schein (2016) explained that organizational culture is best thought of as layers like those of a cake. The most visible layer on the top is the tangible things that represent the culture, in our case value propositions and other forms of marketing communication (Schein called these 'artefacts'). Underneath that are the behaviours of people, which include the things that relate to what we explored in the previous chapters on competency such as taking action, communicating customer insights and evaluating actions. Underneath behaviours lies an invisible layer of norms, which are the unwritten rules of conduct in the company, things that are expected to happen as a matter of course such as prompt response to customer complaints, collaborative working, proactive problem solving and so on. The final layer is made of values, which are the guiding principles and orientation of the business, such as trustworthiness, attention to detail, and passion for the customer.

We can see from what Robson said above that he recognized the power of norms and values to affect everything the business does. Robson also recognized that the norms and values in many organizations follow how the CEO sees the business and how it should be run. It is the CEO's world view that typically drives the values and norms in the business. This means that the image the CEO has in their mind of what the business should look like and how sales and marketing should work can have productive or very unproductive consequences. Here's a great example of how leadership norms, shared values and beliefs have a positive influence on behaviours, from chief commercial officer Bob:

> So I have a phrase within my business that I call 'do different'. It's something I have used for the last 15 years. If you 'do different' you've got more of a chance of having success in the marketplace, you've got more of a chance of having fun in terms of what you're doing and you've got more of a chance of getting the boardrooms of your competitors talking about you.

In this example we have a simple, easy-to-understand statement of norms and expectations that sets the cultural tone of the organization in terms of being different to the competition.

TABLE 10.1 The general structure of organizational culture

Things Behaviours	Visible
Norms Values	Invisible

On the other hand, problems and division can occur when an organizational leader has a particular view that differs with colleagues about what is culturally acceptable and what is not. Leadership beliefs shape the organizational conversation and conversations shape action. In this example, a director of the organization was sceptical of the idea of Brand. Consequently it was off limits to talk about and develop branding ideas and action. Siobhan, marketing director in higher education, shared this example with us:

> Historically there has been an issue about our brand, and developing brand strategy and brand awareness. Under our old director brand seemed to be a bit of a dirty word, because it was deemed something that belonged in the commercial world and not in the higher education sector. As such no one ever mentioned the word brand. As a result I think we've really suffered from sort of our lack of commitment and attention to an overarching brand strategy.

This is a clear example of where what happens in the organization and ultimately in the marketplace is shaped by the particular ideas and preferences of the leader who then expresses them as expected norms and behaviours. Indeed, marketing experts Professor Malcom McDonald and visiting Fellow Peter Mouncey of Cranfield University observe that:

> CEOs and MDs are increasingly accepting that they must take on the role of chief marketing officer if they want to create truly customer-led organizations (McDonald and Mouncey, 2011, p 57).

It is therefore clear that the culture and leadership of the business needs to be fundamentally market oriented if the pursuit of differentiation is to be treated seriously. Indeed, V.A.L.U.E. competency indicates and at the same time relies on market orientation (Gebhardt, Carpenter and Sherry, 2006; Narver and Slater, 1990):

> Market orientation is essentially an informal organizational culture, a shared mindset assuming that value creation for customers is the key driver of business profitability (Frosen *et al*, 2016).

A V.A.L.U.E. competency culture is an innovative culture

It's one thing to recognize and describe the culture in an organization and another to define the type of culture you need to produce the value competency performance you seek. Readers will no doubt be familiar with all sorts of cultures that business scholars, pundits and gurus claim are essential for success, such as a winning culture, a 'can do' culture, etc.

Formal academic studies have identified many types of cultural attributes. Handy (1993) identified cultures that were dominated by power (where authority and control is in the hands of a dominant leader), role cultures (highly bureaucratic organizations), task cultures (where team adaptability is the norm), and person cultures (in which people and their development and well-being matter). Quinn and Cameron (2011) identified clan culture (emphasizing the nurturing role of teams), hierarchy culture (emphasizing efficiency and doing things right), market culture (focusing on competitiveness), and adhocracy culture (emphasizing being adaptive, risk taking and being first movers).

Johnson *et al* (2017) gave us the cultural web as a way to capture the symbols, structures, stories, routines, and worldview in different organizations. Each culture has its own style, strengths and weaknesses; however, when it comes to the right culture for pursuing differentiation in B2B we believe there is something that is essential for the creation of effective value propositions and stand-out marketing and that is a *value culture*, which is an organizational culture that encourages and supports innovation and differentiation.

We take a broad view of the idea of innovation and so for us innovation is not only the introduction of new devices and technologies, it is the task of introducing any new idea or method that creates value for the customer. Producing differentiated value propositions is therefore an innovative task. It stands to reason therefore that to create differentiated value propositions you need a culture that supports innovation. It is also crucial to understand that value propositions are not just a communications task done *after* the fact, designed to simply grab the customer's attention and pique their interest in products and services by promoting distinctiveness and brand promise. Value propositions are *seminal* and reflect the business model of the organization. Value propositions are thus innovative concepts that define and drive the essential design elements of every product-service solution which the customer seeks and the firm needs to deliver to win business.

The work of Hogan and Coote (2014) suggests a number of important cultural norms and values that need to be in place to support innovation and we can see that many of them resonate with the competency elements we have outlined in the previous chapters:

- openness and flexibility;
- good internal communication;

- good interfunctional cooperation;
- taking responsibility for action;
- taking sensible risks;
- being commercially astute.

Innovation applies to every aspect of sales and marketing, from visual and copywriting creativity to product-service innovation and business model innovation (Chesborough, 2007). Furthermore, innovation relies on doing things that create customer value at the same time as being commercially grounded. Ideas must be customer relevant and commercially feasible.

The importance of commercial grounding is something that Bob, chief commercial officer of a building supplies company, drove home when he told us:

> The question needs to be asked, why are there usually no marketers operating at board level within the organization or going on to run a business? And that's because most marketers don't understand the commercial realities of business like people who've got a finance or sales background. Commercially grounded people understand the beat, they understand what's actually going on within the business and most marketers don't.

What Bob is telling us when he talks about understanding the beat is that a V.A.L.U.E. competency culture needs a commercial mindset in the company. Without a commercial mindset value propositions become solely creative imagery and wordsmithery. This means that to be truly differentiated in a B2B context you must be able to quantify the proposition, not just create distinctiveness and an abstract brand purpose. This belief has to be embedded in the culture of the business.

With these thoughts in mind we can picture the layers of a V.A.L.U.E. competency culture as shown in Figure 10.1.

We can see, as Robson emphasized, that the foundation of an organizational culture that pursues stand-out marketing rests on a leadership idea and commitment about the right behaviours, norms and values that support V.A.L.U.E. competency.

It will be clear by now that we believe that market differentiation and avoiding sameness therefore depends on the market orientation of the CEO, the board and in turn co-workers of the business and that this orientation (norm of working) indicates the culture of the firm. Indeed, Narver and Slater (1990) described this type of organizational culture by emphasizing the three elements of customer orientation, competitor orientation and

FIGURE 10.1 Appropriate cultural conditions support V.A.L.U.E. competency and achievement of stand-out marketing

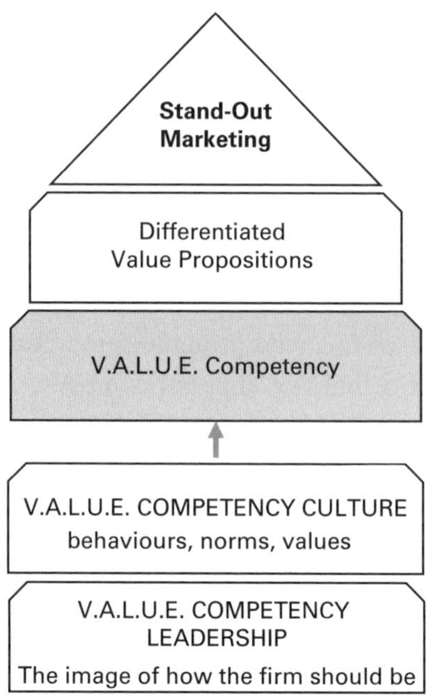

interfunctional coordination as essential values, norms and behaviours of the firm (Homburg and Pflesser, 2000).

In a nutshell, V.A.L.U.E. competency is generated and thrives in a V.A.L.U.E. culture which relies on the engagement of employees and how they learn and respond to customer needs. All of which rely on the vision and behaviour of market-oriented leadership that values deep understanding of customer-relevant differentiated value propositions and the means to produce them.

TIME OUT FOR THOUGHT

Take five minutes to reflect on what we've covered so far. Does your company have an innovative culture? On a scale of 1–5, where 1 is poor and 5 is excellent, how would you score your company on the innovative culture factors of openness, communication, cooperation, responsibility, risk taking and commerciality?

The importance of employee engagement and organizational learning

The key for creating an innovative organizational culture is ensuring that employees are engaged and that the company is effective at learning from the marketplace. It seems intuitively right that there is a link between employee engagement and the performance of the company; indeed, business researchers Liat Eldor and Eran Vigoda-Gadot (2017) identified that:

> employees have a critical impact on an organization's innovation, flexibility, competitiveness and success... and those who are strongly engaged with the organization are proactive, promote innovation and invest efforts in improving the outcomes of their organization.

Other researchers such as Bailey *et al* (2017) underscore this link between engaged employees and innovative work. So, the traits, behaviours and attitudes we need for an engaged innovative culture should include the following:

- self-starters who have resilience in the face of knock-backs;
- support from colleagues and supervisors;
- continuous feedback and dialogue;
- trust in leadership and a voice that is listened to;
- flexible and imaginative non-routine ways of working.

These factors mean individuals typically go that extra mile to achieve success which in turn leads to higher company performance. Going the extra mile gets noticed, as financial services CMO Heather pointed out:

> So I have a woman on my team that has been here four or five years now in the old business model of being a support structure only. She was a doer. So anything that came to her, she got it done. She had a great reputation for getting things done and she did. And I could count on her for anything.

Clearly this person was highly engaged and her engagement was inextricably bound up with the culture of the business.

In parallel to employee engagement we need a culture where the organization as a whole learns. This is key to supporting the Learner competency we introduced in Chapter 7 with the key traits, behaviours and attitudes being:

- a whole company approach;
- being close to customers and markets;

- continuous feedback and dialogue;
- open mindedness;
- adaptability.

VP of Sales Kirk shared his views on the importance of this when he observed:

> At Company X they never were arrogant to the point where they felt like, we've got it all right.

Crucially, it is important to appreciate that a learning company is one that has a culture of market- and customer-oriented learning.

Things that undermine a V.A.L.U.E. culture

The challenge we face when talking about achieving the right culture is that it can all seem a little bit utopian and idealistic. In reality people don't always fit the culture, leaders set the wrong tone, departments don't always work in harmony. So if you have any form of bad behaviours and attitudes in your organization it should come as no surprise that your chances of developing a V.A.L.U.E. culture and competency that leads to value proposition differentiation are massively reduced. Here are some key problems to identify and avoid:

- dogmatic leadership;
- sales and marketing function dysfunction;
- lack of commerciality and whole company perspective.

Telco president Robson is unequivocal in terms of the blame for bad behaviours and attitudes, which he claims lies right at the top of the organization. Dogmatism can also be reinforced by recruiting in the image of oneself. Consultant principle Herbert explained how cultural values, norms and behaviours simply get imported from one organization to another so the prospects of innovation and differentiation are greatly reduced:

> I think there's a certain amount of institutionalization. The more you work in a particular environment, the more you become part of it.

The technical term for this issue is 'enculturation', where you carry the values, norms and behaviours of the culture you were part of into the organizational culture you are joining and where you are reluctant to adapt to a new culture. The opposite is 'acculturation', where gradually you adopt a new culture.

In conclusion, we can see that culture creates a playbook of expectations about the way things should be done around here. These ideas are based on what people believe are key factors for success. Typically the CEO ultimately determines what goes in the playbook. They aren't necessarily written down and they all relate to values, norms and behaviours. The pursuit of meaningful differentiation needs to be recognized as culturally important and then reflected in the values and behaviours of the organization.

So now it's over to you. The following exercise is a way of diagnosing the culture of your business to see if it aligns with a V.A.L.U.E. competency culture.

READER ACTIVITY

Do you have a culture that supports V.A.L.U.E. competency? Thinking about your organizational culture, how would you score your company against the factors listed, where 1 is poor and 5 excellent?

TABLE 10.2 V.A.L.U.E. culture self-assessment inventory

Culture Factor	1	2	3	4	5
Open-minded leadership					
Market orientation					
Customer orientation					
Open to new information					
Information is shared freely					
Commercially grounded decisions					
Takes sensible risks					
Leadership is trusted					
Supportive management structure					
Supportive colleagues					
Flexible working					

(continued)

TABLE 10.2 (Continued)

Culture Factor	1	2	3	4	5
Clear values					
Common values					
People go the extra mile					
Personal development is encouraged					
Bad behaviour is not tolerated					
Effort is given to aligning activities					
Colleagues feel engaged					
Innovation is the norm					
Blaming is uncommon					

References and further reading

Alfes, K *et al* (2013) The relationship between line manager behavior, perceived HRM practices, and individual performance: examining the mediating role of engagement, *Human Resource Management*, **52**, pp 839–59

Bailey, C *et al* (2017) The meaning, antecedents and outcomes of employee engagement: a narrative synthesis, *International Journal of Management Reviews*, **19**, pp 31–53

Bersin, J *et al* (2017) The employee experience: culture, engagement, and beyond. 2017 Global Human Capital Trends: Improving the employee experience, Deloitte Insights

Chesborough, H (2007) Business model innovation: it's not just about technology anymore, *Strategy & Leadership*, **35** (6), pp 12–17

Deshpande, R, Farley, J and Webster Jr, F E (1989) Organizational culture and marketing: defining the research agenda, *Journal of Marketing*, **53** (1), pp 3–15

Deshpande, R, Farley, J and Webster Jr, F E (1993) Corporate culture, customer orientation and innovativeness in Japanese firms: a quadratic analysis, *Journal of Marketing*, **57** (1), pp 23–37

Eldor, L and Vigoda-Gadot, E (2017) The nature of employee engagement: rethinking the employee–organization relationship, *The International Journal of Human Resource Management*, **28** (3), pp 526–52

Ellis, P D (2006) Market orientation and performance: a meta analysis and cross-national comparisons, *Journal of Management Studies*, **43** (5), pp 1089–107

Frosen, J *et al* (2016) What counts versus what can be counted: the complex interplay of market orientation and marketing performance measurement, *Journal of Marketing*, **80**, pp 60–78

Gebhardt, G F, Carpenter, G S and Sherry Jr, J F (2006) Creating a market orientation: a longitudinal, multifirm, grounded analysis of cultural transformation, *Journal of Marketing*, **70** (October), pp 37–55

Handy, C (1993) *Understanding Organisations*, Penguin

Hogan, S J and Coote, L V (2014) Organizational culture, innovation and performance: A test of Schein's model, *Journal of Business Research*, **67**, pp 1609–21

Homburg, C and Pflesser, C (2000) A multiple-layer model of market-orientated organizational culture: measurement issues and performance outcomes, *Journal of Marketing Research*, **XXXVII**, pp 449–62

Hunt, S D and Madhavaram, S (2006) The service dominant logic of marketing: theoretical foundations, pedagogy, and resource advantage theory, In *The Service Dominant Logic of Marketing: Dialog, debate and directions*, eds R E Lusch and S L Vargo, M E Sharpe

Johnson, G *et al* (2017) *Exploring Strategy*, 11th ed, Pearson

Khan, W A (1990) Psychological conditions of personal engagement and disengagement at work, *Academy of Management Journal*, **33** (4), pp 692–724

Kirca, A H, Jayachandran, S and Bearden, W O (2005) Market orientation: a meta-analytic review and assessment of its antecedents and impact on performance, *Journal of Marketing*, **69** (2), pp 24–41

Kohli, A K and Jaworski, B J (1990) Market orientation: the construct, research propositions and managerial implications, *Journal of Marketing*, **54** (2), pp 1–18

Macey, W H and Schneider, B (2008) The meaning of employee engagement, *Industrial and Organizational Psychology*, **1**, pp 3–30

McDonald, M and Mouncey, P (2011) *Marketing Accountability: A new metrics model to measure marketing effectiveness*, Kogan Page

McLure, R E (2010) The influence of organizational culture and conflict on market orientation, *Journal of Business and Industrial Marketing*, **25** (7), pp 514–24

Narver, J C and Slater, S F (1990) The effect of market orientation on business profitability, *Journal of Marketing*, **54** (October), pp 20–35

Quinn, R E and Cameron, K S (2011) *Diagnosing and Changing Organizational Culture, Third edition: based on the competing values framework*, Jossey Bass

Schein, E (2016) *Organizational Culture and Leadership*, 5th ed, Wiley

Senge, P (2006) *The Fifth Discipline: The art and practice of the learning organization*, 2nd ed, Random House

Shuck, B (2011) Four emerging perspectives of employee engagement: an integrative literature review, *Human Resource Development Review*, **10** (3), pp 304–28

Spector, P E *et al* (2006) The dimensionality of counterproductivity: are all counterproductive behaviors created equal? *Journal of Vocational Behavior*, **68**, pp 446–60

Wernerfelt, B (1984) A resource-based view of the firm, *Strategic Management Journal*, 5 (2), pp 171–80

11

Using V.A.L.U.E. competencies to stand out from your competitors

In this chapter we will:

- revisit the purpose and aims of this book;
- introduce the golden threads competency that leads to high performance;
- provide a competency framework for achieving stand-out marketing;
- demonstrate how V.A.L.U.E. competency can be used for recruitment, selection and personnel development.

We started this book with a purpose. Our goal was to identify the competency B2B organizations need to stand out from their competition. We found that the competency of outstanding sales and marketing professionals which lead to superior departmental and organizational performance could be categorized into the V.A.L.U.E. competency framework. The personal competency set out in this framework is vital for producing market differentiation and the ability to swim away from the Sea of Sameness. V.A.L.U.E. competency underpins the task of B2B value proposition differentiation and is particularly relevant to:

- directing the behaviours for stand-out results;
- measuring individual sales and marketing performance;
- recruitment, selection and development;
- aligning stand-out marketing competency with generic competency;
- communicating the norms and values of the organization.

V.A.L.U.E. competency is not wishy-washy theory. It is about the demonstrable behaviours that relate to the ability to make good decisions, creatively solve problems, navigate the organization to get things done, interact in positive prosocial ways, adjust assumptions and behaviours to changing circumstances when needed, demonstrating the ability to listen and learn, showing the ability to change the rules if needed and to make balanced judgements. These are differentiating high-level competencies that operate above and beyond the knowledge of sales and marketing techniques and market sector knowledge.

By thinking about marketing in terms of V.A.L.U.E. competency we want to call out and challenge the contemporary obsession of believing that the future of marketing lies in digital marketing. We are *not* saying that the digital marketing skills such as SEO, SEM, understanding 'search frictions' in web page design, marketing automation and so on don't matter. Of course they do. What we *are* saying is that these relate to level one competency not level three competency. Think of it this way. Many of us will have had the experience of visiting friends or family in hospital. The doctor is evidently highly qualified in diagnosis, surgery and a medical specialism; however, it is the doctor's competency in terms of the way s/he deals with people and situations that sets them apart and makes them stand out. In this regard we talk of the doctor's 'bedside manner' rather than their technical ability. Doctors have to handle the patient, their friends and family as well as the disease (Hariharan and Padhy, 2011).

As Daniel Goleman (1998) pointed out:

> the skills that distinguish star performers in *every field* is not IQ, advanced degrees, *or technical expertise*, but... self-awareness... integrity; the ability to communicate and influence, to initiate and accept change – these competencies are at a premium in today's job market [our italics].

This is what we mean by stand-out marketing. Stand-out marketing performance relies on much more than being good at marketing technicalities.

The relationship between skills, competency, culture and leadership

A central theme in this book is the distinction between skills and competency and we want to emphasize that our focus has been on the identification and development of senior-level competency that goes beyond the operational tasks of marketing planning, segmentation targeting, and positioning and managing the marketing mix. Excellent operational marketing skills in themselves do not indicate the presence of a commercially aware entrepreneurial mindset that would gain respect and recognition as a C-suite player.

It should also be recognized that marketing professionals obviously don't operate in isolation, they work within a particular culture and are guided by a specific type of leadership. We believe that this culture and leadership needs to be value oriented. This means there needs to be a clear organizational commitment to a deep understanding and pursuit of commercially grounded customer-oriented differentiation. In particular, the culture of the organization needs to have V.A.L.U.E. competency-based professional practice embedded in its values, norms and behaviours.

Golden threads of stand-out marketing

When we looked across the elements of V.A.L.U.E. competency it became clear that there are some golden threads which linked them together. Our golden threads pull V.A.L.U.E. competency together and are evidence of the ability of someone to work with the V.A.L.U.E. competency elements as a whole; they indicate a high degree of self-awareness, pragmatism and creativity. Our golden threads also demonstrate judgement, intuition and acumen. In that sense they are performance differentiators and are identified as:

- Contextualization – communicating and adapting to different contexts.
- Curiosity – having a proactive and continuous interest in the world.
- Dot-connecting – connecting disparate pieces of information into coherent themes.
- Balancing – manipulating alternative perspectives to make sound judgements.

Our golden threads are included with individual V.A.L.U.E. competency maps we provide at the end of this chapter. Golden threads can be used like a 'tie-breaker' when scoring individuals who perform equally well on a particular V.A.L.U.E. competency. They are the differences that make a difference. They are what makes someone stand out.

Bringing this all together we can show V.A.L.U.E. competency, with value leadership and within a value culture. Stand-out marketing will only exist in your organization if it mirrors this model.

FIGURE 11.1 Stand-out marketing, competency, leadership and culture

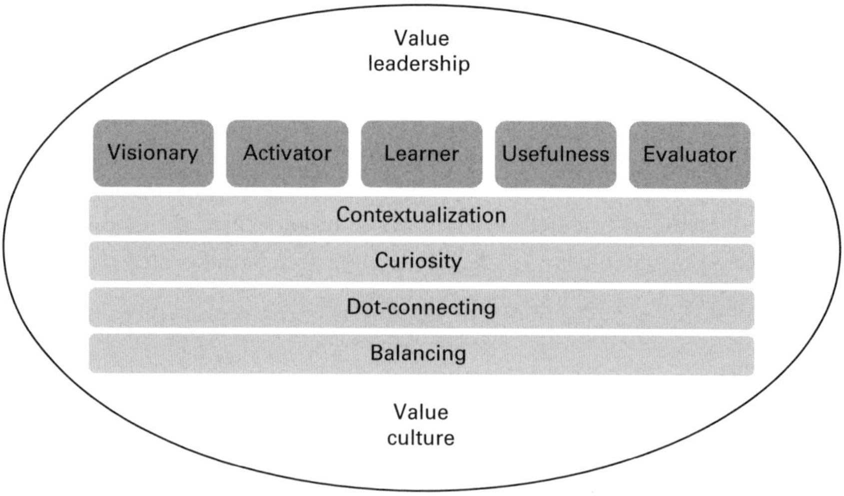

This model shows how V.A.L.U.E. competency sits within a positive organizational environment. This environment is made up of a value culture and value leadership that places importance on creating customer value in the pursuit of meaningful differentiation. Cutting across the individual V.A.L.U.E. competency elements are our four golden threads which are vital for each V.A.L.U.E. competency element to reach its full potential towards the achievement of stand-out marketing practice.

Who is responsible for competency mapping?

The responsibility for deciding on and mapping competency in the specialized area of B2B market differentiation and value creation must be led and driven by the senior sales and marketing leadership team with advice and support from the HR team. It would be a mistake to delegate this task entirely to the HR team alone because they will be one step removed from your B2B marketing reality. The framework we set out provides the basis of a critical competency map that can be integrated and aligned to the more generic competency sought by your organization.

Identifying behavioural indicators of competency

Behavioural indicators are evidence of competency. To establish evidence of competency a candidate or current employee needs to provide specific examples of their thought and action. A good way to do this is to get the people whose competency you want to assess to explain their experience and abilities by following what is known as the S.T.A.R. approach in their responses to your questions. This means the individuals being assessed should be able to demonstrate their competency by explaining the general situation or context of the action, the specific task that was required, the specific actions that were undertaken and the result of the actions. For example, a situation could be a six-monthly customer review meeting, a task could be to introduce and develop a new value proposition with the customer, an action could be presenting an initial proposal and engaging in dialogue to customize aspects of it, and the result could be getting a deal signed with the customer.

V.A.L.U.E. competency mapping

Each V.A.L.U.E. competency is mapped with a scoring system. The scoring system rates participant responses on a scale of 1 to 5 where 1 indicates definite rejection and 5 indicates outstanding. It is important to have a clear purpose and aim for the competency map. In this case we are interested in competency that supports the pursuit of differentiation and value creation and demonstrates stand-out marketing.

Purpose: To ensure sales and marketing activities result in stand-out marketing by producing differentiated value propositions that increase market share and company profitability.

Aim: To identify evidence of senior-level sales and marketing competency necessary for swimming away from the Sea of Sameness.

Method: Assessors and interviewers ask questions that examine each area of competency by probing for evidence of the required behaviours.

Six individual competency map templates with behavioural indicators follow below (see Tables 11.1–11.6).

TABLE 11.1 Visionary competency map

	Definite Rejection	Below Average	Average	Above Average	Outstanding
Competency	1	2	3	4	5
Visionary					
Sees the bigger market and organizational picture, demonstrates foresight, demonstrates perspective-taking, anticipates issues and problems, uses imagination to provide fresh perspectives.					
Behavioural indicators					
Outside-in					
Awareness of long-term implications and market trends. Understands customer pain points and needs. Understands our role as a supplier in the world of the customer.					
Farsight					
Understands competitive position of the business and implications of threats and opportunities over 10-year+ horizon.					

Sucessfully identifies key issues and resists short-termism and reactiveness.	
Zooming	
Ability to view events from different perspectives and connect specfic instances to the bigger picture.	
Predicting	
Anticipates future moves of customers and competitors. Sensitive to weak signals from customers and markets that others miss. Is able to generate scenarios of plausible possible futures.	
Imagining	
Develops and communicates scenarios of plausible possible futures. Asks what if and explores possibilities, encourages the act of supposing, can create and move ideas between different contexts.	

TABLE 11.2 Activator competency map

	Definite Rejection	Below Average	Average	Above Average	Outstanding
Competency	1	2	3	4	5
Activator					
Makes things happen. Proactive and assertive. Sensitivite to organizational politics and uses organizational understanding to ensure goals are achieved.					
Behavioural indicators					
Balanced advocacy					
Considers likely support and resistance to proposals. Accurately assesses priorities in relation to organizational goals. Provides a balanced perspective of company and the customer needs and expectations.					

Listening

Elicits information and opinions from face-to-face interactions. Brings assumptions to the surface.

Listens to different opinions without bias.

Negotiation

Confers with others to reach a solution. Explores possibilities and alternatives that work for all parties.

Tenacity

Holds to a position or plan until it is achieved or can sensibly be relinquished.

Keeps direction regardless of obstacles and stays on target.

(*continued*)

TABLE 11.2 (Continued)

	Definite Rejection	Below Average	Average	Above Average	Outstanding
People centricity					
Conscious of the feelings and perspectives of others. Values them as people not just as a job title.					
Contextualization					
Understands the particular circumstances of the person they are dealing with. Shapes value propositions that resonate with them, be it external customer, or internal executive.					
Shows ability to understand dynamics of diverse interest groups and bases of power.					

TABLE 11.3 Learner competency map

	Definite Rejection	Below Average	Average	Above Average	Outstanding
Competency	1	2	3	4	5
Learner					
Shows a desire to learn new things and undertake self-development. Shares knowledge freely. Critical thinker who is aware of assumptions made by self and others.					
Behavioural Indicators					
Curiosity					
Seeks new ideas. Looks under the surface for causes and influences. Asks questions. Doesn't jump to conclusions.					

(continued)

TABLE 11.3 (Continued)

	Definite Rejection	Below Average	Average	Above Average	Outstanding
Proactive and engaged					
Committed to continual learning. Grasps problems speedily, involves others in problem framing and solving. Keeps an eye on future developments.					
Reflective					
Self-critical. Thinks back over personal performance and seeks improvements. Ability to think conceptually to develop solutions.					
Fearless experimentation					
Ability to step outside comfort zone. Has a mature perspective and learns lessons from failures.					

Creates innovative solutions and experiments with new ways of doing things.		
Growth mindset		
Has eclectic interests. Inquisitive about new management ideas. Takes on board new ideas from diverse sources. Gathers information from a wide range of sources.		
Receptive		
Open to new ideas and ways of working. Willingly embraces critical feedback.		

TABLE 11.4 Usefulness competency map

	Definite Rejection	Below Average	Average	Above Average	Outstanding
Competency	1	2	3	4	5
Usefuleness					
Demonstrates strong customer focus and understanding. Asks tough questions about the relevance of ideas and solutions to the customer.					
Behavioural indicators					
Connects the dots					
Identifies patterns and connections in diverse customer needs and market activities. Sees the similarities between different customer attitudes, behaviours and situations.					

Makes connections between the needs and solutions found in one situation to new situations.	
Learner	
Makes use of investigative skills to understand customer problems and context. Creates helpful models and diagrams to explain complex customer and market situations or problems.	
Customer centric	
Demonstrates concern and understanding for customer needs. Maintains and develops positive customer relations Focused on providing high-quality service.	

(continued)

TABLE 11.4 (Continued)

	Definite Rejection	Below Average	Average	Above Average	Outstanding
Disciplined					
Tenacious. Thorough. Sees things through to completion.					
Flexible and adaptable					
Changes approach and style to suit the context. Open to alternative ways of doing things.					

TABLE 11.5 Evaluator competency map

	Definite Rejection	Below Average	Average	Above Average	Outstanding
Competency	1	2	3	4	5
Evaluator					
Makes realistic, accurate judgements. Recognizes and works with strengths and weaknesses.					
Behavioural indicators					
Integrity					
Models high standards of behaviour and transparency. Demonstrates honesty.					
Balanced advocacy					
Active listener to other points of view. Willing to change postion on issues in the light of new information. Supports the right thing rather than personal interest.					

(*continued*)

TABLE 11.5 (Continued)

	Definite Rejection	Below Average	Average	Above Average	Outstanding
Connecting the dots					
Makes commercially sensible connections between costs and actions. Understands the consequences of decisions for different organizational functions.					
Persusasion and poltical nous					
Gains commitment from others across a spectrum of interests and levels of authority.					

TABLE 11.6 Golden threads for stand-out marketing

	Definite Rejection	Below Average	Average	Above Average	Outstanding
Competency	1	2	3	4	5
Golden Threads					
High level competency which connects individual V.A.L.U.E. competency elements. Indicates a high level of overall judgement, intuition and acumen.					
Behavioural indicators					
Contextualization					
Recognizes the idiosyncratic nature of each business situation and adapts approach accordingly. Resists applying prescriptive solutions in every circumstance.					

(continued)

TABLE 11.6 (Continued)

	Definite Rejection	Below Average	Average	Above Average	Outstanding
Demonstrates an ability to alter personal behaviour and approach to suit the situation.					
Curiosity					
Never assumes to know all the answers. Spends a lot of time asking questions.					
Dot-connecting					
Makes insightful connections. Thinks systemically and grasps implications of impacts in one area on another. Makes complex things sensible for others to see and understand.					

Balancing

Recognizes competing tensions between ideas, people and proposals. Skilfully manages optimal outcomes.

Considers all aspects of a situation with fairness and objectivity and takes into account self, others and the organization.

Afterword

Stand-out marketing competency draws on ancient ideas that are still relevant for today's B2B organizations.

In ancient Greece, Athena, the goddess of wisdom, was accompanied by an owl and that is why today we talk of the wise old owl. Competency is wisdom in action. In the final analysis that is exactly what stand-out marketing is about. Wisdom. Stand-out marketing draws on a savviness about the world of B2B marketing that is earned from the school of hard knocks, or the university of life. It is business knowledge gained from doing the job, not only reading about theory.

The idea of competency is also connected to something ancient Greek philosopher Aristotle called 'Metis'. Metis is described by academics Andrew Pressey, Alan Gilchrist and Linda Peters as a 'triumvirate of intellectual virtues' (Pressey, Glichrist and Peters, 2016). For Aristotle, Metis was made up of three aspects: techne (technique or practical ability – know what), episteme (knowledge – know how and why) and phronesis (wise judgement). Phronesis is all about so-called 'grey hair' experience (Maister, 1993). Digital marketing falls under techne. Stand-out marketing is all about episteme and phronesis.

To really understand the idea of professional competency we must also explain what we mean by the term 'profession'. A profession operates in a system or 'ecology' 'that is sensitive to the actions of competitors as well as

FIGURE 11.2 Owl of Athena

themselves' (Murphy, 2014). In B2B marketing this means that professional marketing practice is deeply knowledgeable about the market or sector, customer oriented and competitor aware. Professions are also defined by the idea of differentiation in terms of task differentiation or specialism. In that sense B2B marketing is a specialism that is distinct from B2C marketing. For example, telecoms sector specialism is different to aerospace sector specialism. Professions are also sensitive to customer or client differentiation. This means it is recognized that each customer or client is unique and requires a tailored response to their unique needs and contexts. Therefore stand-out marketing competency is evidenced by a clear grasp of the task of B2B customer value creation and the application of the Value Stack (Kelly, Johnston and Danheiser, 2017). The Value Stack model we introduced in Chapter 2 draws attention to the unique needs of each and every customer, different industry verticals and individuals in the buying decision group.

In sum, professions are defined by people with a common world view such that a profession can be recognized as:

> a set of practices whereby professionals have a certain job to do and do so in a certain way. This involves their 'thinking' as well as their 'doing' (Murphy, 2014, p 14).

A profession is characterized by people who have a proprietary body of skills, unique culture, an emphasis on service that includes a subordination of self-interest to general interest, an autonomy that isn't rule fixated, and evidence of expertise. Professional competency reflects an expectation of how things should be done and is directly linked to an 'anticipated performance-related outcome' (Waseem *et al*, 2018).

Stand-out marketing

There is a difference between the competency we need to generate stand-out marketing and the competency we use during customer interactions and service delivery. Our aim in this book was to focus on the competency needed to support swimming away from the sea of sameness. To that end we set out to identify the competency that enabled the creation of stand-out customer value propositions and solutions in the first place.

We have avoided listing the attributes of service, relational and consultative competency sought by B2B customers in their everyday supplier interactions. Selling relational competency as a value-added customer service is the subject of competency-based communication featured in the work of Golfetto (2016; Golfetto and Gibbert, 2006) and Ritter (2006).

The ability to swim away from the Sea of Sameness and create meaningfully differentiated customer value is entirely dependent on being able to understand AND appreciate the business lives and experiences of customers. Sales and marketing professionals must understand and respond to what is going on in the world of the customer and the role they, as suppliers, play in improving the business life of the customer. This means that sales and marketing must be concerned with understanding subjective experience as well as objective analysis and decision making. Marketing professionals need to be more critically aware of the invisible paradigm that guides their practice of brand management and marketing communications in order to avoid being trapped in a management worldview that over-emphasizes reliance on data analytics, lag indicators such as satisfaction surveys, abstractions such as brand purpose and undue faith in customer/consumer research objectivity.

Marketing professionals must also pay attention to their sales colleagues. This is necessary to create a virtuous circle that links external market performance and internal effectiveness. Marketing professionals need to proactively engage with real customers and real sales people. The reports from sales about the lives and experience of customers need to be taken seriously and not dismissed as one-off anecdotes by marketing. These reports and stories need to be understood in a qualitative and systematic way because they contain clues and weak signals about emerging changes that will be of the utmost importance for your business.

Senior-level marketing competency is about demonstrating leadership and entrepreneurialism. To stand out and have any chance of getting respect and a seat in the C-suite you have to be more like an anthropologist than a digital technician. Someone who understands people and commercial organizations rather than someone who is skilled in using software applications. Norman, head of marketing, brought this distinction home when he told us that experienced sales and marketing professionals are people who can explain 'because'…:

> Nothing other than experience has taught me what those becauses are.

Giving a 'because' is the experienced ability to tune into and explain the things that are going on in the customer's world, why they matter, and how things might be in the future. Stand-out marketing happens because the right people, with the right competency, are doing the right things in your organization.

References and further reading

Burgoyne, J G and Stuart, R (1976) The nature, use and acquisition of managerial skills and other attributes, *Personnel Review*, 5 (4), pp 19–29

Goleman, D (1998) *Working with Emotional Intelligence*, Bantam Books, New York

Golfetto, F (2016) Communicating competence: an experiential communication approach for business, IMP 2016 Conference Paper

Golfetto, F and Gibbert, M (2006) Marketing competencies and the sources of customer value in business markets, *Industrial Marketing Management*, (35), pp 904–12

Hariharan, M and Padhy, M (2011) Emotional intelligence of doctors, *Social Science International*, Jan–Jun 27 (1), pp 15–22

Kelly, S, Johnston, P and Danheiser, S (2017) *Value-ology: Aligning sales and marketing to shape and deliver profitable customer value propositions*, Palgrave Macmillan

Le Deist, D F and Winterton, J (2005) What is competence? *Human Resource Development International*, 8 (1), pp 27–46

Maister, D (1993) *Managing the professional service firm*, Simon & Schuster, London

Murphy, B (2014) From novice to expert: a phenomenographic study of chartered accountants in Ireland, Doctoral Thesis, Sheffield Hallam University (United Kingdom)

Pressey, A, Gilchrist A and Peters, L (2016) Managing Metis: Using Aristotle's Nicomachean ethics to understand the expert professional services buyer, Conference Paper. 32nd IMP Conference, Poznan, Poland

Ritter, T (2006) Communicating firm competencies: marketing as different levels of translation, *Industrial Marketing Management*, (35), pp 1032–36

Sanghi, S (2016) *The Handbook of Competency Mapping*, 3rd ed, Sage

Waseem, D, Biggemann, S and Garry, T (2018) Value co-creation: the role of actor competence, *Industrial Marketing Management*, 70, pp 5–12

INDEX

The index is filed in alphabetical, word-by-word order. Numbers within main headings are filed as spelt out, acronyms are filed as presented. Locators in roman numerals refers to information within the forward.